pei

*from early childhood to
adulthood. Her recollections and
attention to detail are uncanny.
Her resilience to adversity and her
comebacks are captivating.
Margarete has poured her
heart and soul into her story.
She is capable of influencing
the reader to believe not only in
the power of prayer, but more importantly,
the act of forgiveness."*

—Ruth Woelfl

*"A well written autobiography,
which shows how to forgive the
abuser and not to blame yourself.
Also, the steps that can be
taken in the healing process by
finding a good therapist and having
strong faith. I recommend
this book for anyone who has
experienced any kind of abuse."*

—Ann Kroeker

FROM VICTIM TO VICTORY

SURVIVING CHILDHOOD SEXUAL ABUSE

Margarete Ledwez

The events described in this book are true and factual as recalled by the author to the best of her recollection. All stories are based on memories of actual events, locales, people and conversations. In some instances the names of individuals have been changed to protect the privacy of the people involved, and some events may have been compressed or chronologically rearranged for literary interest. All conversations are based on the author's recollections and are not intended to represent word-for-word transcripts but are presented in a way that evokes the essence of what was being said.

All Scripture quotations, unless otherwise indicated, are taken from the Holy Bible, New International Version®, NIV®. Copyright ©1973, 1978, 1984, 2011 by Biblica, Inc.® Used by permission of Zondervan. All rights reserved worldwide. www.zondervan.com The "NIV" and "New International Version" are trademarks registered in the United States Patent and Trademark Office by Biblica, Inc.®

ISBN 978-1-958407-05-9 (Hardback)

ISBN 978-1-958407-06-6 (Soft Cover)

Book design by designpanache

ELM GROVE PUBLISHING

San Antonio, Texas, USA

www.elmgrovepublishing.com

Elm Grove Publishing is a legally registered trade name of Panache Communication Arts, Inc.

Contents

Preface

This autobiography is a story of a life of restoration and these are my personal memories as I could recall them. The writing of this book developed from a commitment to healing and an exercise for the regaining and exposing the deep thoughts and hurts buried somewhere deep within me. Portions of my forgotten and segmented past incessantly tried to disclose themselves with sudden unpredicted triggers that disturbed and frightened me. These unexpected triggers revealed themselves, confusing and mystifying me throughout my life as a child, and subsequently into my marriage. They became intolerable, agonizing and perplexing during my life, both physically and mentally, to the point of defeat, blurring and challenging the foundation of who I was and how life should be. On countless occasions I considered and even believed I was mad, as I anguished and didn't comprehend or recognize where my fears and triggers originated.

My story gives light to the facts as I remember them knowing my parents tried the best that they knew how in their world, struggling with things they did not know how to control. I know I loved and depended on them as I grew up in that tiny household, although with much confusion, into adulthood.

In my case even the unthinkable circumstances were confirmed as I will relate to you in these pages. These lines to freedom are written not to dramatize abuse and glorify fear but to relay the power of God, and to show His guiding, forgiving and cleansing power. It is written for healing and to give hope to those who read it, as I show how deliverance, restoration and confidence was revealed and imparted to me.

This love story is a summary of how God met me in my time of profound unfathomable needs. It relays how I was lovingly nurtured as I was supervised and carefully directed by God even when I was not aware of the power of Him in my life.

This story gives hope to those who are sexually abused and to those who have overwhelming fears and it teaches how to forgive and work through those issues to freedom. It is especially for those who do not know where the origin of their hidden deep pain comes from. The journey is sometimes long and difficult, but I encourage you to go back and with God excavate every memory so you can become free as you were designed to be.

I pray my restoration opens doors for you the reader, to see what God can be in your life: healing, loving, forgiving and guiding. God has done all these things in my life as I have walked with Him on this awesome most marvelous journey.

FROM VICTIM TO VICTORY

Prologue: The Nightmare

Praise be to God and Father of our Lord Jesus Christ, The Father of compassion and the God of all comfort, who comforts us in all our troubles so that we can comfort those in any trouble with the comfort we ourselves have received from God. For just as we share abundantly in the sufferings of Christ, so also our comfort abounds through Christ.

2 Corinthians 1:3-5

I awoke suddenly, audibly crying! Weeping uncontrollably and sobbing, my head was spinning with disbelief. I knew instinctively it was true, as I finally recognized that face.

I kept crying out, "No! No! No!"

"Why?" I questioned again repeating with searching words. That constant strength in my life held me tight as I felt his strong arms around me. This night's actions took him by surprise and with startled eyes, he prayed he could make it go away by keeping his tight grip on me.

After years of the same constant characterless nightmare, I could decisively focus, and see that once illusive face. With that unclouded revelation, came a tidal wave of suppressed, censored memories. The recollections were appallingly worse than I ever could have imagined, leaving me shattered with responsive feelings so raw that I couldn't describe them. Why didn't I know this? Until then I disbelieved that a person could block life-changing events, only to recall them many years later. I could not deny the facts now as they clarified within me while my emotions were bruised, and my heart ached with devastating sadness. It never occurred to me that this could have taken place in my life! I could not imagine or believe this was a shrouded part of my forgotten past.

We scarcely slept that night as crazy irrational deliberations swirled around in our minds. We began so many conversations that had no conclusions. The images confronted me, over and over as I once again was transported back in time to become a helpless and wounded young child. I suffered and experienced the pain, betrayal and helplessness!

With great determination I composed myself during the day, weeping repeatedly. Confining my emotional breakdowns to the concealment of my bedroom became a daunting assignment. Being on the defense all day, I never knew what would launch me into an out-of-control spin. Evenings would find us withdrawing to the refuge of our bedroom shelter, trying to make sense of the remembrances and the sensitivities they evoked. We often retreated to our sanctuary as the children matured and were grateful that they would invite their friends over and entertained them regularly.

Our bedroom was designed and became our retreat from the household. A large dormer with a huge window created a cozy nook. We sat there oblivious to the warmth of the fireplace. Our concentrations were distracted and scrambled as we mourned our former tranquil lives. The lights of the enormous ships on the canal one block away were visible through our high arched window, as we stared into the distance.

This waterway had been an element of our lives since we were children, and we enjoyed the weighty massive structures repositioning themselves from one bridge to another. At every bridge crossing, the ship would stop all traffic, putting everyone's lives on a sometimes lengthy pause. Reflecting, I can view my life on an unannounced suspension for a designated time as I waited for my bridge to let me resume life; I hoped it wouldn't keep me waiting too long.

I would have to process all of what I knew as well as deal with the deep untamed emotions. I felt hate and anger towards this man in my dreams and was overcome with betrayal. How *could* he, and *why* did he? It was problematic because of who he was, and I could not force myself to visit his home for a long time. We visited often in the past. What was I going to do?

For the first time, all the perplexing and anxious feelings that I experienced during marital intimacy made some sense. I was learning where and how their roots started. Currently the only comfort I had was discerning I wasn't abnormal, weird, strange, different, or even crazy. There were explanations for the sensitivities I wrestled with all my married life. This person left enormous wounds, entombed deep within me! I suspected and recognized that his actions were unforgivable at that time.

To make sense of it all, I needed to summon up my earliest childhood memories. I would try to rummage through every conceivable recollection and try to figure it out! When and where was this nightmare's origin born? God would have to grant me resolution, courage and concentration. He is at present and was constantly before, my go-to dependable friend, even as an immature young child.

1. Hipple Farms

Retrieving and accessing every element of my lifespan, the earliest recollection happened to be a celebrated, sunny day with the feeling of delight as I lived it. Each day while at the farm was an undiscovered experience.

The sun shone intensely, only to be interrupted by the odd, cotton-like cloud, flawlessly and impeccably poised in the sky. While I watched, they moved ever so slowly overhead giving such little relief from the scorching heat of the sun. The farm workers toiled, sometimes with audible groans, and were repeatedly seen with handkerchiefs wiping their sweaty wet brows.

I was gratified that I could recapture in detail such a favorable memory, and it gave me energy and momentum to continue my investigation into my past.

Those daylight hours that my parents took my brother Mat and I to work with them were pleasant days. The elevated swaying grass was positioned to be on guard and the protector of the maze of paths we had trodden while engaging day after day in our paradise. As you will uncover, paths remained a mysterious and an intriguing necessity in my life, as continually drawn to their undiscovered, and unexpected end. I treasured and enjoyed walking down them greatly as they carved their way into that present landscape. At that moment, they narrowed and wound through the giant grass of the adjacent meadow. I enjoyed not seeing the end of a path from its beginning as it didn't blemish the sense of the unfamiliar and unknown revelation. The grasses persistently grasped for the sky, and they made a great camouflage for our short, undeveloped bodies. Mat my older sibling and I bounced along them only disclosing tufts of red and blonde hair in a rhythmic repetition.

It was the most wonderful aroma….grasses, fresh picked fruits, wooden baskets, and the lunches at noon, "Yummy." A potpourri created in a time never to be repeated in my life. It was something you could not manufacture and happens in a time and place, unexpectedly, as your senses are stimulated, and brain activated to eclipse. They are stored in your memory bank forever to be withdrawn at will, or to surprise you again in a most unexpected time. It was a moment to be enjoyed for many countless years; more than I would have ever imagined at that childish age of almost three.

I watched as the farm workers carefully arranged old wooden crates behind the conveniently stacked mountain of containers. They were struggling to shield their tired, sweaty bodies from the heat of the noon-day sun. Lunch was commonly the highlight of our long days, except for sneaking away to explore some unknown place.

The quiet and sometimes commanding talk was soothing as we listened sitting with our homemade "Zwieback," in hand. This is a Russian Mennonite bun with a small, tiny bite size bun sitting on its top. Baked that way, it is perched as if to portray it was the more prominent of the two, yet both being equally important, although not at all equal in size. As we ate our bun and our homemade plum jam, it was relaxing, and we delighted in the close fellowship. We felt nestled in as it created a comfortable and safe environment.

Watching as the other farmhands drank their tea, they seemed to put excessive importance on equal time while passing the cup from one to another. This cup was aluminum, but some cups were also carved ox horns. The straw is made of metal with a flatter bottom like a miniature golf club. It serves as a miniature sieve for drinking the tea.

It was a tea that they brought in this distinct cup and poured hot water over it from a bulky old metal water pot. It was heated on the old wood burning stove at the farmhouse. I questioned why they shared a cup instead of everyone bringing their own. My parents brought coffee in a jar and their own cups. While conversing, the workers would sip the tea and continuously pass it from one to another. I wondered why our mom and dad never drank this apparently coveted drink. I was young and I never thought of germs. Germs were not talked or thought about much back in the late 1940s and early 1950s. Germs certainly manage to curtail much of our activities in the 2000's and after.

Many years later I found out that the drink was a Mennonite tradition, and my mom was not nurtured with this habit. I don't know where the tradition came from, but a lot of the Mennonites that have come from South America still take part in this habitual drink. They get together evenings and share their *maté* as a group, chatting, chewing their sunflower seeds, and playing games. I have been at these evenings but never partook in the specialty myself.

Our mid-day break was over too quickly, and the farmhands packed up the remains of their lunches. We watched as our mother got up while adjusting her wide brimmed straw hat and walked over to the baskets. As she picked up the container, she urgently called out to us. *"Mateus und Grete, kommt mal her!"* This is German for, "Mateus and Grete, come here."

We ran over and to my delight found a family of mice. Apparently, the young were born in the basket as the stacks of containers sometimes lay in the fields for many weeks. The adult mouse looked trapped and quite harmless, so I could not help but reach into the basket and pick it up.

OUCH! I was bitten by a mouse. The little pinch can still be recalled, but even more the embarrassment of everyone unsympathetically and hysterically laughing as I held my finger and cried. It is still a vivid memory. Of course, years later, I too saw the humor in it.

It was there years ago that I decided that crying just drew attention to yourself and I didn't cry when I was hurt, at least when I could help it. You can imagine the bottled-up tears that would flow when they were finally released. Physical pain never set off those dreaded tears, although emotional pain certainly did. You would think that with this kind of memory, I would protect my children from similar humiliation that without a doubt they have experienced.

Once when I disciplined our son, my heart ached with him so much that it was a matter of laughing or crying. These two emotions were so close that before I knew it, I reacted. I was young and didn't realize what I have learned since and let the emotion of laughter loose. I could have very well cried, as that is what I felt like doing. To cry would have been an example of sympathetic compassion instead of humiliation. His heart was broken seeing me laugh at this inappropriate time and my heart ached at my reaction. It taught me a huge lesson for the future, though keeping those emotions straight has not always been easy.

Back then my brother Mat being older, consoled me and we chased the mouse out of the box. For a moment it felt like we rid the world of mice, once and for all. Later, my dad retrieved a mouse that was caught in the trap in our basement. Mouse traps were normal in those days because everyone I knew had mice in their homes. To display them to your children as my dad did, was just plain gross. The gnawed, arched mouse holes in the wide baseboards were just like the ones you see in pictures, or on the old cartoons. Despite being repulsed by the mouse, I was made to touch the dead bloated body. The trap had caught the mouse just below the neck. It was an ugly sight and every time I heard that trap snap, I could visualize those bloated mice. I'm not squeamish at all, on the contrary, but I still would preferably not see the mice agonize in a trap with the life squeezed out of them.

The farmhands focused on their jobs once more, so Mat and I strolled down one of our paths. We were hidden, and well guarded by the high grass on each side of us while it accompanied our every move. Before we knew it, we had gone too far from everything familiar. Merging onto a path someone else made, we knew we should not be there. It was a place our parents showed us some time before with strict verbal warnings, "Never to go there alone." Of course, the warning came in the German language. German or English, it didn't matter and would not have kept us away.

How beautiful it was, looking like a picture of peace and serenity! We have spoken of this wonderful place countless times. Even as an adult, my husband and I drove there to try to recapture it visually once more. It had the characteristics of my memories but lost its personality and charm after so many years. It appeared somewhat deteriorated by time or was it just because it did not measure up to my childhood imagination. We met the owner of the farm, the son of Mr. Hipple senior, who was so kind and invited us to investigate this place any time, satisfying our curiosity.

My husband and I were invited there that day by Linda who had arranged to have, "certificates of immigration to Canada," presented to some of those who lived and worked on the farm after immigrating to this beautiful country, Canada. Maria, Linda's mother was acknowledged as the oldest living member in the group. It was for our 60th year, as we emigrated in 1949. Dean Allison the MP of Lincoln was invited to extend the congratulations and give out the certificates. It was an awesome day reminiscing and speaking with Mrs. Klassen about the good old days as she reminded me of so many things I had forgotten.

I focused once again to what my brother and I saw so many years ago. Mat and I came to a small clearing where our view was unbroken. There was a tranquil and calm, but a sizeable pond directly in front of us with an island in the center of it. The island was accessible by a narrow wooden plank bridge. Ducks nestled near the shore of the small island as they ruffled their feathers and groomed themselves after their family swim. Occupying their cool retreat as though they had squatters' rights; their movements caused ripples dispersing from the roots of the oversized weeping willow. The tree cradled the pond with its branches reaching low towards the water while reflecting their shade.

It was the kind of place I would go to at a moment's notice, clearing my mind and refreshing my spirit. If there was such a place now, you would find me there often in freedom of expression and meditating. Now that I am grown and time has taught me a few constants, I realize scenes, experiences and smells that I enjoyed as a child also comfort me as an adult. This fact is also true about those dark experiences; they have given me haunting, unsettled, anxious feelings as I travel through this same journey of life.

Our new quest felt so safe, so tranquil, and so welcoming as we enjoyed this forbidden place. We had no choice but to enter the picture. We would have looked perfect on the canvas, if you were painting that scene. It is the style of picture I would appreciate to be able to paint, imparting the serenity perfectly harmonized with my recollection.

Curiosity was a part of my nature and I ventured on. To the right of the glassy pond the freshly cut grass path wove into who knew where. Running through it, I could faintly hear my older brother's warning in German. *"Margarete komm zurück,"* translated he said again, "Margarete, come back." As I ran on ahead, I knew he would follow being the older and responsible sibling. The path left the tall grasses and once again ahead of me lay the peaceful pond. The cut grass looked so pristine, and this place was magic to my young eyes as I quickly scanned the area and again spotted the bridge. What a great place to go, still running while getting out of breath, I arrived under the shade of the weeping willows after crossing the bridge. Panting, I took a small break to look around. The ducks were sent into a flurry of quacking and fluttering as I neared them. They collectively retreated to the middle of the pond as their serenity and time of grooming had been abruptly broken. I turned my clammy body to see where they were going. Feeling a little deserted, I spun just in time to see my brother step onto the wooden bridge behind me. Taking no notice of all the commotion or of the slippery moss and greasy duck droppings, he took one step to cross over the bridge. His responsibility was to harness my disobedient spirit. With a short, loud yell, he slipped and went flying into the water headfirst. The pond was deep, and I watched him franticly gasp and sputter and then he vanished underneath the water. Terror and panic gripped my heart as I turned to go back to the slippery bridge. I saw his arms once again and then he was out of my view permanently. What could I do as we couldn't swim? I screamed uncontrollably and was overcome with indescribable instincts of terror, loneliness and fear. Unexpectedly out of nowhere came a person to help. I could not recall who they were. The person lay down on the dirty slimy bridge and started feeling under the water. I observed quietly and frozen as even their upper body got wet as they partially immersed themselves into the pond. It seemed to take forever, but they finally reached my brother and I recollect that someone pulled Mat up and slid him onto the bank. I don't know if artificial respiration was used, but I know my brother coughed and spit up a lot of water.

Finally, he was able to sit up. Apparently, someone came to look for us as we were nowhere to be found in the barnyard or fields around it. Hearing my screams, they ran to the source of the sounds and located me at the edge of the pond. Why could I not recall who saved my brother. I was good at blocking horrible dramatic times in my life even from that young age and could not recall who it was.

The skid mark on the board was all we could see as we looked at the bridge while crossing to go back. We were forcefully ushered back. My wet drenched brother cried uncontrollably as we returned to the farmyard. Being young, I assumed this was because he was scared that he would get into trouble. Of course, he was crying because of his frightening experience and a spontaneous reaction of nerves. His clothes were dripping, and our feet got muddy as we weren't wearing shoes.

The lane back to the workers was a dirt road. My parents' car was parked in the hot sun on the side of the lane beside the field. This was so the workers and especially our parents could keep an eye on us. I am sure we were made to realize the dangers of what we had done. My parents would not know that my brother was trying to keep me safe. I do not recall being disciplined for our actions, but as usual, we were sent to that hot car to spend the rest of the day away from harm. The windows were left open so we could feel that warm, welcoming intermittent breeze. We spent many hours in that hot vehicle always waiting for the opportune time to escape. Nowadays a parent would have been in trouble if they left a child in the vehicle for that long. The other farmhands had pity on us and often gave us water to drink. Those were different days and we lived by rules of necessity. There was no one to babysit and no daycare; everyone took care of the youngsters as needed while working. Our parents couldn't afford to pay for a babysitter even if there would have been someone available.

I realize at this time that I could have avoided the whole thing if I had listened to my brother. I assure you that this was only one of the many times he warned me, but I did not listen. My parents often agreed that I was a spunky, happy child until the age of three. Then something happened to make me a very sad and cautious child. Why didn't they wonder why I changed so noticeably? The sadness drove me deep within myself, to somewhere safe, somewhere hidden away from the hurts of reality. It felt like a secret hiding place.

Every day was a new experience for me as a very young child. That summer, the clothes I wore, or didn't wear, according to my parents, were part of the game of, "How long do I keep them on." I certainly didn't want to dirty my clothes in the mud puddles or water that I continually seemed to find. I played and got what I wore dirty, so I figured I could take them off and keep them clean!

Our days were spent playing and keeping busy in the farmyard. One of our favorite things to do was just behind the farmhouse. Wondering just how to reach those wrinkled, dried untouchables, we peeked over the tall grass with care. Near the house were the rustic clothes lines, and nearby, an old, wobbly wooden chair. This was a very sunny hot side of the main farmhouse. It was a perfect location for drying laundry, as well as drying those marvelous treats. The flower gardens, as wonderful as they were, never demanded our attention as the fruit did. We dragged the weathered chair over with anticipation of reaching the high planks loaded with the drying fruit as the aroma made our mouths water. The planks were elevated so we could not reach the many trays they held, as well as protecting them from animals. I constantly wrestled with my taste buds and the stringent orders, not to touch the approaching winter treats. It was a dried fruit buffet. All summer the grandmother worked diligently to provide fruit for the family throughout the bitter drawn-out winter. She may have possibly in addition dried vegetables, but I only recollect the apples, plums, pears, and apricots, all remaining to be my favorite to this day. Abruptly we heard an aggressive shout and the elderly lady, still wearing her stained apron, came running in our direction shaking her over-sized wooden spoon in the air. She had been missing a good deal of her harvest and we had been warned to keep our distance. With our mouths full and our hands clutching our favorites, we jumped off the chair into the flower garden. We could always hide in the high flowers until her anger subsided. I couldn't appreciate why the next time she saw us she forewarned us, but never held a grudge or showed anger.

I have since recognized that at her age she was a grandmother and of course, that is just the grandmotherly thing to do. As a matter of fact, I think she might have enjoyed the reality that we loved her dried fruits with passion, as every grandmother enjoys when young people covet their creations.

I wish we had grown to know her as a person. Everyone's life was very busy back then, and this grandmother did not have the time to play or talk with us. In those days, just as now, unless you make it a point to relate, you will let people pass you by only to have regretful thoughts about not getting to know them. These days, grandparents take the time to play and spend time with their grandchildren and form bonds that last in ways long after the grandparents are gone.

The multi-colored flower garden was fragrant with all the perennials displaying their finest unfolding beauty and scents. The tall sunflowers were also prepared for the winter by drying them. I never cared for them as much as I did the dried fruit, probably because at my age I was not able to crack them open and separate the meat from the shell. The plants themselves were extremely tall and everyone seemed to take great pride in their stature. There were discussions about who had the tallest sunflower plants. The hollyhocks, which grew all over the area, reseeded themselves where they pleased. The native to Canada delphiniums, and daisies added even more splashes of color. There must have been a lot more varieties in this garden, although I can't recall them all. A direct path led you through the garden to the side door of the charming, weathered white annex to the old farmhouse. The front door was never used and it was overgrown with shrubs, grasses and trees.

I don't think anyone cut the grass around their homes back then or was it just that way in the places where I had been. The people we knew were too tired from work to put energy into their uncut yards. This is one reason the pond looked so groomed; its grass was manicured until suddenly meeting with the tall wild grasses. I recall from childhood that high wild grass grew where there were no gardens, paths, or dirt roads. I think, therefore, there were so many paths carved into everyone's yards. It was easier to walk on a well-trodden path than struggle through the natural tall ground cover.

I don't recall the fragrance of the flowers, although it was one of the most beautiful gardens to look at. In my album of mental snapshots, I can enjoy the garden at will. The love of gardens has stayed with me throughout my life. Hollyhocks still stop me in my tracks and take me to another place and another time, to the old farmhouse.

My most beloved garden style to this day is called an English garden. I sometimes forget that it takes years of consistency, of letting the seeds fall to reproduce and develop into this kind of splendor. I, of course, want to achieve this look in one or two seasons at the most.

When a tree is just a sapling, I see it in all its glory, beautiful and mature years down the road. I visualize everything mature and aged; although when I plant them, they are undeveloped and small. Planting everything close together gives me the immediate more mature garden appearance. Soon my plants need thinning and spreading out. This has enabled me to distribute and share countless plants with many other gardeners, new inexperienced ones or just ones requiring a helping hand with additional assortment of plants.

2. Left Behind

The workday ended and our inner clock created an awareness of the time! We were drawn back to where the stationary car would take us home. We panicked as we searched everywhere for our parents, discovering there was no car, and no parents! They were generally nearby on the farm, working in a wide-ranging area where we last saw them. The farm appeared forsaken. Eventually, someone emerged from the farmhouse and informed us that our parents had left for home. No one offered to take us to be reunited with them. We had never been permitted to be on our own at the farm without our parents!

With a feeling of abandonment, we decided to head for home by ourselves. The general direction was through a bush, an exceptionally wet bush and two fields. I was afraid of getting lost and was reassured by my brother that he could make his way to get us home. I was barely three, but Mat was just a little older and wiser. We left the lengthy dirt laneway of the farm and headed into a field. I could not see where I was going as I was used to walking on delightful paths that took no effort. These prickly grasses were high and made me itchy and scratchy and I could not see over them. My brother, a measure taller than I, could just gaze above them to adjust our direction. We reached the edge of the meadow and stood in front of a mysterious and dark looking forest. It appeared shadowy and scary, full of underbrush and murky water. Not wanting to enter this creepy place, my hand was taken, and I was pulled along giving my sibling much protest. Our shoes got wet, making me more tense. Would the water get deep, and would we see other dangers? It was a very hot summer and some areas of the water had dried up, nevertheless, I was frightened and didn't feel good about this. My shoes got so muddy, and my feet became very heavy and difficult to lift. Crying to myself, with the odd audible sob keeping myself from looking frightened, Mat's tugging kept me going. We climbed over branches and fallen tree trunks that lay anchored in the water, but most of the time the water was only up to our ankles.

Reassuring me that we would be there soon, my older sibling finally shouted, *"Siehst du!"* meaning, "Can you see!" We were nearing a clearing on the other side of the woods. The sun had lost its intensity as we stood under the canopy of the forest yet giving us a glimpse of daylight. We were peering at the opening in the forest and saw another field in the distance. I was informed this was the last open area to cross as he started yanking once again. It was an unbearable task for Mat to drag me through the tall grasses, never mind the tiresome marsh. When would it end? I was so tired and scared by now, assuring myself that we were lost forever. Meanwhile, Mat started to shout with excitement as we were now on the other side of the woods. We were almost home! There were many ruts in this field, and we stumbled over most of them.

"Only a little further and you will be in the grapery," I was repeatedly told. Of course, that in our mother tongue, German.

Our house was between Highway 8, an old Indian Trail, and the green lush grapery. The vines were so tall and dense that I could not see past them. My brother took me further down the vineyard and told me to look straight down the row. There I could see the roof of our house. It seemed to take forever to walk that row, but we trudged on. We came to the end of our yard and there to the left of us, was the outhouse. I disliked the smell of that small structure but was so relieved to see such a familiar landmark. Just past the outhouse was the small white farmhouse we lived in.

Our parents were outside and entirely oblivious to the fact that we were missing. They were upset and we heard yelling. We struggled through the forest and came back home by ourselves, and nobody cared or noticed. No one said anything about my muddy wet shoes and dirty dress. It seemed there was something bigger and more important to occupy my parents. I don't know what would be more important than knowing where your children were. There was a policeman speaking with my parents and voices were raised even more as my dad spoke. I have no idea what transpired that day, but I was told later that someone stole something from our house. The officer left and that is all I know about that day. The thoughts of my brother having the courage and knowledge to get us home, is something I am grateful for. Our parents had to have been very upset to lose sight of the safety of their children. They usually kept us close at their sides unless they were working on the farm.

3. The Sharp Knife

The house was full of that familiar aroma, the baking of buns. Mom said they would be ready soon. Their scent would not stop beckoning me and I was overtaken with the compulsion to consume one. We would be able to taste their soft warm consistency very soon. Irresistibly, they were cooling on the counter beside the old-style farm sink. The family was enjoying a quiet peaceful evening together in the small living room at the front of the house, when our mom came in to join us.

Realizing there was no one in the kitchen with the freshly baked goods, I ran to help myself. I reached for a long sharp knife to cut that bun in half. Then I would continue to make it perfect by spreading some homemade plum jam on it. This was a jam that had been cooked down to become thick, no "Certo" needed to make it a perfect consistency. It was laden with chunks of plums, which by the way, I didn't like. It is still my favorite flavor of jam to this day, although I puree my plums to get rid of the pieces of fruit.

Being conscientious, I minded what I was doing, after all, this was a sharp bread knife. I heard a loud command to put the knife down. I watched my parents use this tool many times, and assured Mat that I could do the job quite nicely by myself! As Mat was shouting to our mother, she yelled back not to let me cut the bun. Responsible as he was, he grabbed the knife away from me. Of course, I was not about to let go and fought for my right to be an independent three-year-old. Well, you guessed it, blood was everywhere!

The finger next to my thumb on my right hand was cut to the bone in one clean sweep. Mat started to yell for our parents, and I started to scream. I knew it had to be serious with all that blood and it was starting to pain.

It caused a great deal of panic in the house. When cleaned up and dowsed with iodine, the throbbing finger was bandaged. I was told once again not to touch a knife. The reason given was that "I could have cut my finger off." I thought at the time how silly that was. I would never cut my finger off, but my brother most certainly could have done just that.

Sixty or seventy years ago we did not go to the doctor or hospital for stitches, so I was just bandaged up and the cut was left to heal on its own. The cut healed well but left a scar that still pains me when I hit the area at the wrong angle or the weather changes. When it hurts, I just think of how blessed I am to have my finger and how well I came out of that situation, mostly unharmed.

Again, now that I see the situation through mature eyes, I know I should not have touched the knife and listened to my older brother. The scar is always there to remind me of my mishap.

As my grandchildren have acquired some of their own scars, we have had a few conversations when they were very young, regarding them. Their scars make a wonderful reminder of an incident in their lives that they would have preferred to avoid. Although this is true, there is always a lesson to be learned for as long as you live, as well as a reminder to improve.

It is difficult to have good insight into oneself while you are trying to unleash deep feelings of your own. While busy tending to the needs of a demanding active family, there are many distractions. I am so grateful that my children were raised without too many physical scars. More profound is my gratitude that they did not grow up with deep subconscious emotional scars that have crippled me for all those years in the past.

4. Triggers Are Born

All memories of farm life eluded me after my mother left and came home with my baby brother. Such a dramatic happening as having a new baby in the house should have been eventful and happy. I would have enjoyed remembering some of the emotion that would accompany becoming a big sister. All I remember is that I turned from a noisy, inquisitive, happy child to one that was fearful, serious, and sad. I recall our family in a black car taking Mom somewhere to have a baby. The only memories that seem to escape my prison deep within me, are ones connected with fear.

As I thought back, I tried to recall where some of my instinctive triggers in life were rooted and born. I became conscious that they began when Mom was away. My bedroom door represented and became a trigger of great emotional unrest and I dealt with this most of my life, until I learned why. As a child the door was left ajar just a couple of inches and the light from the hall would be left on. My bedroom was dark. I could envision a dark figure standing in front of the crack in the door, then it moved towards me. Even though it provoked panicked and terrified feelings for years, I continually looked at the door to see if someone was there. I couldn't stop looking at the crack in the doorway. I did this for many years later, even well into my marriage. I could only have the door open all the way or closed. The frustrating part was that I did not know why I felt that fear of a partially opened door and I continually had to stare at it. My husband was so gracious for many years, closing or opening the bedroom door and not knowing why I needed that. It feels so freeing now recalling this and knowing where this fear originated. I thank God for a man who tried to understand me even when I did not understand myself. The partially open door became my first trigger.

The first recollection of my baby brother George was when he was about a year old and crying. I was watching him in his crib as he was making that dreadful sound while tossing his upper body from side to side. I felt his distress to the extent that a small child could. Lying there with a brace attached to his shoes and his feet pointing outward, I tried to cheer him up and talked to him gently to stop him from making that terrible wailing noise. Although he was young, we were initiating a pattern for our childhood. In the future he would need my assistance more often than I would have guessed or wanted. This time I would climb right into the crib with him.

The crib was an old metal one with arched rounded ends filled in by hollow tubes. It had also been mine before he was born. Being confined to the crib when you wanted to walk must have been so frustrating. His feet were in high laced up shoes, which in turn were bolted to a metal bar that pointed his toes outward and stretched his feet in the same direction. I don't know how long this brace was worn, but when we moved to the city, he wore them only at night.

5. Yates Street East

The move from our country farmhouse, which we had known as home, took place without any recollection on my part. I not only had a little brother George, but also a little sister Helen, and where did she come from? There was no memory of a baby, or Mom going away to have one. It was like my world was full of the unknown. I couldn't find myself or anyone to help rescue me from my mental absence of reality. I know my parents would have been there and they must have fed and clothed me, as well as having played with my siblings, but why didn't I retain these times!

My thoughts went back to what I could recall. Our basement apartment in town was at the back and bottom of a huge old building. It was on Yates Street East, in St. Catharines and we accessed it by an alleyway between our apartment building and a large office building. Being on a slope, our basement apartment was a walk-out at the back. It had a roofed porch with a large wide, wooden planked deck.

Oversized sliding doors flanked this spacious outdoor living area. They were old, massive barn doors, with gigantic industrial rollers on top and large old hardware. The wide doors were used to close off the loading access, of years gone by. Goods were unloaded from boats docked at the old canal, which we now know as Twelve Mile Creek. At this time, we overlooked an old foundry. We played in our shelter even when it rained to elude our mother's tension. She was easily agitated at the slightest commotion and the energy of our playing.

During thunderstorms Mom made us huddle quietly in a corner with her. I found out years later that Mom became fearful of thunderstorms when she was young and living in Germany, where she and a girlfriend took refuge under a large old tree during a terrible storm when they were only twelve years old. The lightning hit the tree and killed her friend, consequently Mom never got over the fear of storms and she tried her best with her actions, to pass this fear on to us. As far as I know, none of her children ever displayed a fear of storms, other fears yes, but never the weather.

We could see the old canal clearly from our porch, and the chain link fence around our yard gave us great views as well. The underside of the Burgoyne Bridge was the backdrop as we looked to the right of our yard. We would be looking at Highway 406 today, when looking straight ahead.

Our building had apartments with a staircase that ran from the basement to the top floor. Our access to the stairs was in a closet, where at the top of the staircase the door was locked.

These buildings were part of the old city and ran together as one building along the street. They were made into three separate units at street level with their own entrances. They were all accessible to each other in the unused basement level.

Years ago, the covered porches were loading docks, receiving all the goods and wares that were sold on the floors above. The ships would unload at the docks of the canal below. The old canal, now with its turbulent waters, rushed a few hundred feet from our door and our parents would have been apprehensive to live there with us, had it not been for the old chain link fence that secured our safety.

Our days were now a huge change from the farm life that we had been used to, as we had freedom roaming in the country and now were scavengers in the alleys and their garbage bins. As children we didn't miss a beat, but rather immensely enjoyed city life as we appreciated the getting out and exploring. No one complained about using our inside flush toilet instead of that old smelly outhouse from the farm.

When you entered our living quarters from the large old porch, you would go into the living room, then into my parents' bedroom where at the back wall a door led to a deserted unfinished basement. The forgotten basement ran along Yates Street and was an unused space. There were apartments all along the street in these buildings with basements like these. We were told never to enter the door leading to this unused basement area. I do not need to tell you why, but of course I investigated beyond the forbidden doors, and apparently my brother Mat did too, but at a different time.

As I entered, the cold dampness overtook my small frame and I shivered. There were large doors to the left, but I opened the one in front of me. It was heavy and made a noise as it scraped on the cement floor, and I pushed until the door would go no further. It opened enough for me to squeeze through, and I cautiously moved forward advancing with fear in every step as the next room was scrutinized. The dim light still accompanying me from behind from our apartment was consoling. I have taken note that in my life, curiosity was the stronger instinct as fear always gave way to it.

The dark place appeared to have stacks of junk in it, or so I thought, recognizing that if some of that junk was in my possession today, I would appreciate them for the antiques they were. They would be valuable relics of the past, especially one being an old worn chair as it looked cozy, and even then, at that young age it called out for me to sit in it. Charm was not a part of my vocabulary back then, but the feeling regarding this old piece of furniture was described by the word and I used its precious lingering image in my first book, *Past Secret Present Danger*.

Another door induced a desire for me to move forward, but should I? Well, take a wild guess. Seizing all the courage I could muster after the minor interruption of my scattered thoughts, I grabbed the huge door handle and proceeded to pull it open. The rough industrial elongated door handles that felt rusty to the touch, made me want to release them immediately. Unexpectedly, a slight crack of light appeared on the other side of the room as I peeked around the door. There were many barrels and wooden buckets to climb over and making my way through what I perceived as more clutter, I stumbled. Fear getting the best of me, I quickly made my way through the debris to the glimmer of daylight coming through a crack. The dark, minute basement window which had gathered many years of street dust, gave me a gloomy dim bit of daylight. As I frantically opened the door, the sun blinded my eyes. My hands quickly covered my eyes and after pausing a moment I peeked through my fingers noticing the outdoor stairway. A heavy black iron railing surrounded the stairs preventing anyone from falling into the stairwell, from the sidewalk above. I was nearing the top of the incline and it took a few steps to reach the sidewalk, where being at street level, I noticed that I had played here many times with my friends. I was elated and felt like I accomplished a great feat, as well as having a wonderful secret. Ending at the top of the street, I skipped down the sidewalk past the grand cement steps that led to the dwellings above ours. Stopping at the long narrow alleyway leading to my safe home, I decided not to tell my parents of this adventure, but I confided in my brother and some of the playmates in the neighborhood and discovered, I was not the only one who had been snooping.

Our alleyway was a safe one, until one day a teen boy stood at the street entrance calling for us to watch him. Holding a cat in the air by its tail, he continuously swung it. The cat was screeching and making strange noises as we ran to tell our mother. You guessed it, by the time she hurried back with us, he had disappeared; we were afraid after that horrible scene and used caution when we left the yard via the narrow alleyway. This was our only way out, and if that wasn't bad enough, we found that our new neighbor, was that same "Boy Terror."

We were told not to look, not to talk, and just stay away from the adjoining side of the yard and it was a tough job at our age not to look over there. Can you imagine challenging your children not to look over to the yard next door and expecting it to be so? All my mind could do was think, "Look over there, what is he doing now?" The never-ending drama displayed in the neighboring yard was consuming to us.

The precious ball that kept us occupied every day went over the chain link fence. While trying to figure out how to retrieve it, a loud voice shouted, "Watch this!" As we looked over, we heard *"Bang!"* The ball had been stabbed with a large knife! We were deflated like our ball and were called into our house to lick our wounds.

The last recollection about those neighbors was seeing their dog laying in the yard with foam coming out of its mouth. Never had we seen such a sight and our mother went to the neighbor's and called the "dogcatcher." This is what he was known as in those days. Soon after we heard the foulest language ever to penetrate our ears as it was repeated in anger and there was so much violence that the police were called. When all was quiet some other men came out to the yard using a long pole with a muzzle attached to it and put the dog in a cage. We had pity on the dog as it seemed so sickly, but still thinking it would get better soon, we were consoled, not realizing the dog probably had rabies and was put down as we never saw the dog again. The neighbors relocated shortly after, and we felt sheltered and safe once more.

For a while the now serene quiet neighborhood was only interrupted by the clip clop of the horse drawn ice and milk wagons. The bell from the wagon signaled for us to hurry and get some free pieces of ice as there were always ice chips to crunch on helping to cool those hot days of summer. These were pieces that dropped from the wagon as the iceman used large picks to carry his deliveries.

We were babysitting our little brother George and as usual he followed us everywhere and wanted to play with his siblings. One day he escaped out of the gate when the milkman was delivering, and in no time, he was up the alley towards the street. We were there admiring the horses and carriage and wondered how it would feel to have a ride on it. As we watched the milkman, he commanded the horses to go forward, and we all heard a *clunk*. Immediately halting the horses, he jumped off only to find, yes, our little brother George under his delivery wagon. Thankfully, he was in the middle between the wheels. There were milk bottles everywhere from the sudden halt and the bucking horses. Carefully checking him over, he picked George up to take him down the alley to our mother. She was already running towards her screaming child and the stunned delivery man. George with his chubby pale face wet from crying, jerked his shoulders with each sob as Mom was trying to comfort her youngest son and we watched as his little body was felt and stroked to make sure nothing was broken. While the milkman was hovering over the two, our mother was trying to console both the man as well as her child; with broken English and a heavy German accent, mother decided her little fellow would be fine. Stroking his thick blonde hair, she held him close and led us back down the alley to safety, listening to the last apologies of the milkman echoing behind us. We learned to watch out for the young ones, but we were only children, and made many judgment calls leading to many other mishaps.

It was fall, the season for me to finally attend school. I was prepared for kindergarten only by being told I was going to school the next day. My brother knew no English when he started school and had a difficult time learning the language as well as doing the schoolwork. Our parents were oblivious to homework and there was none done in our home, never mind helping with schooling and this became evident as we struggled on our own and got poor marks and even failing our assignments.

The day I started school was a disaster as it started with my mother and brother Mat walking me to school. I felt so alone as they both left; even my older brother was not going to my school as I went to St. Andrews Ward School in 1953 and he would come by after attending Memorial School to pick me up and we would walk home together. I had learned a little English from my older brother and the children in the neighborhood while playing. It was helpful to know what the children were saying.

My school was on the other end of town from Mat's school. Mat had to do a lot of walking every day, and at noon we went home for lunches, eating quickly under pressure to get both of us back to school. I have no memory of being in a classroom or who my teacher was at this school, only of the fear and loneliness that I felt. I was still in kindergarten when I was told that I would attend Mat's school, since my school was closing.

The kindergarten class was a new addition to Memorial School on Welland Avenue, and it was bright and cheery. I was fond of my teacher and seemed very content for the remainder of the year while making many friends; it was a secure feeling to go to the same school as Mat and I enjoyed the semesters spent in kindergarten. I was taught to tie my shoelaces on one of those bulky, brightly painted wooden shoes, I now recognize as primary colors.

There was a girl in my class whose dad was a doctor, and she often wore beautiful dresses with hand smocking that made such an impression on me.

I didn't know what the embroidery was called until I was grown up, and later as an adult and grandmother it gave me great pleasure to smock my granddaughters' outfits. Smocking is still deemed to be unique to me, even now, as it did when I was five years old. I had no idea at the time the labor of love it took to make my playmate's dresses, as she had many of them in various colors. Fifty years later it still requires the same amount of work, and I was so appreciative to a friend in our church Mary, for teaching me this ageless and extraordinary form of needlework. She will have a special place in my heart for imparting her knowledge of this delightful, long-standing craft to me.

Grade One was completed at the same school. I had what I considered an elderly teacher and can still see her standing over me. The location of the classroom and a lot of details of this moment are still well defined, even now. The room was located at the left front corner of the school facing it from Welland Avenue. The classrooms were situated around a substantial open auditorium area.

While learning to count to one hundred, I was not comprehending and seeing the pattern, and I was not able to repeat the numbers. I kept turning my numbers around and expressed them in the wrong order. We had been informed to practice at home with our parents. That of course could not happen as my parents did not know how to count in English themselves. I can still recall the scene clearly. While sitting at my desk, I was asked to count to one hundred and I just could not do it. It was explained to me repeatedly until the teacher was frustrated beyond her constraint as she marched over to me with a strap while I was seated. She commanded me to stretch out my hand towards her, right there in front of my classmates. She must have assumed I was trying to be defiant while I obeyed and stretched out my hand and she brought the strap down on my hands three times. OUCH! That was a humiliating sting. After beginning to cry without end in sight, the teacher got furious, and I cried lacking any control while she got angrier and angrier. This was the last straw for her, and I was sent to stand in the hall to stop crying. Once I started to cry, I could not control this emotion, and this has been one of the constants throughout my life. A half hour later I was commanded and pulled back into the classroom before another class came by the hall for rotation. She declared she did not want to be embarrassed by me standing outside her class crying. My parents were never told about the strapping, but I longed for my parents to have helped me in my schoolwork but was never assisted or even encouraged. Although this was not a good experience and there were many other ways of handling the situation, I held no anger towards the teacher. Instead, I blamed myself for not being able to learn and was embarrassed about it.

There were pleasant times playing with my friends after school and discovering more about our city playground. My brother and I did not even walk home together most days as we would go our separate ways to play with friends.

I had a playmate whose parents lived above a restaurant they owned on St. Paul Street, St. Catharines and we had such an awesome season roller skating from one end of town to the other. Having visions of this, I hope we were courteous to the pedestrians. Our roller skates were the old ones which you clamped onto your shoes and tightened with a key. After our heated, prolonged excursions, we headed for her restaurant where her mother would give us both an ice cream cone. The oriental family was the sweetest and treated me with such kindness. We were also allowed to go to the back entrance of their apartment on the top floor. Not really into their home but up the back stairs to the fire escape. It went up about five floors from the ground level at the back. The restaurant's location is now the Meridian Center walkway area. We talked and many times played with her yo-yo on those back stairs.

The city buildings all looked so chaotic from the back. The small landings had many little shack-like structures perched on them. It just appeared so untidy but from my point of view as a child, so attention-grabbing. I never drive on the highway behind the city without reminiscing to myself and constantly admiring the cleanup that has gone on in the last few years. People that aren't comparing it to the past, wouldn't agree that it looks distinctive and orderly now, but you should have seen it then. Of course, I experienced it up close and not from a distance.

Another classmate whose company I delighted in spending time with, was from the other side of the tracks, the advantageous side and I assumed she had everything a person could ever want. We played together on many occasions in her family glass business on King Street, joy riding on the elevator, we snacked on things I never had before or could afford. I experienced the interior of a store from angles most people didn't see.

A much-loved memory is a birthday party for my friend that was held at her home, and her parents picked me up after checking with my parents of course. Many times, we travelled past this home as a family, and I felt like stopping to say *hi,* even though we hadn't seen each other for so many years. I find it so fascinating how childhood friends remain in your heart throughout your whole life, awaiting to be a rekindled bond at a moment's notice. These were the kind of people you just want to touch base with and see how they were doing.

There was a sizeable train set in their lower level, which etched its way into my mind. This was the most elaborate and magical train set depicting reality in ways I had never seen before. So much so that when we had our son, we surprised him with a train set. I enjoyed working on it with my husband. Developing the landscape, making the bushes, trees and mountains was a delightful past time and my visions of what my kids would see, was nothing but a dream come true.

My friend's birthday party was wonderful, and I had experienced a new way of life, if, just for one day and it would kick start me to dream bigger dreams. Coming from a needy family wasn't something I was aware of until sometime later, but I already knew we could not buy many things that others could afford, but never knew we were poor.

For my birthday I invited my friend to play with me at my home. It was a wonderful day for me one of the first of rare days that I could invite a friend over to my house. We never expected to have any of the trendy toys everyone else took for granted, and so it was certainly wonderful when I received a T- shirt with the hero of the time, "Davy Crockett," on the front of it. It was trendy! Everyone at school was singing the song, "Davy, Davy Crockett, the King of the Wild Frontier." The whole family appreciated my trendy gift and made a big deal about it, but as usual, all good things come to an end and so did my special day. My friend and I played many times that summer at her parents' place of business. She had to go to work with them on many occasions and spent time there until closing.

Behind the buildings of downtown, Mat and I investigated the garbage in the alleyways, and we found boxes of office waste. Every time we came home with more carbon paper, our mother became hysterically angry; what child could understand this reaction until having their own children? You know how the old carbon paper would have transformed clothes, hands, and everything else it would touch. We found small pencils and old fountain pens, only to be commanded to throw everything out except for the pencils, as they were valued as a useable and a necessary item. After some time, we learned not to bring these precious items home but play with them there in the alleyways behind the stores, wondering how she knew, we never understood how our mother always knew of our activities.

Getting home from school at noon, became more and more difficult as we only had one hour to get out of school, stop in at least two laneways, get home, eat lunch, only to run back to school, reaching it always on the sound of the bell. I learned to loathe the sound of that bell after lunch. Of course, a little over a year at this school was too long and we were transferred to another school in town, but at the far end of our city.

Walking to Robertson School gave us no time to hunt for anything. It left us disconnected with no friends once again. Our home life was still strained with an internal never-ending war and every area of our lives was in upheaval.

We loved the parades downtown and there were many small ceremonies with bagpipes and marching bands. The little park beside the now CKTB building, known now as, "The White House," had many wreaths put on its monument as we stood and watched and I had no idea what it was all for, but it brought out a lot of uniformed people and I enjoyed the activities. Later I realized the largest gathering was a Remembrance Day ceremony at the Cenotaph, where the wreaths were so exquisite, and I wondered why no one ever stole them. After all, they were just lying there out in the open, even through the night.

The few months in grade two at Robertson School in 1955 were uneventful, except for being unexpectedly called into the principal's office. The serious look of the principal and the secretary in the room, was very intimidating. They asked me many questions about a little girl that lived near us. I knew where she lived and met her in the neighborhood many times. The principal asked how often I saw her and what we talked about. They also wanted to know what age she was and if I could convince her to start school. I responded that I would try to convince her to come to school with me.

She lived in the oversized, shabby looking two storied house that was encompassed with verandas, and was once a beautiful house, but now run down and unkempt looking, giving a foreboding look as it stood in the distance by itself. I had spoken to this little girl a few times when she came up our street with her brothers. We could see her house when we looked to the right, down the hill at the end of our street. I had such compassion for her even then, for I knew she was not cared for and loved in the same way we were.

One day her dad came looking for her as she was hanging out with us on the front steps of our building. Swearing with angry overtures, he rode up with his bicycle, a view I will never forget. It was a dark, hand painted bicycle with a large carrier containing a cardboard box mounted on the front, in which my tiny-framed friend often sat as her dad rode around town. He was of small stature, but I feared him and this time he was especially scary, and his anger was out of control as he picked her up by her ears and jerked her into the carrier. I was in awe that ears could be used that way, as our mother only pulled ours for discipline and we thought that was painful enough. I wondered if ears could fall off and I decided he must have been very worried about her, although I knew that this was not the way to act. I remember thinking how thankful I was, that her dad was not my dad.

The day arrived when I was supposed to take her to school, but there was no one to join me except my brother. I had to report to the office regarding my absentee neighbor, and that was the end of seeing this little girl for many years. They moved to another location without any notice. As an adult we crossed paths again, or should I say she crossed my path like a bulldozer. I say this as she has been in need for one thing or another most of her life as she has made some unwise choices and fallen on hard times.

While we were living downtown, we seemed to adopt a gentleman who came from Germany, but I don't know how he met our family. After living in Canada a while, he was joined by his soon to be fiancée. My bed was just inside the bedroom in the traffic area where everyone walked and one evening, I peeked as they got engaged. Naturally, I was supposed to be sleeping like my other siblings.

This couple had such a powerful impact on us children and I considered them a gift of love. We have spoken of them many times and still see them occasionally. They were so kind and charitable to each other, as well as to our family. This is the first time in my life that I noticed how couples in love acted towards each other. It was evident that our parents had some marital problems, although what was really happening, we as children did not understand. Ernst and Rosa took us for walks and babysat us at times. Having no relatives around, we had never experienced an aunt or an uncle. All our family, grandparents, aunts, uncles, cousins, everyone lived in Germany. My dad's mother and relatives were captured and taken to Siberia where they now lived still prisoners. Our uncle Gerhard lived in Winnipeg, Manitoba, and was married also starting a family of his own. Mom's family lived in Germany, but no one could afford to travel that far in those days so we didn't grow up knowing what an extended family could be like. I believed this young couple was our family.

For Christmas I received a doll buggy from them, which had a canvas top that had been painted a soft attractive cream color and looked like new. It was secondhand, picked up from somewhere and they fixed it up and painted it to look awesome. My little sister received a little wooden highchair with an old doll dressed in a newly sewn outfit. It was the best Christmas that I can remember, not just for the toys but the feeling we all had of harmony and love.

Having orange crates for their end table didn't seem to destroy this couple's initiative to improve their lifestyle, because soon after, they were able to afford to move to another apartment. It was in a better part of town, and they were able to buy some new furniture. Visiting them was always a family treat and we loved their modern furniture and above all, their young attitudes. After they started their family, there was always time to make us feel special and make our visit a time of joy. They later moved out of town and although we saw them from time to time, their absence left an immense hole in our lives. We missed their attentiveness while living close to our family.

There was another family in our lives at that time who had twin girls and an older daughter who was getting married. Not until years later, did I find out that my parents received them into their humble home when this family first came from Germany. The Bleich family slept at our place where they were made to feel welcome, and Mom proved over and over to be a compassionate and giving person in this way, as she loved helping those in need. This family thrived in this land of opportunity and soon moved out and improved their lives. The first encounter with twins I had, was their daughters. They looked identical and I was always trying to figure out how two people could look so alike. They seemed very close, and I wished for a twin that looked just like me. I would never be lonely if I had someone like me around. Naturally, wishful thinking did not create reality and that didn't happen.

Bleichs took me for walks to those beautiful areas behind our fenced yard where the paths led to the sizeable Burgoyne Bridge. It was the largest bridge I had ever seen up to that time. Below the bridge lay so much hidden beauty, as there were paths with flowers that led to under the bridge and continued to a rock garden park. With much kind heartedness they led me as we walked this amazing place.

We were in touch with this family for many years until my parents gradually pulled themselves and us away from them. Again, we were left with so many unanswered questions regarding relationships.

Those exceptional gardens beneath the bridge are accompanied by memories of me running their paths with the other children. I can still smell the ground cover, and low flower patches along the stone paths, and amongst the rock boulders as well as the blooming fragrant bushes.

I am not proud of the time we cautiously and quietly snuck up to get close to the oversized box used to sleep in under the bridge. It was a shelter for the homeless beside the pillars of the bridge and we kicked the boxes with the homeless napping in it. They were aroused and terrified while crawling out with angry scowls on their faces so we all ran as quickly as we could to get away, although there was no danger. Granted, being children, we did not realize that they were harmless.

We had been told never to go down there under the bridge, so we thought they were bad people. Never to go on our own was the rule, but naturally we did not listen. Our impressions of these people were that they would hurt us as they looked unkempt. I have become more compassionate and changed my attitude towards the less fortunate by now, being knowledgeable of how harmless they were and how life has taken a bad turn for them.

They had nothing but a box to sleep in, even in the bitter cold winter, snow and all. It was not like today where there are shelters for the homeless in different areas of town. Sometimes they had an old mattress, dragged from the furniture store close by and carefully placed into their huge cardboard box. Often there were smoking fire pits with empty cans lying around. We also saw a quantity of empty alcohol bottles, and wondered why people would live like that?

I could not understand that at my age, but I remember wondering who loved them and where were they? Now I have the knowledge that life is not always fair, and everything is not always in our control. I am thankful for what I have and how we can be more understanding to those around us, especially those less fortunate.

Occasionally people would drive by with a huge truck and clean up everything in sight, and we noticed that it didn't take long before it was all back again. I remember considering and speculating where they slept in between.

It was not long after our cruel act that our mom gave us some sandwiches to take to the homeless, providing we all stayed together. It was as if she knew we had to make a wrong, right. We were so excited with anticipation as we walked down the path to under the bridge, and as we neared, we saw everything had been cleaned up once again and no one was there. Our hearts sank as we placed the sandwiches down on the cement foundation under the bridge near to the blackened remains of their campfire. We hoped they would return to eat the sandwiches as we sadly and quickly ran back to report to our mother, and she suggested that someone would discover and enjoy them.

On a frigid, blizzardy, winter's night, we were ordered to get out of our warm beds, and when barely dressed we were dragged up the alley to the street from our warm safe apartment. Where were we going at this time of night? It was late and dark and cold.

As we crossed the huge bridge, my hands and legs felt sharp biting pain as the wind blew freezing air under my dress and coat as the driving snow blew around our young bodies. We questioned our mother often as to where we were going, only to be answered with sobbing and crying. She must have had a hard time carrying our little sister, but we didn't think about that at the time. Realizing only the weight of pulling our little brother George along, Mat and I just hoped we would soon be there; not sure where that was. Without a doubt a child can be made to go just about anywhere, as in total confusion, we blindly followed where we were led, and we trusted our mother every step of the way.

As we reached the other side of the Burgoyne Bridge, I was a little relieved. The blowing snow, bitter cold and poor visibility had given me the most insecure feeling while walking across its massive length. I was seeing through a child's eyes, and it felt like the wind was trying to blow us right over the rail. Next, we walked across the train bridge and continued down the road, finally turning onto a side street and then into a driveway that I recognized.

We arrived at our friends, who used to live at the Hipple farms too. Mom knocked anxiously on the door. Freezing and shaking, the door could not have opened quickly enough. Our friends, the Klassen family, lived in a mobile home park, but it was so late that it seemed like an eternity for the man of the house to answer the door. With a startled look, and a questioning face, he quickly ushered us into his warm sanctuary.

With so many questions directed at our mother, we sat down bewildered and mystified. They did not want us to know anything, so, consequently sent us to the next room, while the talking continued for hours, or that is how it seemed to us. My mother must have had great confidence and trust in these people to come all this way by foot with her young fragile family, especially on this cold blizzard night.

A considerable time later my dad knocked at the door, and another prolonged talk took place I kept peeking around the corner to see what was happening when the conversation got quieter and I never understood what transpired, except that I saw my mom and my dad on their knees at the end of that night. It didn't make sense to me, but I always remembered that they were on their knees praying. I wondered what kind of desperation drove Mom out of the house with her family in tow.

Later we all went home in our family car. It was a much warmer drive home although the car was not upholstered and heated like the cars of today. The seats were wooden and hard. I discovered years later that Dad accused Mom of having an affair with someone who used to drop by for lunch often. It would have been difficult to do this with the children always there for lunch. My parent's marriage was one of mistrust. Years later I would find out why.

6. Impacted

But I pray to you, in the time of your favor;
in your great love, O Lord, answer me with your sure salvation.
— Psalm 69:13

George and Helen were baptized at Grace Lutheran Church sometime during our stay at this downtown apartment. George wore a bright white shirt and bow tie with his black pants, and he looked like a miniature man, as that is what most men wore in those days. Helen was adorned with a beautiful light blue chiffon dress and an over-sized ribbon in her thick wavy hair, and she looked so lovely, and I wished I was that beautiful too. Usually, children were baptized as babies and then were confirmed to profess their faith. It was a time where Grace Lutheran Church took interest in our family while Mom and Dad were taking steps towards raising their family for God.

There was an exceptional young man who went to Grace Lutheran church where my younger brother and sister were baptized. This committed person picked up Mat and I for Sunday school. Our parents never came to church with us but that never bothered me at this time in my life, as mother always got us ready in our best to go with this stranger. Sunday after Sunday we would wait for him at the bottom of our alley. It was the beginning of my love affair with God. I say this because it was the first time I was able to go to church and get to know who God was. I learned to love Him and yearned to meet with Him even as a child.

We didn't have the latest styles; rather clothes bought at the Salvation Army, or something Mom had made. This being true, they were always clean and crisply pressed.

Our shoes were polished in a traditional fashion every Saturday and then purposefully lined up in a straight row by the outside door, in the rustic old porch. We were left with the feeling that this was something to be proud of, and to this day it gives me a sense of fulfillment to polish my shoes. The transformation that occurs with just a little bit of elbow grease and polish, always amazes me.

Even more remarkable, was the difference God made in our lives with this young man doing as God prompted him to do. My brother Mat and I were so impacted by this person who was willing to pick us up, and then teach our class, never missing a Sunday. Week after week we learned to hear God's voice through his deed and words.

One Sunday we waited in the alley for our ride to Sunday school as usual. Suddenly a pigeon flew overhead, and you guessed it, the droppings landed right on my shoulder. I ran inside where the stain was quickly worked on, and in a few minutes, I was ready for our driver. I looked up to him, admiring him not for his looks, although he was probably a good-looking gentleman, but for picking us up. It took sacrifice on his part as he also had to pick up his wife and daughter for church before teaching our class.

Another Sunday morning as we were waiting for our ride to church, a policeman startled us and asked to see our dad. Taking him inside to our parents we wondered what would happen and he let Dad know there was a complaint, that the pigeons were let out to fly around. It was against the law to raise pigeons in town if you let them fly freely. We all went to the pigeon house just off the large, covered porch and watched as the policeman checked things out. My father was telling him that our pigeons never got out to fly around town like many others, but we were served pigeon on Sundays for dinner instead of chicken and it was true, our pigeons were totally closed in by a large, cubed structure made of chicken wire. It was so large that an adult could walk in it, but I don't know if they flew free or not, but my brothers say they did. The officer just repeated that he was sorry, but you could not raise pigeons in town, and that was that. Our driver arrived to take us to Sunday school, and we left still upset about the visit.

My heart was crushed, and I felt defeated when I found out that we were relocating again. It was not that we were moving to the country, I cared less about where we were going, but had concerns about our ride to Sunday school. Being reassured by our driver that nothing would change, I felt at peace.

Still in grade two, it would be difficult to attend yet another school, making different friends and having a new teacher. Our parents were oblivious and certainly didn't care what time of year they moved us from one school to another.

It was around this time of my life that my consciousness of who I was and what God was to me generated an awareness that I truly needed Him. During one of the lessons taught by our driver and teacher at Grace Lutheran Church, I asked God to be in my life and love me, forgive me of my sins and be my best friend. Our teacher explained the plan of salvation in such a simple way that it became very clear as to what my actions had to be. This was not done loudly or vocally but in the quietness of my heart and mind sitting there in Sunday school. With my head bowed, I realized that I was a sinner and God would forgive my sins if I asked Him. It was such a revelation to me and changed my life forever. No matter what, from that time on, I went to God for everything. He filled such a void in my life and for the first time I received unconditional love. This fulfillment happened in the quiet places of my mind and heart, giving me a genuine impression of being loved that made a difference in my reality. Sitting peacefully in my chair at the end of Sunday school I had a life changing conversation in my head with God. The lesson was on love and our teacher laid out the plan of salvation and gave an invitation to his class. I felt I could confide in no one of my deep hurt and hidden pain but God. God wanted to set me free. With this revelation of God came more knowledge of battles I needed to fight and win.

There were triggers that I had no idea about and I went through a terrible inner battle of noticing men's pant zippers. You might think this strange, but it was a compelling thought pattern that embarrassed me, although I could not stop thinking about this one area. Even sitting in front of my Sunday school teacher as part of his class, I had these terrible thoughts and couldn't control them as it was a secret inside me that even I did not know about. What did those feelings mean? It was confusing, bewildering, and fearful. Why did I feel this way? Every man hid something that made me feel terrible and guilty, but I couldn't understand it at my age. I would listen to the lessons and become so blushed from my thoughts, although my thoughts went no further than that fly and zipper, but why! I was so uncomfortable, and this crippled me with anxiety and the fear of danger, but I worked diligently to control my mind and thoughts, becoming very successful at it.

7. Despair

I was completely disheartened when our Sunday school driver had to stop picking us up as his family was expanding and there was another child on the way. It just became too difficult for his family, especially since we were now, so far out of town. I was just starting to grow in knowing what God wanted and who He was to me, and now would have to leave Sunday school.

My despair gripped the most inner part of my being. I didn't know the God I had met could perform miracles, and cause situations that I could not even dream of. Being unaware that God was in control, I went on with my life as best as I could.

I felt crushed, but never blamed our driver in my heart. As an adult I would have loved to tell this man what he imparted into my life, and how he directed me towards a path of transformation and healing, but trust that my God will let him know how much his good works meant to me, and how he impacted my life with the introduction of God.

I was angry with my parents as going to Sunday school was the one thing that I loved and looked forward to. God made me feel alive and good about myself. I felt worthy because of Him. I was just getting to experience God and didn't know if He would stay with me, if I didn't attend Sunday school.

We now lived on the second floor of a two-story farmhouse, and this is where our dad worked as a farmhand for the Wiley Farm. It was on the opposite end of town from the church and from where our driver lived, and I felt isolated and lonely without Sunday school.

My mother loved moving furniture around, so we slept in every bed-room at one time or another. It was a freezing winter and for the first time

I realized I didn't like the cold of this season. That winter, the four of us kids got the measles. We were all put into the largest front room together. Heavy sheets were hung over all the windows, and we were told never to look at the daylight or we would go blind. This was a challenge of course and we went into the hall and looked out of the large window at the end of it and waited. We didn't go blind immediately, but the children tattled on each other and of course we got our punishment, a spanking and a yelling at, then there was nothing to do but wait to go blind as Mother assured all of us that this would happen. After a couple of days, I forgot about going blind and went on with life as I knew it.

Often experiencing loneliness, I was setting the printing press of my life to copy the same habitual patterns and feelings to live by. These patterns would be repeated while I did not even realize the kind of foundation that my surroundings were creating. I recognized much later, as God showed me how to discipline myself to correct my behavior.

As I lay in bed at night, terrible sounds came through the heating vents from downstairs. It was my mother crying bitterly for hours and I lay in bed assuming I was the cause of her crying. After some time, my father would go to console her and I could hear them talking in the empty, echoing room downstairs. The downstairs apartment was vacant, and I could never understand totally what they were talking about, but I felt like it was my fault. I believed to be the cause of those arguments between my mom and dad, and continually felt unloved by my mom as it seemed she just did not like me. The tormenting cries persisted while we lived there, continuing night after night! To my surprise, my siblings don't recall any of this as they slept through it all. I had a very difficult time sleeping and even when I fell asleep, I would wake up intermittently and lie there awake for hours. I was afraid of something, and continually looked for the light on the other side of the partially opened door.

The door being ajar bothered me to such an extent, that I woke up and immediately had to focus on the door to make sure everything was as it should be. Was someone standing at the threshold? The habit of staring intently at the door stayed with me for years, even as an adult when I couldn't figure out why I did this or why I was afraid of seeing a shadow of someone in the doorway. It is now controlled, and I say to myself, "No, there is no one there so I don't have to look at it." I must say, I still prefer doors open or closed. At this time, it is only an instinctive response that can easily be rationalized and put into perspective. At the age of 70, I can wake up and not even think of looking at the door, "Knowledge brings freedom," and I am so grateful for that. God's perfect will is for us to be free, but for myself it was a grueling task to acquire this freedom through knowledge although God was leading me towards conquering this restriction in my life. I had so much to let go of and had to learn and mature into that knowledge and freedom.

When I was young, telling lies was an uncontrollable habit. They seemed so real at the time that I was telling them, so much so that there was not even the slightest prick in my conscience for lying. We had friends over one day and I told many stories of kissing a boy, and it wasn't even true. To my parents it was an outrageous thing to talk about, even to say you kissed! At supper time my brother told my parents, and they became very angry. My mom and dad got into such an argument at the table after telling me how bad I was for saying those things. My mother left the table in tears. I had done it again. Why couldn't I be different?

I felt like no one loved me. It is difficult to describe why a person would feel so totally rejected. I was a normal child living with a financially and emotionally struggling family and it was nothing too dramatic. As time went on, the causes of who I was becoming were revealed to me, but not without many desperate hours, searching and weeping as reality became all too clear.

Mountainview School at that time was a two-room school, not like the city school with auditoriums and two levels, in comparison it looked like a house with a bell on it. The winter's day was cold, and our water had frozen, but my older brother Mat went to school, and I stayed home. Upon arriving at school, the teacher asked my brother if I was sick, and he told her about our water problem. She asked if he washed his face with water and he replied," Of course, yes, I did." She was interested to know how he did that without water, and he said, "I melted some snow." This sounded doable to the teacher, so she sent him on the long walk home to bring me back to school.

We could stay home any time we felt like it. Going home to pick up his younger sister was not an easy task. We had no phone to call for a ride, so we walked to and from school in the coldest weather. I quickly got ready and went to class with him after he stated that the teacher expected me at school.

Thinking about it now, I believe the teacher knew I needed the class time. She was not so concerned about our faces being washed, rather about our education. She showed patience and concern when caring for her students and I liked the kindness of my teacher.

Her thoughtfulness showed at Christmas when the class drew names for a gift exchange and I do not know who I drew, but remember who pulled my name. The day had come, and we all opened our presents, after which we were dismissed to go home but I hid mine. My brother of course would see that I had received a little black car, which by the way, he liked. The following day the teacher asked everyone what he or she received for a Christmas gift. Being so disappointed and embarrassed about my gift, I said I could not remember what I received. Back then a car was an unacceptable gift for my gender and finally seeing the embarrassment on my face, she asked my brother what I got. He boldly reported that it was a car, and I did not like it because it was a boy's toy. She totally agreed and asked who brought the toy and why it was a boy's gift.

The boy conveyed his mother forgot to check the name and bought a boy's gift, and following that, the teacher displayed wisdom and kindness to my classmate. She made sure he did not feel guilty about this situation, saying it was all right and not his fault. She asked if I could bring the toy the next day and in the morning upon handing her the car, she handed me a wrapped gift. Opening it I found a beautifully illustrated book written by Beatrice Potter, called *Peter Rabbit*. It is so unexpected how little things touch you so deeply. They become a part of who you are and what you love as an adult. My grandchildren were all started on Beatrice Potter's video that I had purchased. I had forgotten about the book I received from the teacher, until as a grandmother I saw the book, *"Peter Rabbit"* again. I recognized it as the same books and video stories that I enjoyed reading along with my grandchildren.

As a child I looked and read that book until it literally fell apart, until Mom forced me to throw it out, as it got so tattered. To this day I wish I could have kept it as it was such a precious gift to me and it was the first book that I owned, and one that was just mine.

School became drudgery for me, especially the recesses and lunch hours, although class time was scheduled and went quite quickly. I told so many lies that I could never have redeemed myself with the students, and how could I expect them to be my friends?

If you have a child that cannot distinguish their lies from the truth, there is more going on than meets the eye. Every child learns the difference between truth and lies, but if there is a compulsion that can't be controlled, there could be something deeper going on. Look at your children from the perspective of not the lie but what is causing it. Big or small, the lie is not the problem, rather what is prompting it as all children go through a time of lying and the growth of curbing and confronting the deceit.

On the farm there was a large, dilapidated barn which was totally collapsed on one side, and of course we were told never to go near it. A raccoon with her kits would sit on the barn boards and clean her young and I gazed out of the two-story window and watched intently as she took such care of them. I sat there wondering how she knew what to do and how lucky she was to have her family around her. I had my family around me too, but why didn't that fulfill my life, it should have been good but the cloud over my head became heavier.

Dad came home from work early one day after he had been chopping wood and the axe struck his head. He made a dramatic entrance into the house covered with his blood. Mom dressed his wound and he healed up nicely after wearing the bandages for quite some time.

On another occasion Dad was going to teach Mom how to drive, so we were all loaded into the car for a little driving lesson. It was such a memorable day as she was sitting behind the wheel and doing fine, when unexpectedly, the car got too close to the deep, wide ditch. The wheels started to slide when she steered the car right into the ditch. Mother, being very spontaneous, stepped on the gas instead of the brakes, ending up adjacent to the grape post. Somehow, she turned the wheel, and we crossed the ditch and ended up on the road again, and what a ride it was!

She quickly got out of the car and took her place in the passenger's seat and announced that she never ever wanted to drive the car from the driver's seat again. From that time on she developed the practice of being a back seat driver and I must say she did a consistently good job at it. If Mom was in the car, you never needed a GPS, as she knew every turn and told you when to make that steering wheel rotate. Dad on the other hand was not such a great navigator, getting lost many times without his co-pilot.

On one occasion Dad announced that we would take a little day trip to somewhere new, and we were excited, but it seemed to be a long drive. We travelled past Yates Street, where we lived before, down St. Paul Street and through St. Catharines, along Queenston Street past the huge General Hospital. I was fortunate not to have seen the inside of this massive building up to this point. The car ride seemed to take forever as we passed by the wide spreading Victoria Lawn Cemetery, and arrived at a bridge.

We had not seen this kind of bridge before, and the gates came down to stop the cars as we could see a huge ship approaching. All the children stood up to see this gigantic monster as it was coming closer into our view. There were no seat belts in those days, so we moved around freely listening to the piercing siren sounding, and we saw the bridge split in the middle as the two sides rose high in the air so the ship could pass through.

On our side of the highway was a store filled with lots of trinkets, cigarettes, and food, it was called Louis Coffee Shop. On the other side of the road was the Clover Leaf where we viewed and enjoyed the collage of signs and how busy these interesting places looked.

We were in awe as we watched the gigantic ship move close in front of us, and it was so massive and high, impressing its onlookers with its size. As exciting as our view was, this very scene would try our patience many times in the future. When the bridge went down, we heard another siren, and we were on our way after the gates opened.

Back then this was part of the Queen Elizabeth Highway, and it was a busy place for tourists on their way to Niagara Falls and locals going into St. Catharines or other parts of the Niagara Region. I was terrified crossing the bridge, wondering if it was safe.

Reaching the other side of the bridge we were once again in the country and passing the Rainbow Inn Hotel, we travelled alongside of some water to Niagara Stone Road. In those days Niagara Stone Road did not take the short cut but you travelled down Stewart Road to a little store and gas station at Strand's Corners, at that point you turned right onto Niagara Stone Road.

Soon we arrived at our destination, and I don't know about the rest of my family, but I thought this was not a nice place. We came from quite a modern home for its time and had running water and flush toilets, but this place lacked a lot of necessities. As we walked through the doors, I realized it was a barn, converted into a house but not yet finished. The first room was still used for the chickens and the next room was used for the family's home.

We visited what I found out later, was an old friend of my father's, from the Ukraine. They were known as the Herbert Ledwez family, and Antonie, Herbert's wife and my father grew up together in the Ukraine in a small German village, which in those days was a part of Russia. As children they went to school together, although only for a couple of years. Children did not go to school very long back then as they had to help support their families. They had not seen each other since they were in Germany, where my parents visited the Ledwez family in the small hamlet of Buelstedt. It was where the Ledwez family settled after their journey and escape from the Ukraine.

My family, who immigrated to Canada in 1949, included Mom and Dad, Mat and myself. My dad knew all the Ledwez family very well including extended family still in Germany. Everyone in this area we were visiting this day spoke German. My brother and I were getting quite accustomed to our English language, and it was strange hearing nothing but German again. As interesting as this place was, I could not see myself living there with no flush toilets, no bathtubs, and no running water. How did they do it?

To give you a little background, Herbert Ledwez was part of a wagon train leaving the Ukraine that was led by John Klassen. The Klassens were also the family we worked with at Hipple Farms. They were also the family where Mom took us on that cold winter night across the bridge. The people of the wagon train escaped from the Ukraine with everything they could carry with them, and they travelled through Poland to Germany.

In Germany the farmers were responsible for the immigrant's livelihood as they worked the farm and did other chores for their lodging. The Ledwez immigrants were given one side of a pig barn to live in. They wanted to be welcome as immigrants in Germany, and Herbert was able to adapt himself and do most jobs well and became the caregiver of his growing extended family. He had both mother and mother-in-law as well as sister-in-law to look out for.

Herbert and Antonie became Christians in this town in a home service. It radically changed their lives and their desires to become freer and serve their newfound God. The couple decided to immigrate to Canada to make a new life for their growing family. When they left the Ukraine, they had two children, Walter, and Lena. Gerda was born in Poland while fleeing. Harry was born in Buelstedt in 1945 and Antonie was expecting Erika as they travelled across the Atlantic to Canada on a refurbished cattle freighter. They landed in Quebec City on July 3rd of 1953 before taking a train to Thunder Bay.

It was disappointing to see so much rock and lack of opportunity, so after a few months they moved to St. Catharines. Their sponsors, the Bulognas, packed all that the family owned, plus four adults - one pregnant, and four children into their car. They travelled bumpy dirt roads and arrived in what I now call, "Little Germany," a small community in St. Catharines near the intersection of Niagara Stone Road and Stewart Road.

I later found out that almost everyone in this unique neighborhood had travelled the same path from Europe to Canada looking for a new start.

8. Little Germany

Before long we were packing up our belongings and moving to this German neighborhood on the other side of the canal, realizing that not even one year had passed since we moved to Wiley farms. We heard promises of a good life and wonderful neighbors and our parents relished the community because everyone knew each other, and they all had their place of origin in common. Some arrived via Russia, the Ukraine, Germany or South America, but all knowing each other from the old country.

We rented the front apartment in a very old house, but nevertheless it was roomy. We called it "Dyck's House," as Mr. Dyck owned it. My parents had a lot of large furniture including a tall, oversized oak kitchen cabinet. It had a metal countertop to work on and sizeable bins that tipped forward and held flour and sugar. On the upper hutch was enough storage for all of Mom's kitchen supplies, bowls and so on.

The house had an oversized yard surrounded by tall chestnut trees, bushes, and meadows. The Ledwez home was our neighbor on one side and a huge old barn stood on the other. The house had a rusty brown tin exterior with two residences, one at the front being ours, and one at the back. We had many adventuresome times living there. As a child I soon enjoyed the great places I investigated, and I learned to hide from my reality. The large old chestnut trees in the front yard provided chestnuts for many projects for us children.

An old wreck of a car was hidden from sight in the thick shrubs between our home and the barn, making a wonderful place to spend time. The abandoned car was overgrown with tall grasses and bushes, so it wasn't visible from the house, road, or barn.

My kids and grandchildren would recognize the look when I say it looked haunted, and yes, that was my first haunted car. We could sit in it and pretend we were driving behind the steering wheel and rummage through the glove compartment all we wanted, as we stored all kinds of stuff in that old car. It was just a great place to spend time and I can only imagine the mice and other rodents that would vacate their home in the car every time we entered it. As children we never thought of those kinds of things.

The old orchard beyond the barn seemed to be a meeting place for the neighborhood kids. We sat in the trees for hours eating cherries. The only time we came down from them was when our intestines growled, and that panicky feeling overwhelmed our bodies. The only toilet paper in the orchard was those large fuzzy leaves, which were almost as bad as those glossy catalogue pages in our outhouses. No one had real toilet paper in our neighborhood. The next day we couldn't resist the cherries and did it all over again.

Many people lived in the back of that old, metal clad brown house at different times. One of my favorite families was so kind to us, and their oldest daughter was Linda. She was younger than I, but a good playmate, and I even had a chance to babysit her siblings at times and delighted myself in it very much. This family was Native Canadian, and we spent many enjoyable hours playing together.

Color wasn't really a point of distinction amongst the people I knew, as we were completely respectful of one another as we all made our way to a better life. Everyone was making their way with pride; in the best way they knew how. We were all from different parts of the world and now becoming friends and neighbors with those around us, and it seemed to me that everyone was important, and everyone helped each other. I was so sad when Linda's family moved away, and I lost another friend.

The Jansen family also lived at the back apartment of this house. They had two daughters. The one had long blonde curly hair and the younger had very light brown straight hair. Since we lived in the front apartment, we became childhood friends for years, but they too moved. Hanging out together as much as we could and enjoying hours playing, we stayed in touch throughout the years, and it was always nice catching up on our families.

My parents decided to purchase a house down the street in this neighborhood. I must say it was the tiniest of homes and it could be called a "tiny house" according to today's TV show standards, but at least we would have our own outhouse and did not have to share it with two families.

It was a very pretty house when we purchased it, all white with a little porch on the driveway side, and it was located on a bit of a slope; the house was at ground level at the front but also had a ground level walkout basement. We moved our beds into our humble home. I don't know how to tell you just how small this house was, but we all slept on the main floor in one room and that was the extent of our upstairs. Steep stairs led down to a basement that appeared unuseable for living.

Our dad thought someday he would change the basement into a living and eating area, but for now the basement was not finished so there was no place to eat or hang out. We still rented one room for our kitchen, at the back of the old, brown tin clad house—Dyck's House.

The Plett family also moved into the front of this house with six children, as they had just arrived from Paraguay. Mrs. Erna Plett was Herbert Ledwez's sister, and he arranged for them to come to Canada, the land of milk and honey.

Every morning we got dressed at our little house and walked across two yards back to our rented kitchen for breakfast, and I remember it being cold many mornings. I think I could have forgotten about breakfast, and just gone to school from our bedroom. In the evening we had supper at the one room rental and then went back to our house to hang out and then go to bed. Every time we wanted a snack, we had to go to the fridge two lots over where the door was locked if Mom wasn't there.

I do not know how my mother put up with that kind of set up, but she did and much worse soon after. I am sure my parents were excited because they would have their own property, mortgage and all. When Dad finished the renovation, we moved the kitchen over to our tiny home. It was great eating in the same house you woke up in. We enjoyed a lot of family times, everything except sleeping was done in this one room at the bottom of the very steep stairs.

One morning in the fall, we were stopped on those stairs and told by our mother to put our boots on. We did this matter-of-factly and sat at the table to eat breakfast with water under our feet.

During the night, water had gathered in our basement and there was more flooding, and the ground water from outside appeared to flow into the interior of our house. Our lunches were made in a hurry that morning and breakfast was rushed, as I am sure mother was so happy when we were out from underfoot that day so she could clean up the mess. Upon arriving home from school, we saw that everything was mopped up and life went on in our usual manner.

It was the weekend and as we came down the stairs for breakfast, you guessed it, we had to put our boots on. Since we were home, we had to help transport pails of water from our kitchen and dump the water outside. It was such an effort that I recall wondering how my mother ever did this by herself.

Since Dad was home too, he decided this could not go on any longer, and he saw for himself what our mother put up with, and then we watched as he took a pickaxe and hammer and began to break a hole in the floor. I can still see it about a foot and a half wide and a foot deep in the shape of a funnel. It was just big enough to get a metal scoop into the bottom of it. We worked all day lugging the pails of water outside and my parents toiled all night as well as all weekend. Naturally everything was put aside, and our priority was filling and taking out the pails of water.

The house felt damp, and we had no place to sit and relax comfortably except on the beds upstairs. My folding bed had to be put away every morning and stored. We were quite happy to catch the bus for school by the time Monday morning came. It must have been an endlessly tiring time for our mom, who by this time I noticed was a compulsive cleaner.

Our house was small, so you would have imagined that everything was in disarray or on top of each other, but not our house, it was always spotless and tidy. Every bed was made, and cot put away, every floor washed, every dish washed, and every article of clothing put in its place. I don't know where we put it all, but everything had its place.

Dad was busy digging all around the outside perimeter of the house and put a tile bed in, as we all hoped it would keep the water out.

The best part of the house for me was the little room outside under the porch, which ended up being my playhouse. It was cleaned of cobwebs and the dirt floor was swept and afterwards I put my doll buggy and miniature set of porcelain china dishes, a gift from Rosa and Ernest in it. I greatly treasured these toys, and this was an appreciated cozy home for my dolls and my brother's cowboy toys.

The boys had toy guns and trucks. Their toys cluttered up my little hideaway because there were so many, as Mat was meticulous with his property. There was no choice as I had to share my space.

I was the senior girl in the family and did a lot of children sitting at home. Of course, not for payment as we never expected to receive money in those days; it was just not a part of our lifestyle.

During lunch hours at school, I envied the kids that could afford to buy their milk, as it came in those nice little glass bottles with a round cardboard cap for a seal. They also received a straw with their milk, something we never got to use. I remember telling many lies at school about our family, how rich we were and what kind of house we had.

My behavior in class was always good and I tried to pay attention but there was still no interest shown by our parents in the schoolwork we did or didn't do, so we struggled on our own.

It was a season of getting to know the neighborhood and some of the children we went to school with. The rules for the playground at Consolidated School were very strict, and I felt anxious that I would get into trouble. Since we were bussed from the other side of the bridge and the school was overcrowded, they decided to send us to another school.

At Ferndale School it was getting to know another set of rules, friends and surroundings. It was maybe two months, and we were sent back to Consolidated School. Can you imagine your child being taken to another school for only a couple of months and then back to the original one? We would not put up with that these days.

Mom and Dad would belittle us in front of other children. Many times, they repeated that we had difficulties learning, and I felt they meant we were stupid. Can you imagine growing up and being programmed to fail? As an adult one of my brothers tells me he still remembers our parents saying some of these things about him. I admire his strength for not accepting those devastating words and letting that seed die in his life. He proved the words to be untrue, as we all struggled to do, despite those cruel, untrue judgmental words, we proved them to be lies and wrong. There must have been a secret ingredient in our lives as most kids live up to their parents' expectations, and we all grew past them into freedom.

Some of the children called us Nazis because we were German and there was still a lot of talk of war in their homes. I wondered why this happened as some of my relatives died or were imprisoned for their convictions against Hitler. Even though this was true, my mother could not let herself believe it was as bad as people said it was. How could her people do such terrible things to as many people as was reported and to that extent?

Such a holocaust is truly unimaginable unless you are in the middle of the experience yourself or see the proof. Many common people in Germany had no idea what was really happening. We were on a trip to Israel a few years ago and while walking through the holocaust museum, I was totally overcome with the reality of this, to the point of running out sobbing. What the children and families went through and endured was so overwhelming and broke my heart. You could see photos of young children, so thin and such sadness in their deep-set eyes. One cannot even imagine their children or grandchildren going through this type of torture and then death. It was the first time that I realized, the importance of not forgetting just how horrible this time in history was, so we might never repeat it.

My parents and all the immigrant families were so on guard about their freedom being taken away. Religious and political freedom was not taken for granted as it is now. We are not standing on guard to protect our country anymore, but just stand by and watch so many of our freedoms being taken away. We do not even realize when this is happening anymore. How can we truly appreciate freedom if we have not experienced its cruel forced and devastating loss? Our hope is to continually hear the warnings of our forefathers' words reminding us to be on guard. I wrote this many years before the turmoil of 2020 and I cannot believe how relevant this is today.

A story depicting our poverty has to do with the kids going to Jones Snack Bar next to Consolidated School, where they purchased bubble gum and sponge taffy at lunch hour. When the bell rang and everyone spit out that huge wad of gum they were chewing, we would step on it and hope it would stick to our shoes. Then, when no one was looking we took it off our shoes and kept it for the next recess. We took recycling to a new level as most kids these days wouldn't even think of doing that. Germs however never entered our minds and we just never thought about it, and we didn't care about anything except being the proud owner of this free wad of gum. It would be huge, pink and sometimes still sweet if you were lucky. Do you have any idea how great it was to chew gum instead of the hot tar off the road?

Still building our immune system, the tar was what we usually chewed. On those hot days of summer, the tar became nice and warm, sometimes to the point of bubbling. This was the optimum time to scrape it and chew it, but we did not enjoy the little pieces of grit or gravel that were intermingled and tried to spit them out.

The road was also our favorite playing ground after a warm rain, and we would be allowed to put on what we called swim wear. This consisted of perhaps a pajama short and little top or anything else you would get your hands on. It felt so warm and freeing to run down the road dotted with warm pools of rainwater, splashing and sliding we ran from one end of the road, to the other, totally elated and enjoying ourselves as we hit each puddle with full impact. The worms escaping the wet ground while crawling on the roads just made the slide easier. The road was not used much as the new section of the Niagara Stone Road was built by now and this would leave us with a very quiet corner of the road to call our own.

Our bus driver was a wonderful, highly respected and loved elderly gentleman Mr. Wherry. He didn't drive our bus too long, as his son took over and followed his father's footsteps. We loved him too as he was always faithful in doing his job and seemed to enjoy the children, even though we were loud, rough passengers. Sometime between grades three and five we got a brand spanking new bus and I felt so proud to be sitting in it. Not only did we love our bus driver, but our affection also included his bus.

It seemed that we got a lot more snow on those cold winter days, and the radio had to be on every morning especially in the winter when the school closings were announced. Our ears were pinned to the radio with great anticipation. Would we be staying home? Sometimes it was not a matter of the school being closed but our bus not being able to make the run, and this happened quite often during the winter months.

On one of those snowy days the bus picked up the students as usual and we traveled our daily route, which led to a very steep hill and as it neared the top, the bus had to merge onto Highway 8. Our bus driver proceeded to climb this treacherous hill with great caution. It was very slippery and layered with ice and snow.

To give you an accurate picture of the hill, you must picture a steep hill with a road cut into its side running from bottom to the top a 30-degree angle. On the outside of the road there were no guardrails, just a drop off to the bottom of the hill. The road was only gravel and dirt until it met at the top with the paved road. You hoped there were no vehicles coming so you could keep your momentum going and merge right onto Highway 8.

We almost made it up the hill when the tires began to spin, and the back of the bus slid sideways off the road towards the drop off. The bus could not go forward or backwards, and I'm sure Mr. Wherry must have felt desperate at the thought of what could happen next, and the lives he was responsible for. Starting to go over the bank with the back tires, it felt like the bus was tipping and ready to roll down the hill, so the bus driver opened the back emergency door and told us to get out and not to stop until we were far from the bus. As we jumped out onto the icy slope, most of us slid all the way down the hill on our rear ends or lunch boxes. I don't know how the girls did this as we did not wear pants but only dresses in those days as most of us could not afford snowsuits but did what we were told.

A tow truck had to be called to pull the bus out. It was so cold but as a child I had a great time as we played in the snow at the bottom of the road and watched the action. You can understand why our bus route was canceled so many times and this was an especially exciting day. We loved getting to school late and it was a great story to tell when we arrived back home that evening. The amazing thing is that our parents didn't even know of the mishap. We had no phone and quite honestly, I cannot remember who in the neighborhood did, but someone must have.

9. The Accident

It was a cold winter's day and although the buses weren't running, we were getting a ride into school. My older brother and I hurried to get ready for school and our dad who we called Pop, was going to drive us. We were diligent about making our lunches, which was part of our regular routine, and you can imagine how excited we were as we had never been chauffeured to school before. At times we watched as the odd car pulled up to the school and dropped children off in the mornings although it was not as prevalent as it is these days, where the streets are lined with the parents' vehicles.

Pop was in the driver's seat, and I sat in the middle seat beside him. My brother got in on the passenger side, also in the front and we were off as there were no seat belts to buckle up in those days. The roads seemed very slippery, and snow covered, but it was a picturesque snowfall.

Our car did not stop at the stop sign as we neared the corner, the harder Dad stepped on the brakes, the more our car slid, and I remember going through the stop sign. What happened next went at such a high speed that the details aren't very clear. As we slid through the intersection, we crossed another car's path. The crash and noise were over! Frantically, Dad assessed his precious cargo hoping he was not responsible for injuring his children. Inspecting me with blood streaming down my face he became very concerned, but not as disturbed as when he viewed my brother's forehead gashed open from top to bottom. As I turned to look at Mat, I could see his extensively exposed skull.

I thought he was dying as he appeared pale, powerless and slow in response, but was able to slightly express himself. The neighbors on the corner observed the collision and someone called the ambulance and police.

A couple of people from the house hurried to the accident site and helped my brother and myself into their house as Dad was not hurt. Someone from the Joseph Schulz family carried my brother into their front room and laid him on the couch. I was not allowed to go in but had to wait in the kitchen as they did not want me to see him in that fragile state. I don't recall anything else about getting to the hospital or seeing my brother or Dad after that. I went into my tuned-out-state, that safe place, as it was too much for me to handle.

Being shorter, my nose was broken as I hit the dashboard, and luckily, not the windshield like Mat. My hospital stay went by without any recollection and must have made for some long days except, for one memory. A nurse took me to see Mat, creating a long walk and I anxiously wondered how he looked. The last time I saw him he looked so hurt and so bloody I couldn't even tell if there were more cuts on his face.

The nurse said, "Just around another corner and there we are."

Shyly, but with great anticipation I walked into the room, and I could see his face. His face was clear except for above the eyes, where his head was still bandaged. We visited a while and I even picked up some toys to play with, but he had to stay quiet and motionless in his bed. I was in the hospital for a week and went to school after that following weekend. Mat was in the hospital for quite a while after my release and I can't remember how long it was. In those days my parents and family would not have gone to the hospital often. Mat's classmates sent letters for him to read and drew pictures for his entertainment. His grade four teacher Mrs. Lyndsy also sent an unexpected fruit basket to our home and asked how Mat was doing. The whole family enjoyed that fruit basket as we had never seen anything like that before. The basket was arranged with many bananas, beautifully polished apples, pears, grapes, cookies and even some candies. We were in awe of such an unexpected, attractive but tasty gift.

Mrs. Lyndsy and her class showed expression of concern, which touched our family deeply, and her kindness impacted me greatly and presented a high marker, as to how school and specifically one teacher can impact a whole family, not just a child. Someone from the school caring about us in this way stayed with me, and this would be the second schoolteacher that impacted my life in such a positive way that affected my adult life. Mat finally came home, and we could still see his raw scar from hairline to eyebrow, nevertheless he was back to his old self.

Winters were active, and we never got bored as there was an important pond down the gently sloped incline across the road from our house. The neighborhood children from youngest to the oldest diligently shoveled it and skated every night. We used our valuable skates purchased at the Salvation Army store, just like everyone else. I put them on in the warmth of our home and walked across the street with my skates on. It was a terrific time particularly when there were a bunch of kids out for a skate on those clear cold evenings.

We could stay out all night without curfews, if we could stand the pain of our frozen toes. Our feet suffered and hurt as they were freezing, but that was nothing compared to when they were thawing out as that was excruciating almost unbearable pain. We hung our socks over the oil stove, our only source of heat in our basement living room. We rubbed our feet when we could stand to touch them until they were finally out of pain, and that usually took an extensive time of diligent concentration on our feet. As bad as that pain was, it never deterred us from going out the next day for more fun, always arriving at that excruciating painful end.

Supper would be prepared in our one room living space. It was where everything that our family did, happened. In this one room there was quite the activity and noise every evening. One of my favorite meals was when my mother made the small sausages, we now know them as breakfast sausages. I only received one and a half sausages as everything we had was rationed and divided up to keep the cost of groceries down.

My mother canned every summer and harvested everything she could from our garden to save money. The first years we had no freezer, and everything was canned. She even canned meat in jars when we were fortunate enough to get an extra rabbit or chicken from someone, and she took great pride in her fruit cellar and knew exactly how many jars she had canned every year. The shelves contained everything from peaches, pears, raspberries, gooseberries, blackberries, sweet and sour cherries, apricots, plums, beans, pickles, beets, watermelon, carrots, crabapples and more. Can you imagine canning just ten jars of each, how much canning that would be? I know I have forgotten some, and she canned many more than ten of each. Our mother did all this besides laboring every day in the summer and fall. She canned all the juices she could get her hands on, and I recall her trying different types like watermelon juice, which most people we knew didn't bother with.

Later, in years to come, we could afford a freezer and you can envision how much was put away every year for the long winters. It is too bad we did not appreciate these foods as quality foods, just because they didn't come from the grocery store in interestingly designed packages. As I raised my family, I took those skills imparted to me way back then, nourishing those special people in my life with quality instead of all those packaged processed foods. They are still enticing us as much now, as they were back then. A great appreciation developed for the long hard hours that Mom worked. All of us realized, hard work paid off and it was a concept not preached at us, but daily shown to us, by example.

10. A Trigger

Mom and Dad took the four of us children shopping. Mat and I were left in the car and the other younger siblings were taken into the store with them. Another car pulled up beside ours. As we kept ourselves busy in the car, I noticed the man in the vehicle staring at me and motioning for me to draw closer and it looked like he wanted to tell me something. Of course, I climbed into our driver's seat to give him my attention. I noticed what he was doing, and I went into a partial state of shock!

That is the only way I can explain it, as I went numb and started to let my mind journey to another place. My older brother inquired what was the matter, as I sat emotionless and frozen. He knew something was dreadfully wrong and quickly looked over to the man in the car next to us and saw that the man was masturbating, which I knew nothing about. We knew you should not expose yourself to others. Dad always said what happened in the family stayed in the family, and never expose yourself to strangers, but we were strangers to this man. The view is as clear today as it was then, and haunted me for many years, from then on. Why it evoked such a threatening and fearful emotion in me, I didn't know. It came back repeatedly for much of my life. It was the tip of an iceberg showing only a little of what was inside of me. It should have been at the most, a very unpleasant experience.

The view of his hand on this private area transported me into another place, one well hidden. I felt so panicked, and the fear was overwhelming as well as debilitating. It seemed to force me to a place deep within, where the pain was too great to bear, and I was found looking on from outside my body.

My brother seeing this man's actions, commanded, "Don't look over

71

there," and worked quickly to lock all the doors. The car doors had to be locked separately as no one had power locks and he worked quickly to secure us. Soon after, the man drove away, and we franticly watched for our parents return. I was slowly coming out of my trance and upon seeing our parents, we could scarcely wait until they neared the car so we could divulge our frightening account. They were both upset and scanned the area to see if the man was still around somewhere, but he was not. After that we were never left in the car alone and commanded under no circumstances to speak of this incident again.

There was endless arguing on the way home, and I could not figure out what it was about, except that I had done something wrong by having noticed the man next to us. Why did I have to disobey and cause trouble all the time? The scene I had witnessed with this man, became a trigger, although that was far from my knowledge at that time.

There was repeated rough play and tumbling with the kids most evenings that continually, without fail, ended up with my mom and dad in loud conflict and arguing. Dad enjoyed wrestling with us, and this happened repeatedly. I was made to feel that I did something inappropriate and of course took the blame on myself; confused and perplexed I was trying to figure out what I was doing wrong. The turmoil of my home and the anger I felt from my mother became a regular part of life, until I started to dread family times and especially dinnertime.

At the dinner table someone would say the incorrect thing and a war of words would start all over again. Over and over my mealtimes were interrupted when I broke down and cried and could not stop, after which I was told to leave the table until I could refrain from crying, which was usually in time to do dishes.

It was at one of those dinners a few years later, when I vowed to change my future and I remember where I sat. I would not argue like this at my dinner table if I had a family. I would let the kids have fun at the table and laugh.

We were not allowed to laugh at the table by our mother's orders and our dad would purposely make his children giggle. Guess who was left in trouble, not our dad, not at first anyways, then we were screamed at until we didn't feel happy anymore. The hurtful war began with another argument, who would have guessed it! I anticipated and dreaded this experience to the point of not wanting to have dinner at home.

Our dad spent time playing with us, but Mom was always too busy doing house chores. I had to do dishes and wondered what it would be like to watch someone else doing them as I did my homework or played as this is what the rest of the family did after supper day after day.

I went to bed wondering if my mother would leave one day, not even considering what would happen to us children. We didn't know the word divorce back then, as it was not common in our circles, until I got to be a young teen.

I went to bed quietly crying myself to sleep most nights as my bed was moved from one place to the other in our little home, always left in a high traffic area. Therefore, I learned to be quiet while crying, as to not attract attention to myself. I have memories of my throat aching, blowing my nose as quietly as possible as hot tears rolled down my cheeks onto my pillow night after night.

I was so grateful to have God to talk to in my broken-hearted silence and I learned to lean on Him for comfort and after much anguish, I would surrender my fatigued body and fall asleep. The swollen eyes in the morning bothered me and now wonder why my mother never picked up on that and asked me what the problem was. My emotions were so neglected when I was a child.

Years later, from this experience I developed a sixth sense regarding how people around me are feeling and I can usually see their pain, not always knowing what is causing it or what to do about it. I made up my mind to be a watchman at the gate of our home in later years. It was my job to make sure that my family was emotionally safe from all that was out to hurt them. If I couldn't protect them from hurts, I would walk with them, helping them heal so they knew someone loved them, always, no matter what happened. Of course, there was the physical safety too and I let my husband take care of that aspect as he was more than qualified to do so.

Years later when my own children would leave for school, I would lay hands on them daily and pray God's protection over them. They depended on this and would not leave the house without their safety covering, even when I was in the basement working, cutting someone's hair, they would call me to pray for them knowing God was their protector and God always did His job well.

Thinking back to my childhood, our big outing for the week was walking to the nearest garage where my dad bought us all an "Oh Henry" bar. It was so delicious and to this present day my preferred chocolate bar is one containing nuts.

On many occasions we went to the mud hole for a swim. The mud hole was a sectioned waterway off to the side of the Welland Canal. It was used to contain the excess water as the locks would fill up and empty into the canal as required. The water would rise so much that I could not walk across until the tide went out. Each person in the neighborhood swam at the mud hole and we had a delightful time there for countless years. We didn't own bathing suits, and no one cared much about that kind of detail, so we wore pajama bottoms for swim wear. The current was more than our young bodies could handle at times, and caution had to be used as we crossed over this channel of water to the other side.

Gerda, a friend in the neighborhood made the most beautiful dolls out of the clay and then we painted them. She taught me how to make them as I worked with her. It took up a big part of our summer, and we got the best clay from the island that was off to the left side of the mud hole. The island had tall reeds and grasses with a path straight through the middle, as well as a haven for snapping turtles. We took pleasure in our crafts, and the diversion of the refreshing water in the heat of those scorching summers.

The fact that amazes me was none of our family could swim until we went to the mud hole and were thrown in to learn to dog paddle and how we didn't drown is beyond me. We would never have let our children swim there by themselves as our parents did. Most of the kids in the old neighborhood learned to swim by being thrown in the canal into the deep end, so I guess we were the lucky ones. We had numerous outstanding experiences at the canal if the preferred people were there.

There were the odd kids who would cause trouble. An example of one was a boy who would push me under water repeatedly until I thought I would die. Every time I went down, I could feel his feet on my head as the soft slimy bottom would squeeze between my toes. Often fighting for my life, I became very good at defending myself in the water even to this day. Do not try to push me under.

11. Dad Committed

We arrived home from school to be confronted with the shocking fact that our dad was taken to the hospital, without any more explanation given. The house felt strange and empty, even sad, as we children had no idea why this happened.

Years later we were told that our mom had him committed to the Hamilton Psychiatric Hospital. My mom must have anguished in a world of turmoil, and terrified at how my dad was going to take this turn of events. She never told us why, but I did figure it out much later. The only one at home with Mom that day was my younger sister, Helen, only three at the time. As an adult she relayed that an ambulance arrived unexpectedly to pick up Dad and he did not concede to going with them, as he became unconvinced and violent. They had to physically restrain him with a straight jacket as he fought them to be released, yelling, and screaming uncontrollably. He was extremely outraged that Mom had secretly executed this confinement and committal to the hospital. With no time to think, he fought as if his life depended on it. My dad was a strong man, and I am sure the attendants had to use every ounce of energy they had that day.

We didn't know what everything meant but understood those angry words as Mom and Dad fought months before as Dad often accused Mom of cheating on him. These accusations weren't true of course, but very hurtful to all of us as we listened and tried to make sense of it all, and our mom must have been very wounded as well. Knowing what I know now, I wish they could have gotten help to leave their baggage behind and heal from their pains. Mom accused Dad and he raged with anger, although we didn't know of what. His eyes flared like daggers, his face got red, and he yelled and pounded his fists on whatever was handy. He never hit Mom as far as I know but I was afraid he would.

Dad also tried to commit suicide at least once. Mom told me years later that he also had lapses of memory. He kept his address in his wallet so he would know where he lived when he forgot. Since we didn't have a phone, a police officer came and told us someone was bringing Dad home because he couldn't remember where he lived. It was soon thereafter that my dad was picked up by an ambulance and confined against his will.

It was such a traumatic experience for my younger sister. Imagine watching while your father is taken away fighting and screaming, as your mother is crying, while fear is gripping you so deeply that you chose not to recall the details until many years later. She had a special bond with her dad, and it was being broken, as she felt she was his special little girl, and she was. I remember Dad spoke fondly and responded kindly to my little sister, and she was the princess in the family, yet her world was being torn apart.

Time passed slowly for us, and it became months since Dad was gone. We missed a father in our home and most of the time missed having food in our stomachs. Our mother took charge and made a point of paying the mortgage on time every month and expressed often of not accepting welfare. That would have been an embarrassment to her, even though we were never in this position before, it humiliated her to be there. That should not be the case of course, but Mom was raised with this notion, and it was a matter of pride.

At first, we didn't get to see Dad much and mother took the bus to Hamilton to see him, reluctant in the beginning she must have been so nervous and anxious wondering how his reaction to her would be. Sometimes friends would take her there and we took care of ourselves at home. When I look at my grandchildren at the age we were and older, I can't believe we were left to ourselves. We took consolation that at any time we could go to our neighbors for help, as they were all reliable friends by now.

12. Unforgiveness

The righteous cry out, and the Lord hears them, he delivers them from all their troubles.
Psalm 34:17

We were left alone a good deal of the time as children, when we began to explore our bodies. We played what we called, "doctor," and this of course was while Mom was out for her visit to see Dad. When our mom got home our little sister exposed us, but I was the only one singled out with harsh words and punishment. I was ordered to my mom's bed after a severe tongue lashing that hurt much more than the spanking. My bed was not available as it was put together during the day. I was told that I would get no supper and that I would never, ever, be forgiven for this. I cried myself to sleep once again wondering why I was so bad. I learned many things when I was young, but one of the most important things was not to say things flippantly or carelessly. I have tried not to leave deep cuts and ugly scars on the lives of my children in that way, although I am sure at times I have failed. I tried not to overreact in various situations, especially with my words. That does not mean I achieved perfection, but I made a conscientious effort to understand the roots of their actions and deal with it accordingly and I learned to think and speak in the sight of eternity. To me it did not matter what the situation was, but what it meant to the soul of the person. It was a long and painful road that led me to that understanding of "word power." I learned it could build you up one minute and in the next second words could be used to destroy you.

Above all, the most valuable part of word power, came upon realizing the power and impact of the words you say to yourself. Still falling into the old snare, I have a method of coming to reality, as the question I ask myself is, "What does God think of who I am at this moment, and what does He think of what I said, saw or did?" This covers a lot of area, and it will all be clearer later as I give examples of this. I learned through many hardships to lean and only count on God's opinion of myself. Not realizing at the time, God was my teacher and rescuer, and He was always close to me and my broken spirit.

Although I told Mom I was sorry for all that I had done, it was never acknowledged, and I was never forgiven. To this day, I think it very hurtful and ungodly not to acknowledge forgiveness, especially when it is asked for. Jesus taught us to forgive one another for our trespasses and we will be forgiven for ours. That is what you need to do, ask for forgiveness and forgive others. Leave the rest to God and his greater knowledge of every situation you find yourself in.

13. God Forgives

For we walk by faith, not by sight.

2 Corinthians 1:7

No matter how many times you must ask for forgiveness, God will forgive you every time, when your heart is sincere. My journey with God is what taught me to know that. He is faithful to forgive, no matter how many times I mess up. Always go by faith that you are forgiven and not by what you hear, see, or feel. Having learned all of this I can recall so many times when my words were cutting, and I didn't use much thought or wisdom before I spoke. It is these times we must forgive ourselves, as well as have God and others forgive us.

It took many years to realize that I had to forgive my mother, even though she had said she would never forgive me. I was journaling my memories when God revealed this to me, and that I must forgive myself for feeling responsible for the turmoil and anger towards myself. When something is revealed to you by God, be sure to do it! It will change your attitude and love towards a person. To forgive Mom released a knot in my stomach, and I no longer had what I now call the "feeling of unforgiveness." The negative feelings towards my mother are now gone. God, as always, is so awesome.

14. God Answers

Give thanks in all circumstances, for this is God's will for you in Christ Jesus.

1 Thessalonians 5:18

God knew the battle that raged in my soul and that my self-worth was low. It took me years to figure out God's ways and to follow His lead. My role models—my parents— were not very dependable, and we were not taught to read the Bible. I didn't have favorite Bible scriptures and verses that would lift my spirit. I learned the Bible stories in Sunday school and how God worked in the lives of the people in the stories. This is how I learned to lean on God and know what his character is.

God answered my prayer, and I would never have dreamed that God would place me, where I could attend church regularly, by myself, without fail. I imagined that I would have to be without God after moving and not getting rides to Sunday school. Here I was, living right beside a church that loved God. I chose to attend the little German church next door. This was where God put me, and I would enjoy my freedom to attend.

My parents discouraged me from going to church and gave little encouragement to be a Christian. Although saying this, I learned a lasting lesson on who God was and what He did because of my mom's actions.

In a time of desperation Mom knew where to turn. While Dad was still in the hospital, something felt urgent and unsettling one evening. Our mother sat us down to sing some songs and we sang out of one hymnal, when my mother told me not to sing because I had such a terrible voice. Up to that point, I loved singing but did as Mom asked. I just listened as she told my younger brother George what a wonderful singer he was. He was a good singer, but then all her children were. She was frustrated with our dad still in the hospital and as a single parent she was providing for her family, but she certainly did not know how to direct her feelings in the correct manner and had to lash out at someone, usually me. I learned that my older brother also felt that directed anger many times. She did this often in her life and we saw unwarranted criticism.

After the singing we were told we had no more food and we always listened to her words as they shredded our self-confidence, so why not listen to her words now. We were continuously listening. She said we should pray, and she asked God to provide us with food. She did not know what else to do and God would have to provide some food. Well, we believed everything else that we were told, so why not that.

We all climbed the steep stairs to bed and said our ritualistic night prayers. "Now I lay me down to sleep, I pray the Lord my soul to keep, If I should die before I wake, I pray the Lord my soul to take." I usually spent many times talking to God about my personal needs after that.

I prayed because in Sunday school I had learned that you talked to God before you go to sleep, and he would listen. No one in our house knew how much I talked to God at night. He became my best friend even though I hadn't yet learned how to express who He was to me. The next morning, we went to the breakfast table as usual, and Mom made us a cup of weak coffee.

We had an outhouse, so the night pot was taken out every morning. I think we all had too many turns taking it out, begrudging every step. We all detested that job above all other jobs. This morning it was my turn and opening the door, I could hardly believe my eyes.

There was a big box of food sitting in front of the door. I called out to the family, and we dragged it in. I recall thinking, "God does listen when we pray!" I felt like I had found a secret formula to whatever I needed, and God used this circumstance to teach us a valuable life lesson. From that day on, I put into my heart that God was a giver of good gifts, especially if we pray and have a need for them.

I realized later that it took a willing participant to deliver the food as God prompted. We never found out who that person was that listened to the whisper of God that night, but that answer to prayer made a lasting impact on my life.

My mother kept up with the singing and praying for a time. I recall that it made me feel settled and secure. Mom attended the close-knit church next door a couple of times, but not regularly. She even went to the front of the church and knelt at the altar where people prayed with her, and she seemed happier when we left. I had no idea at the time why, but I always enjoyed accompanying her, so pleased that she chose me to go with her every time. The others didn't come, maybe because they didn't want to, or maybe Mom just needed time away to think. Perhaps she couldn't experience some things if she brought the family along to worry about. I know now God was calling her and had a plan to fulfill in her life, but she had a hard time following through with what she thought God required of her and her life's reality. At times she would disregard God and other times let Him lead her life and sometimes He was a positive force within her but sometimes she would even speak like she was against God. It was puzzling to know how to pattern my life, so I decided to always… ask God for myself and find out just what He wanted me to do.

15. Childhood Memories

Winter was leaving and I enjoyed the rebirth and scent of another spring. My spirit and soul rejoiced at the smells of the mosses in the woods and the budding trees. With birds singing outside I felt like a new fresh start to life had once again begun. There was a lot of time spent searching for new and interesting things everywhere.

That Easter, I made my own Easter egg nest. I anticipated that the Easter bunny would use it to surprise me. I put the nest right by our back door in hopes that the bunny would see it on the way in, but it was still unfilled the next morning. In defense of the Easter bunny, he continuously left something inside on the kitchen table for us and we appreciated the goodies. Saying that, I was overwhelmed with disappointment as I investigated my nest and found it empty. It looked so soft with its cover of fresh green moss, and I desired to keep it, but Mom insisted I throw it out. My disappointed heart quietly broke without a sound, and the nest was gone.

Looking for different birds was a favorite hobby of mine, and as I walked in the woods I would try to recognize the birds from a book at school. As much time as possible was spent looking for birds and their nests as well as observing their habits. I understand the excitement people feel when experiencing nature in their own special way.

Everyone has their unique thing that creates excitement, and deposits gratification within them. Wise is the person who knows and takes time for these small rejuvenating moments in their lives. Take the time to discover what revives your spirit and you will develop so much more to contribute to life and the people in your world.

There was an unexplainable joy within me when I could spend hours in the outdoors. This was so evident that my mother would accuse me of being up to something. I had that twinkle in my eye when I came home, and I could not explain that twinkle. It came from within only when I was outdoors, and I knew it was wonderful to be alive. The only other experience that compared to this feeling was having a crush on a boy. Without a doubt you have felt the euphoria of a new crush or the experience of first love and can compare.

Some say it can happen because of eating chocolate, but the outdoors did the same for me. There was a freedom that I could not experience anywhere inside our house, and no place that I had been up to that point except for maybe church, but in a different way. Going back to our visits with our dad in the hospital; the visits were very rare for months and our lives seemed in turmoil. There was no arguing between Mom and Dad anymore and the focus seemed to be on us children, but the house seemed empty, and we missed and longed to see our dad.

Children as usual, had a way of being honest and in many respects cruel at the same time. We were repeatedly taunted about our dad being crazy and in the mental hospital. Years ago, mental illness was not as understood as it is today, although there are still so many mysteries to discover about the illness. Growing up with a reality of someone in my family being, "crazy", as they called it, haunted me even into my thirties. The haunting of this gripped my life with a debilitating fear.

Mother told me that Dad had to have shock treatments to forget some things. I didn't know much as a child about shock treatments except that it was supposed to put my dad on the road to recovery, which hadn't happened yet. It was months and we were getting discouraged seeing our mother getting tired and worn down with all the responsibility.

She got little jobs washing dishes at the hotel restaurant, called the Rainbow Inn. It was not far from home, and this was good as she did not drive, and all travel was done by foot. She had to depend on friends to give her rides to Hamilton and they never disappointed her. Mr. and Mrs. Janzen drove Mom many times and they also took us children in later months.

Every time we visited Dad, I battled that very lost feeling. It prevailed in the way of not belonging anywhere and was accompanied by fear. Mat also disliked the trips with great passion, as he had to be responsible for all of us on those long visits to Hamilton. Whether we were left at home or taken along, we were his responsibility. When we visited Dad, we stayed outside as it was summer, and we were never allowed inside the huge haunting building. Our parents didn't miss a chance to go off by themselves, and as children being left alone, it was considered a time to play. As I matured, I realize these were conjugal visits as well as private talks for Mom and Dad. Mat must have felt helpless as we played and ran on the endless grounds of the hospital. His responsibility was to keep us together, and he articulates of it being a stressful and wearisome time for him.

While Dad was in the hospital, back at home there were many trips to town. Each meant a five-mile walk one-way and it was so exhausting as we walked to the city. We were excited and ran ahead only to be called back many times as our little sister's legs could not move her as quickly as ours. Being dressed in our Sunday best to go into the city, we had our customary stops.

One was the Salvation Army second-hand store where we looked for many treasures. Although there were a lot of "must have" items, the answer was always, "No," except for clothing and necessities. I don't know why, but I loved looking in the book section. We were not taught to pick up a book and read it at home and did not have many books in our small house. The older the book the more I liked it, but I was rarely able to buy a book because of it not making the necessity list, I was thrilled when I could work and buy my own. My brothers continuously looked for the great toys. Mat developed a good eye for interesting toys, which he thought had value. When he worked and was able to, he bought what you could say were collectables. I would say our younger brother George also learned to collect, as he accumulated slot cars and other items in years to follow.

We also stopped at a grocery store just down the road from our secondhand store. It was a huge store and we never bought too much because we would have to carry it all home. Even the clothing got heavy for our young undeveloped arms.

There was a German delicatessen in town, and we stopped at it faithfully. We loved going in there to listen to the chatter that went on, always in our German language. Our mother would order a very, very small order of liver sausage, now known as liver pâté. We all loved it and couldn't get enough of the rare unaffordable food. My mother also loved blood sausage, and we ate this creamy red sausage only until the church next door introduced a theory into our lives that God forbid us to eat blood. After that it was very seldom seen at our table. Eating jelled blood is a disgusting thought right now.

On the way to the deli, we passed a well-known bakery. There was a minister that preached occasionally in the neighborhood church next door who worked at the bakery.

Sometimes the bakery would give him the old pastries and breads. The refuse was put in a large paper sack, kind of like our leaf bags today. He gave this bag to our neighbor Herbert Ledwez, who also attended the church next door. Of course, it was supposed to be feed for his chickens and other animals. Before it ever got to the chicken coop, every child in the neighborhood was alerted to the arrival of the goody sack. There were doughnuts, French pastries, Danishes, Poppy seed cake, not to mention the breads and sausage pastries. My pick was always one of those great Danish pastries, sometimes fresh and sometimes very stale. This fact was totally irrelevant to us, and the truth was that it was an overwhelming experience with food. Every time the sack arrived it created an awesome garage party while it sat in the garage open waiting to be fed to the livestock.

Herbert was a real hero providing us with these goodies, he could have paid the dollar or two for the feed and just kept it for his chickens or his family. Instead, we are keeping him in our thoughts forever as the joy he provided for us was long lasting. It is wonderful to bless people who cannot financially afford it and in this we were truly blessed.

It was a sweltering summer, and the seven of us were forced to sit in the hot car on our long drive to Hamilton without air conditioning. I assumed Dad was much better, and I could not figure out why he couldn't come home, as he appeared healthy enough. My brother and I disliked going there so much as our parents went off by themselves. Of course, now we understand, Mom and Dad had a lot to discuss including Dad's illness and they needed some privacy.

The grounds were green and lush with many trees and bushes providing many places for us to hide. It was a wonder that we didn't happen upon our parents on one of the runs around the park. Our younger brother and sister would continuously ask us where their parents were, and we quite honestly could not tell them. My older brother took the main role as the caregiver and continued his never-ending job.

Mother would bring picnic lunches and we would spread a blanket and enjoy a picnic as a family. Many times, people would walk by, and they were patients in the hospital and our dad would tell us about them. One of the men was trying to run away continuously and had someone walking with him. We were told another man was there for many years and would never leave this facility. I remember thinking that it was so unfair to him, and could that happen to my dad?

We were very happy to stay home and babysit in a controlled setting when possible. They were long days, and everything had to be spotless when our mother returned. We had our chores to do and after doing them we went out to play, although I was not the oldest, the responsibility of the other children lay heavily on my shoulders. There was never a moment of total peace and contentment, and I could never do things right and please my mother.

In later years my older brother told me of his battle with responsibility in our home. He felt like it was up to him to keep everyone in line. The younger siblings, on the other hand, had a great time whether they were left at home or if they went along to visit Dad.

16. Coming Home

That fall, our dad was released to come home, although I don't know exactly when, but realized it was before Christmas. We felt like a normal family again and everything seemed to go just fine. Dad was happy that our mother had kept up the payments on the mortgage and it was talked about at great lengths. We all got the impression that it was prudent to pay off a mortgage as quickly as possible, and that it would be one of the most satisfying and rewarding acts you would achieve. This approach to the mortgage stayed with us as a beneficial pattern followed throughout our lives. We were diligent regarding this task and tried to pass this down to all our children as well.

Pop talked daily about building us an addition and that winter plans were made to build onto our existing home. All these years, Mom and Dad had no bedroom for themselves, which must have been challenging for them. The new build would start with a room downstairs at the back of the house, and it would be the new kitchen. Later Pop would build another room above it for a bedroom. We would wait for the build and live our daily lives as usual.

Our clothing was clean but never in style. We wore socks that were darned, even though this was not in fashion at that time. Our clothes had patches and that certainly was way before its fashion, and they also looked well worn and that was to be expected since they started out being secondhand from the Salvation Army Store. I dreamed of having clothes like everyone else and constantly wished it were so.

I have seen at the age of my young teen granddaughters, that they want to look like everyone else, as it provides you with a great sense of belonging to your group of peers.

My hair was also a center of daily strife and was put into braids even though braids were not in style. The hair style was especially upsetting because my little sister had her hair short and in different styles all her young life. Helen had beautiful thick healthy looking brown hair, but mine was fine, blonde, and almost white.

We were allowed to stay home from school with no or little excuse, and most of the siblings took advantage of this. For the life of me I don't know why, but I chose to go to school. Even though it was not my favorite place to be, feeling isolated and lonely, I would rather go to school than stay home.

After this time major changes were made where I slept at night. My bed was in the hallway and later as a teen, in the living room on the floor. The hall wasn't pleasant because everyone walked through it to go to the front bedroom or to the back bedroom when it was built. They walked through only after the bright lights were turned on over my bed making me feel like I had no space of my own.

Later when I was a teenager it was much more troublesome sleeping in the living room, where I dragged the single mattress, and made my bed with the sheets and quilt, and brought my pillow in. It felt good to have a place to lay my head, only to pick it all up again the next morning. It made me weary to be on the floor in the living room instead of a cozy bed as I would have to get it all out of the front room before everyone's day started. There was no place to go during the day when you wanted to lay down or have your own space. It was like visiting somewhere, and you didn't have a place to call your own.

When I was a young girl and sleeping in the hall, I needed a place to hide my snakes. I caught them in the rock pile outside at the side of the house. Not knowing where to put them, I stuffed them in a canning jar and put them under my bed in the hall. My mom wouldn't have let me bring them in the house and I loved collecting snakes up until that time. Dreaming about snakes crawling all over the hall and in my bed, I was terrified by my nightmare. The next day I let them go and never collected snakes again. I often wonder what variety of things children hide in their rooms thinking it was their private sanctuary.

I enjoyed a pair of secondhand runners that I was fortunate to find at the Salvation Army. Shoes make a difference, and I had the sensation of kicking like a colt let out of the barn for the first time. This is what wearing a new pair of secondhand white, canvas runners with thick soles on them, made me feel like. After purchasing them at our favorite secondhand store and scrubbing them till my knuckles were red, I put them out in the sun to dry. They turned out spotless and after the white shoe polish was applied, they looked like new. What a feeling of pride when I wore them to school the next day. They gave me a sense of accomplishment and great pleasure for weeks to come as my glance fell downward upon them, and I still feel a wave of warmth, as I think about my second-hand white canvas sneakers.

After school we changed into what we called our play clothes, and that included our shoes. Then we watched as Dad continued working on building the new room for us at the back of the house. We would access this room through a door at the rear of our basement, which had been our back door to the backyard. The kitchen would have a hand operated water pump inside on the counter. We could then pump the water up from our cistern into the sink inside the new kitchen. Right now, we had to get our water from the outside pump with a pail. As you can imagine our small, everything room would now only be our living room. Our refrigerator and stove would be in the newly built room and became the preparation area.

What would we do with all that space? The all-purpose room now became our eating area and living room, and it held a pullout couch and coffee table. It was still our parent's bedroom until the second story was built in the future. Mom decided to keep the table and chairs for the kitchen in the living room as the new room was too small for everything. The couch was flanked with lamps on side tables and there was even room for a plant or two. Mother loved plants and had more than enough of them. The room also held an oil furnace and the same steep set of stairs leading to the bedroom. One thing with this new room was that you had to take a step up into it, as we wanted to avoid the previous water problems of the basement and it made the room drier. As you exited to the outside, you would walk onto our cement slab over the cistern.

The cistern was another story. A hand pump beside the new indoor sink pumped the water into the house and we were as modern as you could get! The yearly task of cleaning the cistern was unpleasant, and I disliked it with a passion and questioned why me. There were dead mice, frogs and spiders in it and the water was always cold with an access opening that wasn't very large and just big enough to fit a small body. I was let down with someone's rubber boots on, into the chilled structure to complete the task, and scoop everything that was left in it into a pail, and then sweep it out with a corn broom. It was a cold wet job no matter how warm the temperature was that day, and I am so glad I don't have to do that job anymore.

17. Little Church Next Door

Surely your goodness and unfailing love will pursue me all the days of my life, and
I will live in the house of the Lord forever.

Psalm 23:6

The small German church next door impacted my life in an unimaginable way. It was made up of a German speaking close-knit community. God provided a life changing miracle for me. No one could have planned that better than God. This was my place of peace, satisfying something deep within me, as God became bigger in my heart than I could have imagined.

The people that attended were familiar to me by that time as a lot of them lived in our neighborhood. I enjoyed Sunday school and loved attending, sometimes with my siblings. My first Sunday school teacher at this church was the pastor's wife, who was calm and gentle in speech, and she taught us numerous Bible stories about Jesus and Bible heroes. Mrs. Erisman was particularly gentle towards me, and I still recollect exactly how she appeared, although it has been numerous years since then. Her soft voice was soothing as she made those Bible stories come to life. Her attire was modest but modern for the time and she looked neatly put together and had her hair in tight curls that accented her smooth pale skin. She passed away so many years ago but has left a positive mark on my life.

I treasured the colorful pamphlets we received every week, and the inspiring stories they reminded me of. Listening to her comforting and compassionate voice, brought a quiet peace to my soul. It was a dream come true to go to the church next door and learn about God.

No one knew that I had made a commitment to God already. I would never have had enough knowledge of the salvation procedure to know the

Christian language to express that. God was my quiet gentle teacher who taught me things I knew nothing about. My knowledge of who God was became stronger as I took the words of Mrs. Erisman to heart and trusted that her nurturing words were truth. The stories taught in Sunday school became my Bible and it was how I learned of God's character and how he wanted us to live.

A young woman, engaged-to-be-married, taught my next Sunday school class. She became "Mrs. Wolff" and she significantly inspired me to have an outstanding Christian marriage someday. I watched intently from our house next door to the church, as she drove away with her handsome new husband on her wedding day. It was just how I wanted to look one day, just as happy. She made me feel very important to her during class and invested into my life and she showed me reason to look forward to a marriage with a good man and find true love like hers. Hildegard Wolff taught me to have confidence in God. I remember learning to grow and trust in God as a powerful friend who could meet my every need. I talked to God constantly about everything and He became the One I trusted. At night when I was lonely and scared, I would talk to God. When confusion took over my emotions, I learned to lean on God for a sense of peace and balance.

Hildegard gave me a wedding photo of her husband and herself and I was thrilled. I have kept it even to this day, as a reminder of the marriage I wanted. It was around this time in my life that I vowed to God and myself that I would marry a Christian. To me that meant that he would love God and love going to church, any church that taught the Bible and I didn't consider the denomination. Denominations were not important to me at all. I decided this after one of those long quarrels about religion that Mom and Dad usually had during a Sunday dinner after I had a wonderful morning in God's house.

Although I have tried to recall it, I don't remember the people in the church assisting us much when our dad was in the hospital. I am not saying they didn't because I know someone brought us food as an answer to prayer, but I cannot recall much help. I think my mom would have blossomed and accepted God's growth in her life if she was embraced with love and some help along the way.

18. The City Dump and Other Adventures

The neighborhood kids had a terrific time that summer as we discovered the city dump. Five or six of us would get together on a Saturday and walk across the Homer bridge, past the Victoria Lawn Cemetery, down Queenston Street, Hartzel Road, and then to the dump. It is now a well-used golf course. In those days you could walk around on the dump property and investigate as much as you desired. We could hardly believe our eyes when sizeable trucks from Loblaws would drive up and dump vegetables and fruit in quantities we had never previously laid our eyes on. Everyone shared what they found, and the bananas were our favorites, and we could not believe that we could be so privileged.

The scene must have appeared comical to onlookers as we walked the three miles home with our goods. We were just a band of kids overloaded with many varieties of useless items. My most desired item to rescue were oversized wicker baskets from funeral homes. Of course, I didn't know where they came from as a child but loved baskets. My brother valued trucks even if they were missing a wheel or two. We felt like we were the wealthiest kids in town. It didn't take long until our mother put a stop to all that garbage, except for bananas and such. We had collected too much junk that cluttered up the area around the house. When I think back it must have piled up more than we could imagine as Mother hoarded and kept everything because of our needs, so we had enough stuff without going to the dump to get more.

The recollection of the dump is a favorite memory of both my husband and I, as he was in one of the neighborhood gangs, as well as his sisters. Mom kept an immaculate home even though it was super tiny, and she knew how to make every corner maximize its space for storage and found a place for those items from the dump that we were allowed to keep.

Harry's sister Gerda, cut her foot so deep that she hobbled home with blood trailing behind her. Growing up the way we did, made us all appreciate the things we have, and all of us still love to get a good deal, or better yet, get something for nothing. Our knowledge of waste was deeply ingrained in all our minds and left us with an appreciation for transforming old things to have new purpose, before recycling became popular.

The dump was the place where an abundance of food lay at our feet, and we learned to enjoy three or four bananas at a time. In our home we were rationed to have only half a banana a week, and that was on grocery shopping day. When you are limited with something you love, it always leaves you wanting more.

In my home I continually felt under the microscope when my mother was around, and it felt like I never measured up. It was a feeling that I could never explain, but it was continually there with me. I must say that everyone in the family did not have the same emotional response, although we all had our own battles to deal with. I believe the younger siblings had a different childhood than the older ones.

I would have to do a lot of the housework and babysitting while Mom would labor in the fields or orchards on the farms. She had a great reputation and set high standards for herself in the work force as well as in her home. Everyone was amazed when they came into our very small house and saw it so manicured.

To keep this house spotless and tidy was such a task, especially since my dad was not a man of perfection, but a rather messy person by nature. He was a chain smoker and smoked in the house. Mom would wash all curtains and walls and ceilings a couple of times a year, but they still got yellow. I suppose this combination of genes is where my inner battle of messy-versus-tidy comes from. I could never understand that battle within me but am very satisfied to have the tidy genes win most days.

One day my younger sibling was not obeying me, and I applied some force to make him obey. I pushed him back and he hit that doorframe Dad had built leading into the new kitchen. I heard the loudest sounds of wailing, as I tried to console George and told him to be quiet; he would not stop crying. Only after telling him that I would send for our mother did he become brave and quieted down, so I could go for help. I can't remember just how I got a hold of my mom, but she did arrive home and Mom and my brother were taken to the hospital. The farmer's wife, Tina, drove them to the hospital and back. Tina Froese was a God-send as we had no other way to get there. George had a broken collarbone which I was sorry for. This was only one of two he would receive, but I was not responsible for the second one. It was punishment enough to be guilty of my actions causing one injury. I learned not to use force on my siblings even though they greatly frustrated me.

The same brother was across the road with the neighborhood kids building a tree fort. I was in my quiet world at home doing chores when I heard yelling from the children as well as someone crying. As the noise approached our house, I saw my brother covered with blood from the top of his head to his waist. I yelled, "What happened?" as I took him inside the house, checking his head at the same time. A board had fallen from the tree where the fort was being built and hit him on the head. I held a cloth on the area where the blood was coming from. After examining it I noticed that it stopped bleeding when I held the cloth on it. Our first aid training was zero and I learned by trial and error. It was a large, deep gash on the top of his head. One of the children was told to hold the cloth firmly and I started to clean him up. You would not want your mother to see a person in such a mess if you were in charge, would you now. Our mother was sent for once again and this time we went to a neighbor's house to phone the Froese farm where she was working. I don't know how long it took, but she arrived, and Tina took them to the hospital to get stitches. It was a bad couple of summers and George got hurt once more.

The kids all came running home to report that he had yet another accident. As I ran to the end of the driveway, I saw him bleeding once again, but from his foot. I cleaned the wound and you guessed it–Mom was called. The farmer was so gracious to us and took George for stitches again. Froese farms was a haven for Mom, I am sure. They were Christians and I am sure put many good hours of positive conversation into Mom's life. She spoke highly of them and enjoyed how they treated her fairly. It was so kind and giving of them to drive Mom and George to the hospital so many times. I must say this family gave more than just being a boss, and we truly felt like they were friends and we journeyed life together, even when not working for them. It is a continuous pleasure to catch up with one of the family members now and again while hearing about their life's journey.

The weight of babysitting was wearing on me. The unexpected accidents showed I was able to act under pressure but the constant reality and burden of keeping the house to my mother's expectations, was defeating and overwhelming. She consistently criticized and belittled me for not keeping the floors spotless. My siblings and their friends would track in and out, with no regard to the consequences when Mom came home. I had to answer to the amount of food that was eaten every day, and the accountability was wearing me down.

My mother must have been dead tired every evening as well as mentally frustrated with her life, although realizing this, I still don't understand her treatment of me as a child. I struggled to be as good a child as possible, all the while never arriving at her standard.

I made a mental note, promising myself, that when I had children, if I could help it, I would not let them feel like failures. In years to come, as a parent, I learned that we can't be all things to our children even if we wanted to. Even though it was never a hardship to be there for my children, I am sure I did not fulfill all their needs and failed them often. I have learned that only God can be all things to all people all the time.

To compensate for my inadequacy, I drew a picture of everything on Mom's dresser before removing them to dust it. Mom wanted all her many items put back exactly as she had placed them. The sketch was so I could get it right just once, but it never happened, not even once.

Mom didn't realize that our place was the neighborhood hangout when she wasn't there. Can you imagine what a haven for the kids in the neighborhood, as it was a place to do as they pleased. I begged my brothers not to have their friends in, as after washing the floor, they never got a chance to dry before someone walked on them, and I used to get so angry that I could not control their actions. They ate loaves of bread or whatever else they could find, and my brother George took a whole loaf of that special white toast bread which we hardly ever got, rolled it into a ball, then devoured the entire thing in one sitting.

The next year Dad built another room above the kitchen, making this a two-story addition. It made another bedroom and now there were two bedrooms plus the hall on the second floor. All my siblings slept in the front bedroom and Mom and Dad finally had their own bedroom at the back. I was in the hall between the two bedrooms. Dad had built permanent bunkbeds in the kid's front room, and it was a great space saving idea.

George slept in the top bunk and Mat in the bottom bunk, and this worked fine until one night the younger fell out of his bunk onto the corner of a table and then to the floor. The table was provided to do our homework on in case we felt like doing it. I remember waking up to a loud crash and painful crying, and when I reached the room just a step away, there was blood everywhere, and what a horrible sight it was. We stayed home alone while Mom and Dad took George to the hospital, and we thought he would die that night. Upon his return we were told of his broken nose, and we believed it when we saw his blackened eyes, and swollen face. To this day his nose is very stuffed up and George had a lot of accidents compared to the rest of us. I suppose you could also say he is very fortunate because nothing has left him permanently impaired, although he has kept his guardian angel very busy.

I learned about a birthmark I had as Mom continually talked about it. My mother would talk about a little spot at the side of my head, at the top of my ear where it meets my face near the temple. Apparently, this was supposed to be a very special birthmark passed down in the family and only a very few special descendants received it. Hearing this as fact, and knowing I was the only child in my family with this mark, meant nothing except that it made a good tale. This was until one of my grandchildren was born with it too, and it made me realize with wonder at the miracle of our gene pool, even to the smallest of details. Dustin, our only grandchild with that red highlight to his hair, inherited this birth mark too. My mom said she would always be able to identify me because of it, and I guess we will always be able to identify Dustin too. Mom always said one in every generation had the mark. It was much better than inheriting flat feet, or freckles as most of us did.

Our lives became constant in the way of turmoil. Every day under the same old pressures of wondering if our parents threatening divorce would happen, and how many more raging outbursts would there be, as I often heard the word divorce. Except for Mat and I, the other children never felt targeted by Mom and Dad's rage, but I still suffered the backlash of their arguments and felt I was the cause.

Dad thought Mom was cheating on him again, but we knew she was not, and Mom would accuse Dad of many other things, but not so directly that the children caught on. I felt shunned and unloved after each of these episodes.

The pain both Mom and Dad were going through makes a lot of sense to me now, as many years later Dad revealed to me of their earlier lives. Knowing the circumstances and their history, I wish they could have reached out for help.

The terrible unending war was too much to listen to at times and I just wanted to disappear into nowhere. There was such mistrust for my mom by Dad, and Mom had so much contempt for my dad. If they only knew or realized where their feelings began, they could have been whole people, not living their lives through their hurts of the past and then retaliation.

Years later, on our trips to the doctor and during sessions before his dialysis, Dad told me of their tormented past years. We spent a lot of un-interrupted time together in his last days, when he was ill and needed to be chauffeured and assisted with appointments and generally everything. They were days that I could only listen without resolve, only to show com-passion.

It is easy to think on the more recent days with Dad after my healing, but I must go back and let you know the progression of remembering all my life, good and bad.

Playing outside was an escape and restored my gloomy moods, and we played, "Cowboys and Indians," with the neighborhood kids. The forts and corrals were made from tree branches and Harry once locked me up, in a stick corral other kids had made. I was an Indian, and he was being a Cowboy. "Cowboys and Indians," was a popular game played, as well as watched on the television. We meant no malice or disrespect by using these names and used them with high opinion regarding who they were, and it is strange how I recall this moment in time with such detail. I didn't like Harry that much when I was young as I thought he was too bossy and loud, although very good looking. The fort was easy to escape from and as quickly as he left, I got out of there.

No matter what we experienced outside our home, we had to return to the fighting and yelling inside those confining walls.

Dad told me on one of our talks, that Mom had married him on the rebound. She had been married before to the love of her life, but he had an affair, and got this woman pregnant. When Mom found out she was angry and visited the woman. She told her she could have the father of her child as Mom did not want him. Mom got divorced shortly after, and being comforted by Dad, spent many hours with him as he was a close friend. Being betrayed to the core, she was destroyed and became bitter. She accepted Dad's reassurances without falling in love.

Dad said they were already very compatible friends and comfortable with each other as they hung out with the same group of people. Burying the past instead of dealing with it, she and Dad moved in together on the rebound. Mom got pregnant and after a terribly difficult delivery, she bore my brother Mat who was over ten pounds. Apparently, the midwife jumped on Mom's stomach to help her have the baby. I cannot imagine that, and Mom swore she would never get pregnant again. Dad said they were happy and shortly after Mom was expecting again. They were married before I was born but I was a much easier delivery although over nine pounds.

When Mom happened to be out one day, Dad got an unexpected visitor, and it was Mom's ex-husband. I didn't know that Mom was even married and divorced until after she died, and I received all her papers. Dad told me their history then, and it was just a few years before he died.

The ex-husband articulated that he wanted Mom back and would raise her two children as his own, and Dad listened until he couldn't control himself any longer and his anger exploded. He physically threw him out and off the yard, with indignant words and loud outrageous gestures. Dad did not tell Mom that her ex-husband had come to visit and a little while later when I was one, they immigrated to Canada. Dad thought he had escaped Mom's past and his secret. In Canada Mom received a letter informing her of the visit from her ex-husband and the anger began. She felt she should have had a chance to make her own choice. Our mom never forgave nor resolved her unrecognized anger, as she didn't realize or see that it was even there.

Dad continuously feared the fact that she would leave him for another man, if she had the chance, as this is what she continually threatened. What a shame to lose all those precious years to such bitterness, as Mom made comments about never remarrying if she ever got divorced. I thought that was a good rule to live by until I found out she was divorced and remarried. It was hard to figure out this double standard, but I realize now having more knowledge of the matter, that Mom was making digs at our dad. She was insinuating she would not marry him again, given the chance, and that is what she was saying.

Mom was very critical about people that had left their wives in Russia or Germany after the war. Families were torn apart, and people couldn't find each other. It was assumed that family members had died during that fierce war. Many of our adult friends found themselves in this situation. They even had children that were left behind as they traveled to Canada. Some did not tell their present wives of the past marriages and caused many broken hearts. Family problems arose when mail arrived, to inform them of loved ones searching for them. War was a terrible time and was overwhelmingly difficult for many people, although being honest with the people you love would always be the best policy avoiding much hurt in the future. Some of these people never ever considered that they would find their families again. Some of those allowed their hurts to follow them into their graves, but they could have dealt with them and forgiven those who trespassed against them. Dad said that Mom could not forgive him and reminded him of his shortcomings and failures daily.

19. Unrecognized Disabilities

I found school difficult, sometimes getting "zero," on my tests. I would do well on an essay or project my thoughts to paper many times, and then see that full marks were taken off for spelling. To have full marks taken off for spelling was repeatedly devastating to me, and I continuously got failing marks, frustrating me as I got the same words wrong over and over. What was the matter with me?

One of the toughest times to endure was when teams were picked for spelling bees, and you guessed it; I was known for the worst speller in the class. Never picked, but left standing alone and embarrassed, I was left to whoever had the last pick, and could have crawled into the cracks of the old creaky hardwood floors of the classroom and disappeared never to return. The reputation I had followed me, but my disabilities were only revealed to me in the very distant future.

Many girls made a great impression on me that year, and I regarded them as having it all, as their clothes were new and modern, and their hair so stylish for the time. I guess I was getting to the age of wanting to fit in with them, but we didn't spend much time together as classmates and I can't remember who my friends were in grades three, four, and five. I felt so alone both at school and at home even though I was surrounded by people. Christmas was always a welcomed break from school.

We still couldn't afford much, so when the buzz in the neighborhood was that Harry was getting a bike, we all knew about it, and the whole neighborhood was more excited than a disturbed beehive. Harry was not aware of the Christmas gift and not too many kids we knew even had a bicycle. This bike had balloon tires and was painted a dark color, as well as passed down from his older brother Walter, and with his gift also came a pair of new rubber boots. We just couldn't wait for the moment that he appeared on the street with his Christmas gift.

In our family we received our gifts from our parents and not from Santa Claus. This Christmas Eve I went to church while Mom decorated the live Christmas tree for her family. After church I enjoyed walking in a light dusting of snow before I went into our house. Even though I attended the Christmas Eve service next door alone, it left me with a feeling of contentment and joy as the snow falling on my face solidified the moment, and I recall, it was the lightest and most beautiful snowfall leaving the impression of a perfect night in my mind. I could enjoy it as perfection for the rest of my life to be imagined from then on; it was the most awesome night of anticipation and peace, and it was Christmas!

Harry tore around the neighborhood even though it was snowing, and he wore his rubber boots, and was the proud owner of his wonderful secondhand bicycle. I recall thinking it was the most coveted gift I would want as a child. To own a bike—that must be very special! I felt his joy as everyone else did, and I stood there quietly watching him tear up and down the street.

In our home, Christmas was meager that particular year, and we received just one gift each. I was surprised when a disappointed feeling unwittingly came over me when I opened my gift and found a sewing basket. I thought to myself, "Why a sewing basket?" It was not a gift that I longed for or appreciated. I had not yet learned to transform all of Mom's pieces of leftover materials into my own creations and at present, not wanting to disappoint my parents, I pretended to like the gift.

My mother sewed my sister and I identical dresses for our Sunday clothes. Mom must have sacrificed a great deal of time and effort, and it was a token of her love for us as time was at a premium. She sewed at night to surprise us with the dresses in the morning, but I was five years older than my sister, and we had the same dresses. I felt like I should have a more grown-up style or better yet, a dress bought at the store.

Mom knitted me a brown and yellow sweater, which I absolutely did not want to wear, but was forced to. My teacher asked me who knitted my beautiful sweater. That question said to me, it was, and looked homemade.

I have since made a full-turn-around and now have a great appreciation for anything handmade. This took some time of maturing, experiencing the knowledge and the dedication of hours it took to finish a handcrafted project, and I do enjoy handcrafted projects that have a professional appearance when possible.

I hung onto the valuable traits Mom taught me, both the good ones as well as the bad ones, like keeping every scrap of material. I became such a collector of stuff as it was so hard to discipline myself to throw out or give away these extras. The thought that I would need them at some time in the future, continuously interrupted my trip to the garbage, or recycling bin. Nowadays I find it much easier to part with items as I can recycle them to stores and give someone great pleasure when they find them. Recycling is the thing to do in our world today.

20. The Bite

I enjoyed fashionable clothes as much as I knew about them, and to wear those modern shoes would have been a dream. Mine were heavy orthotic shoes because my feet were unusually flat. The laced shoes contained thick metal, "cookies," now called orthotics, and they are now constructed of plastic and much more comfortable than they used to be. George and I were checked by the Society for Crippled Children once a year. They also provided and paid for our new shoes annually. Though disliking these shoes, I know they saved my feet from a lot of pain and discomfort. As an adult I endure much pain because of my flat feet, as I sometimes refuse to wear the correct shoes. The Society only paid for my shoes until I was thirteen, but before that age, I had my feet checked by physicians who thought I should have surgery when they stopped growing. After investigating this, our family physician decided there would be more pain after surgery than before. Although I was not able to wear those wonderful black patent leather shoes as a child, I did wear heels as a teen and thereafter. My feet have pained me most of my life and I am one who likes to sit with my feet up rather than stand. In the mornings they are so stiff that I can hardly bend them until I get them moving, and it looks something like a duck walk.

The Society for Crippled Children also picked George and I up for a Christmas party every year. The first evening made me nervous as our family wasn't very social, and our skills weren't developed by any stretch of your imagination. The Society provided a wonderful turkey dinner.

We certainly did not eat turkey at our home until I was married. I'm not saying my mom didn't make delicious meals, but a turkey dinner was not a German meal, and foreign to her until later years, as well as probably too expensive to buy.

I learned during the first Society for Crippled Children Christmas dinner, that I did not know how to eat with my knife and fork. Carefully watching others, I took those skills home to practice until the next year when they were perfected. I was very comfortable at the beautifully presented table the following year. George and I even though shy, came home from our outing very enthused.

We received a gift from Santa Claus at the party and this was also foreign to us. Santa was not German as we celebrated Saint Nicholas Day on December fifth, when our shoes were polished like never before and then put outside in front of the door. Saint Nicholas would fill our shoes with fruit or candy, but if you were a bad girl or boy, you would have a shoe filled with coal. Thank goodness we never got coal in our shoes, although I do know a child that got coal and I can't believe the disappointment and bruises for life that this action would leave. Back then, Santa was not as influential in the world or our lives, as he is now.

The show and tell current events or news of the day at school were a challenge, as we did not get the newspaper. I wasn't the only one with this problem as the rest of the bus kids were in the same position although this didn't make us feel any better about our situation. We didn't live the lifestyle of most of the children at school. We were all first-generation immigrant children from the wrong side of the tracks, listening to the radio for our news. Most kids did not want to hear the news, instead they wanted to see the cutouts of newsprint that were brought in daily, and we felt our news did not measure up to theirs.

Renate lived in our neighborhood, down one of those paths and was older than grade school level. Most of the immigrant children were put back into grade one to learn the English language. Some of them were teenagers or pre-teens and being put back this far must have been so humiliating. Their parents never spoke English at home and so English never came easily to them.

This young lady captured the hearts of the teachers at Consolidated School. She was intelligent, beautiful, and worked hard. She was going to quit school after the year when she could speak English, as she needed to get a job to help the family financially. Being the eldest girl, it was common practice in most families we knew. The teachers wanted her to enjoy the grade eight graduation as she did so well. Her teacher bought her the most beautiful blue chiffon graduation dress and shoes to match. I remember seeing her at school that day and thinking how gorgeous she looked for her graduation. It was the talk of the neighborhood especially amongst the females. She was a naturally beautiful girl and now looked like a princess and I had never seen such an attractive dress before. The school and teacher presented her with such a personal uplifting gift as they gave the time, effort and finances to reach out to a young person in this way. This still leaves me with warm fuzzy feelings today. Their efforts transformed one ordinary girl into a princess.

That fall I would be bussed to Eastwood School on Stewart Road. The bus route would be broken up and we wouldn't see a lot of the kids we rode with in previous years. Even my younger brother and sister would be bussed to Bethel School in the opposite direction from Mat and me. We would make a lot of new friends from Read Road and Lakeshore Road area.

During that summer I did a lot of housework and babysitting as Mom labored on the farm. I took care of my younger sister who was going to school the next year, but I don't remember much about our time together.

I spent time sewing doll clothes and creating many hairdos on my dolls, but I didn't play with them as much anymore, but rather used them to create fashions of my own. On one occasion my mother showed me some caring emotion. She thought I had done a great job in making a doll outfit.

Mom brought her boss in to have a look at my creation. I remember the outfit well; it was a pink two-piece with a skirt and top. You must realize everything was done by hand, because my little toy sewing machine was broken, and I was banned from using my mom's. She was so protective regarding her sewing machine and everything else she owned. No one could touch the sewing machine, even though it was old, and you had to peddle it with your feet to make it run.

The dolls all got their hair done every Saturday and were dressed in their best outfits for the weekend, and then put away. Most of the time I was given the impression that my hobby was a waste of time, and I should do chores around the house.

Eventually I found a place to have fun at my friend's house, where it became an escape, and where I learned to dance. I visited her when I could and once, I went to see Lorraine as she had just lost her sister to an illness. I thought I would spend some time with her. We didn't see each other often as she went to the Catholic school and wasn't allowed away from home much. She had a busy working mom, who was opposed to having too many kids in the house at one time, just the same mindset my mother had.

Lorraine and her mom went inside the house and asked me to come in for a visit. As I caught the screen door, Rex the family dog suddenly lunged at me. He was black and mean, but he was normally tied up. I let out a yell and they turned and came running back to me hollering at the dog. His large white teeth had penetrated my right wrist both on the top and the bottom. I was shocked and went into my "tuned out" state. This state became so familiar to me in my life. All I can say is that it was a state of being where I seemed to be removed emotionally, and not able to feel. I was in a place where I could not be hurt.

With overwhelming apology, they wrapped my wrist carefully after applying a cream. I said I was fine, and they drove me home. My parents had gone out for groceries with the younger siblings, so not feeling well, I went straight to bed. With no word to my mom or dad about my misfortune, they went to work the next day before I got up in the morning. We still didn't have a phone, so Lorraine's mom drove to our place to see how I was doing. I had removed the bandages for the day, so it was not obvious to anyone. I remember Mom being concerned and I don't know why I refrained from telling my parents. Rex was euthanized, and the rumor was that he went mad because his owner, and best friend had died. Even though he had bitten me, I had compassion in my heart when I thought of him missing the person he loved most.

21. Music to My Ears

We diminish arguments and every pretension that sets itself up against the knowledge of God, and take captive every thought to make it obedient to Christ.

2 Corinthians 10:5

Across the road from Lorraine lived the Joe Schulz family, also from the common town in Germany. His wife Tilly was very kind. The family lived in our neighborhood along with both sets of their parents and all siblings. Their daughter Ruth was a favorite playmate of mine although she was a few years younger. She had lovely red hair and was a spirited child with parents who loved and admired her very much.

Ruth and I took accordion lessons at her home and the accordion was found to be a great instrument of harmony and yet expressed tempo, an enjoyable discovery for myself. It was an overwhelming job carrying that accordion through the neighborhood to the Schulz residence for lessons every week. The teacher usually gave me a ride home after class, and it was so appreciated. I enjoyed the accordion but was not encouraged in our home. Every time I rehearsed my material for the next week the family and Mom told me to put it away. Not understanding, I tried to make excuses for their actions. Maybe in the small space of our home that incongruous musical noise might have been too much. It saddened me to the point of crying and falling asleep with the accordion still strapped to me.

The roadblock to practice stayed with me into my adult life as a parent. It was the deciding factor in letting my children make noises in our home, musical or otherwise, at any time night or day. I had learned a lasting lesson from this experience as I enjoyed the sounds my children made, as music to my ears. I have to say there was a lot of music in our home from trumpets and drums practicing, to bands jamming through all hours of the night and this remained, always to be, a sweet sound to my ears.

When I was young, the walk to Ruth's place was an adventure. There was a well-trodden path at the back of our house that took me past our family's double seated outhouse.

Then you would pass the garbage pile. It was where we dumped everything and burned what we could. The kids loved burning garbage except for the stench. When your nostrils became accustomed to the smell, there was no hesitation. The fire pit was also accompanied with too many parental warnings, although that never stopped us from burning more garbage.

We were not supposed to put sealed cans and such in the fire, but my brothers thought why not? Suddenly, we heard a loud bomb-like sound, and something flew out of the fire. The syrup can torpedoed all the way over to the neighbor's place, where they thought the house was being bombed. There was an empty lot beside us, so you can imagine how far the can flew. Nothing could be kept a secret in this little village and when our parents heard, they banned us from the fire pit after our elderly neighbor explained to our parents what happened. It barely missed his head and hit the building. We were grateful for that bit of grace and did not put closed cans in the garbage again.

At the back of our lot was a very small grapery and the path hugged its property line. Then you passed a few intriguing sheds made of any recycled material in post war fashion. Not one scrap of anything was wasted. You could imagine what it looked like, as one piece of wood was nailed beside a scrap of metal, next to an old door continued by some old timbers, odd pieces of lumber, tin, old wood boxes, chicken wire clad with scrap wood, paneling of sorts and more represented the adjacent wall. There were about four sheds in a row, all joined together. When you passed the sheds another path to the left took you to Ruth's house.

It was so interesting to follow as I learned to appreciate and love those days of simplicity. No one ever minded that you were walking right in front of his or her back door.

An old man lived in the house at that turn. Visiting my parents now and again, he didn't appear well groomed. His clothes were soiled, and his beard was very shabby and overgrown, all the while maintaining a compassionate look in his eyes. He looked different than everyone else and again, Mom's compassionate side showed as she invited him in at times. I never got to know his personality or character, but Mom thought he was a good man, so that said it all.

These paths were so well used that you could find your way on them even after dark although there were no path lights in those days. Continuing, they led through some old orchard until it reached, what I call the city of sheds. I say this, not to be disrespectful because none of us had better and made do with the little we were blessed with. It looked like a small street of sheds to me.

I had a memorable visit at one of these shacks, as I found it so warm and so cozy inside. There was a little stove, wood or oil, I don't know, also a large pot of soup cooking on it. The place was jam-packed full of all kinds of pans, trunks, a small table, and a couple of old worn-out chairs. A lantern hung in one corner, and radiated a beautiful warm glow, into this one room family home. The family of five that lived in this tiny, tiny little place, had just come to this country to be with their relatives. A daughter older than I, was their youngest. Her name was Selma and we got to know each other better as I got older. We soon got to know Selma's mom as "Kleine Oma." (*Kleine,* meaning small in German.) She was short in stature, wore a tightly pulled bun at the back of her head but as I recall, there were always loose strands of wavy hair around the circumference of her sometimes flushed, but round face.

When she spoke, you had no choice but to listen and follow instructions. I often wonder how children recognize these personality and character traits in people and how do I influence the children around me. She was such a workhorse and could do a man's job any day, and did so, every day. Everyone gave her respect for the honest person she was, both in word and in deed. She never minced words, and you always knew what she was thinking. At times she also told you, what you should be thinking. She held no grudges and took life as a matter of fact. What you see is what you get, was her attitude.

One day a couple of years later I was walking this path when I saw her with a huge, long knife in her hand. I stopped and wondered what she was doing as she was standing over a cow laying on the ground with its belly so large that it couldn't get up. Kleine Oma took that knife and stuck it right into the blown-up belly of the cow and I was shocked! It was like a balloon loudly popped and the cow's belly was deflated. When I ran home to tell my mother, she told me the cow had been eating the wrong thing and it caused it to blow up with gas. Mom said it would have burst if Kleine Oma didn't do that. Later the cow was just fine, and I marveled that it could be after a knife was stuck into it.

I didn't get to see inside the other sheds, but I'm sure they had to be stuffed with the most marvelous collection of this and that. Every item deemed as a valuable one that would be needed soon.

The village was made up of people who had lost everything. They struggled to make it through the war and learned to hoard everything they could get their hands on. As I passed this unique little part of my "community playground," I turned to the right and there was the home of my friend Ruth. It was just a basement in the ground with just a waterproof floor above it, but much larger than any of us in the area were used to.

As you entered the stairwell and went down into a large open area, the basement greeted you. Along the front wall of the basement were other rooms. The one I remember most, is the kitchen. I think everyone that knew the Schulz family, and ever met Tilly, knew that she could feed an army any day of the week at a moment's notice. She was renowned for her bountiful and good tasting food. I am sure there are fortunate people still using her recipes to this day. I was taken back as I entered her kitchen as there was always something new to be eaten. You must get the picture; it was a large stove and table all covered with, "The food of the day."

One day it was fried smelts which I just loved, so I ate as many as I felt like having. We were rationed at home, so I thought I hit the jackpot. I often wonder how she kept up as everyone in the village did the same thing, eating without borders. Her place was never one commanding order but rather of total comfort and relaxation. Everyone who entered sensed this mood of contentment.

Later that year Joe Schulz finished the upper main floor of the house.

It was the most modern and best looking home in our little village and it was a "semi." They lived in one side and rented the other side out. Joe built Oma Schulz, Kleine Oma, his mother, a new house too. I was sorry to see no one living in the tiny shed as it deteriorated after being abandoned.

Joe built a huge swing at the back of his home, towering at least fifteen feet in the air. It had ropes attached to the top where it was secured to a four-seater box built of wood. I was a spectator at the time waiting for my turn, while I watched Selma and Ruth swinging as they went extremely high. It looked like so much fun, but suddenly, the rope broke, and they went flying. With screaming, the bystanders ran to the spot where gravity and the wood carrier met. Everyone was relieved to find there were no injuries. Joe never repaired the swing and to my recollection it was never used again. He was too traumatized by the accident and grateful that no one was injured, and he would not take a chance on that happening again.

There was a dirt road across from the Schulz home, an extension of Eastchester Road, and it was freely used by everyone to get to the canal. The grass on the side of the road was tall and flanked with orchards. When nearing the canal, you saw the tall, treed canopy over, the shorter brush shaded beneath. There you found a steep climb on a well-defined path, to one of my favorite spots, the deep end of the canal. As compared to where we swam as younger children, in the shallow end or mud hole, here the water was well over our heads.

This is where I really learned to swim and not just stay afloat. Quite unexpectedly, I was thrown in the deep water just like everyone else and forced to learn to tread water and move my body forward without time to think. We hung out there as much as possible.

It was the first place we headed for after working those hot long days in fields and orchards. It was a meeting place for pre-teens and then as teens. Naturally, it took the place of our galvanized tub in the middle of the kitchen floor for bathing. I found the canal water a refreshing change from the recycled tub water, which everyone in the family used. It was a great meeting place, or at times, a place of quiet solitude. We built rafts and constructed primitive diving boards, never knowing if they would survive until the next time we were back.

I found many interesting things at the canal, one of them being a playboy book. It was hidden in the trunk of a huge old tree. Along with this we found condoms everywhere. Not knowing what they were, we thought they were balloons. Being informed would have been a good thing, rather than to be so naïve.

It was an amazing place to do some bird watching and wander through the forest. We found a lot of bird nests, which I learned to treasure even into adulthood.

From our back door across the church yard beside us, lay another well-trodden path. It took us across the Ledwez back yard and angled left towards Eastchester Road. It passed an old well and continued across a vast field. It took us to another farm. You must get a picture of what this excursion was like as it took effort, and you had to want to go to the farm or else it was too far.

I went to this farm many times not wanting to miss out. The mother of the home was a giving woman who never failed to have time for us as she was not like our mom who was always cleaning the house.

White, sliced, store bought bread, was a never-ending commodity at their home. It was accompanied with a sizeable jar of strawberry jam. This jam was also purchased at the grocery store and was an item we never saw in our homes. Remember, everything we saw at our tables was home made, and second class, or so we thought at that time. We would make sandwiches and watch TV to our heart's content and for a time, the whole neighborhood gathered at this home. None of us had a television set so this was such a treat.

There were only three children our age in this home, but often had at least six kids at a time watching television and snacking with them. The strawberry jam sometimes ran out. In these inopportune times, a new jar of orange marmalade was put on the table. I have to say, it stayed there for quite a while, as the immigrant children did not acquire the taste for this jam, and we still don't like this flavor to this day.

The family had many relational inadequacies, but none of us thought more or less of it. I didn't even realize my own family was dysfunctional. I was told many secrets by my friend who lived in this home. Those details are theirs to tell and my story is mine to tell, although, their secrets added to the confusion of my emotions.

The language I heard made me uncomfortable even as a child and into my teens. Hearing so many swear words affected my mind. They just circled round and round in my head as I was so used to hearing them in the context that made them powerful. Since I chose not to use these words, it was a massive battle not to think them and control my thoughts. I felt dirty having these words in my mind and I was in a constant persistent combat. God helped me to overcome this by giving me an idea. It was to pray for whoever I was swearing at in my mind or pray for whatever situation I was cursing. I did this faithfully knowing God was directing me. In just a short time, I found that I didn't think swear words as much and I felt in control of my thoughts again. If you keep praying when you have evil thoughts, you will stop having those thoughts. You must remember that God is more powerful than his counterfeit and you will be the victor with Him on your side. This was overwhelming and effective in my life, and I still use this method even when I have the wrong feeling towards someone.

Back then I associated everything I heard and felt, "to not receiving love." I was thinking with a child's mind. I remember the desire to have someone to love being so strong, that I prayed to God for my own child. I knew I would take good care of it and love it as I should. I was not even clear on how to have a baby, and I never imagined that sex was a part of it.

I thank God for protecting me in this confused time of my life and keeping me safe until I could make informed and mature choices. I just love the fact that God was there for me to talk to every night, no matter how I felt or how confused I was. He filled my need for love every time I talked to Him.

22. On the Corner

Rod, a bachelor, lived down our street at the corner of Stewart Road and Niagara Stone Road; he regularly welcomed the neighborhood kids to come over on Saturday mornings to watch his tiny television in his very small home. We would sit on the floor in front of the television and be mesmerized. Rod's place was intriguing in that there were stacks of records from floor to the low ceiling. He had a lot of neat things.

Occasionally, we would hear a loud musical sound coming from Rod's place. Every child within hearing distance would drop what they were doing and run at high speed down to the little cabin at the corner. Rod had a captain friend who worked on the ships on the canal and couldn't be around too much because of his job. The captain trustingly stored an oversized "music machine" in one of the sheds at Rod's place where it was well cared for. When he visited, he would play this monster machine. As we watched, the cymbals clanged, the drums banged, the piano played, the horn instruments blew, and we stared on in wonderment and were amazed by this unique machine.

Watching television at Rod's ended for me when we got our own TV and I preferred to stay home to watch. The boys all loved getting together as a group to hang out, but as I was the only girl, I stepped back into my own space.

Years later, as my husband and I enjoyed the Balls Falls Festival, our ears caught that same sound we heard as children. We followed it and discovered that same musical machine in a building. The captain's wife was still giving people the opportunity to enjoy it's music, although the captain had already passed away. It gave us both so much pleasure to view this relic from our past, to know it was still cared for, and sounded just as it had over sixty years before. It is said to be the last steam calliope in Canada, and we were privileged to enjoy it many times in our youth.

The Jeffery family also lived at that corner just to the right of Rod's place. It was a super tiny house. It was as small as our home before Dad built the addition. They were a larger family as there were seven children. There were two cottage-size bedrooms with bunks, and I don't know where they all slept.

Mrs. Jeffery continuously invited us in, even though she often didn't feel well. She made the best butter tarts I have ever eaten. I have eaten many since hers, trying to find that special magic that her tarts had. After she baked them, the tarts sat on the kitchen table, and we were allowed to eat as many as we wanted. Occasionally she would say that they were having company and we should leave a few. It was so different than my place where everything was hoarded.

Betty Ann Jeffery was around my age, and we hung out, but the two of us were kept busy doing chores and neither place was great for getting away from family. We did some school projects together as we lived in the same neighborhood.

Many years later, Mrs. Jeffery visited my mom on a cold evening. As she was talking, she started to cough, so much so, that she could hardly catch her breath. Not being able to breathe, she kept on dragging on her cigarette as if that would cure her cough. It wasn't caring or compassionate of my husband and I, but we started to chuckle, and we had to go to another room not to embarrass ourselves, or her. It simply struck us as odd that she would keep on taking a puff of her cigarette while coughing so badly and not being able to breathe. Probably being the only luxury she allowed herself, as the family was also struggling financially, she kept up her habit. I feel so heartless now thinking about her suffering, but then I just saw what took place in front of me – a very compassionate woman who could not breathe because she was smoking,

My mother asked her if she would like to have a bath, as she didn't have an inside bathroom. My husband had put a bathroom in the house for my parents by then. Take note that this was years down the road from where my life story is currently. She took a relaxed bath and I thought it was so kind of mom to offer her this rare indulgence. I guess Mom must have remembered how it was for her, when we had nothing, not even an inside toilet.

Halloween supplied us annually with many candy kisses, and a few other varieties and every bit was appreciated. The candy apples made by Mrs. Kitcheman in our neighborhood were my favorite. We had to get to her place quickly before they were all gone. This was so different than these days when everything must be prepackaged, and bought, as well as checked by parents before the children could even think of enjoying them.

We gathered old clothing from around the house and were dressed as what we called, "Bums." That word was politically correct back in those days. There was never a time when we didn't dress ourselves and we took great pride in our costumes, as we blackened our faces to make them look dirty. Our parents never went out with us. We formed gangs to hang out with as soon as it was dark any time after five and came home by ten. We didn't have candy to hand out at our home and we never considered ourselves to be cheap or strange. It was just not expected in any of our homes.

We walked all the way to Highway 8 where the Canadians lived, and the treats were bountiful. Then we walked a long way over Homer Bridge, past Victoria Lawn Cemetery, and past Consolidated School, to a densely populated area on and around Queenston Street. The treats filled our now heavy pillowcases as we knocked on door after door. The cloth bags got so heavy after a while that I just wanted to go back home. The walk was exceptionally far and if the older group weren't ready to go back, you just had to wander back by yourself. As we got a little older, we made our own group of younger kids. I was the only girl for a long time, as Lorraine wasn't allowed to go out for Halloween. We knew nothing of the origin of Halloween and its dark side, so we enjoyed it to the fullest, just indulging on the goodies and good will of everyone who passed them out.

The Ledwez family moved just before Harry's seventh grade ended. His dad built a new home at 580 Geneva Street in St. Catharines. It was the same neighborhood where Harry's best friend Marvin lived. Marvin also had a sister Erna, and his mom was my first Sunday school teacher at the neighborhood church. They had a bachelor named George who lived with them.

It was the biggest deal when George got married to a wonderful lady from the west, Helen. They married in their later years, but not too late to have a precious child. They were blessed and thankful to God for their son and the community looked up to this man and revered him to be righteous.

Alexander Schultz and his wife, as well as family, lived across the street with two of their grown children Gertrude and Ernie. It seemed like the German people liked living close to their friends as it gave them the village feeling.

Gerda, Harry's sister was admitted to the Sanitorium Hospital with Tuberculosis (TB). She spent a year in recovery, and it must have been awful as a young person to lose so much time of her life. Although the Ledwez family lived on Geneva Street at this time, the TB was traced back to their cow in the old neighborhood. We still lived there and were notified about the TB and told not to drink unpasteurized milk.

Everyone in our neighborhood drank unpasteurized milk purchased from the owner of the neighborhood cow. Herbert and Antonie Ledwez used to be the proud owner of our lifeline but now it belonged to the Plett family. Subsequently, the neighborhood community was transformed with the regular appearance of a new face, the milkman.

We didn't have to endure making our own butter anymore. I might add, it took a lot of arm muscle as you shook and rolled the large jar filled with cream until it became butter. We also did not have to have fresh buttermilk, as I disliked it. Everyone had to be checked for TB after that, especially the Ledwez Family.

While Gerda was in the hospital, she made Harry a bulky beige sweater with a beautiful large brown deer amongst the trees. It looked like a Mary Maxim sweater with a zipper. Harry loved that sweater and kept it until he was married. His inexperienced wife washed and minimized his sweater into a child size misshaped form. She felt saddened but could not bring it back to life and has pondered often, of the labor it demanded to make this attractive gift.

I missed Gerda when she moved. She spent hours talking with me and hanging out. We talked at church or in Sunday school, which made me feel included. Gerda owned all the paints to decorate our carefully shaped mud sculptures. She knew about design and new trends in clothes and jewelry. Gerda was an interesting person to spend time with then, and still is to this day.

23. Babysitting

No temptation has overtaken you except what is common to mankind.
And God is faithful; He will not let you be tempted beyond what you can bear. But when you
are tempted, He will also provide a way out so that you can endure it.

1 Corinthians 10:13

I appreciated baby sitting and dedicated myself to the children that I cared for, and it was a respectable income for that time. One day Mom and I were in our front yard, and a man just happened by, announcing he was looking for a babysitter. I asked my mother, who was right beside me, if I could go and she said yes. The man looked unkempt, and his car was a total mess with rotted floorboards giving tours of the road. We had no idea who he was, where he lived and what time I would be back. Upon arriving at the house, I felt very uncomfortable. It wasn't because the family was different than we were, but the place was dark, untidy and unkempt. I was not used to a disorderly house like this one. The man and his wife seemed nice enough and left soon after, already having put the children to bed giving me little to do.

Books lay all over the house, so out of boredom I picked one up to read. The sex acts were laid out in such detail that I couldn't have mistaken the facts even if I knew nothing about this stuff. I was learning lots and it was captivating, and was mesmerized until after reading a while, I was jolted back into reality.

The actuality was that I was consumed with terrible thoughts and didn't feel good about myself at all. I wanted to hide from God but didn't know where to go. All I could think about were the sexual pictures branded in my mind. To this day I could retrieve them and could have a very clear picture of my readings, but do not choose to, as this was an overwhelming task for me to overcome back then.

I made up my mind that with God's help, I would never read that kind of material again, even into my adult life. I prayed that God would help me. Then the thought of cleaning the house came to my mind. It must have been God because only He could have ordained so beautifully something else to occupy my mind in such a dramatic way.

I immediately picked up the garbage strewn around, tidying as I went. After collecting a large pile, I headed for the garbage can which I assumed was under the sink. Mentally torn between going back to the books again, I thought with God's help I would not read that kind of material again.

I put all the garbage that I had gathered on the counter and went for the garbage can. As I opened the double doors under the sink, a huge rat stared back at me from on top of the full garbage pail. I screamed and slammed the door, which stayed ajar about an inch or so. I got a chair and secured the doors by putting it in front of them to provide a solid barrier, or so I hoped. I didn't even want to sit on the couch as maybe there was another under it. I sat with my legs up on a chair all night, just waiting for the man and woman to return.

They arrived home very late, and I was frightened all night and thought about that rat, and others that might be close to me. How did these people live and sleep here? Even then, I didn't know their names–how bizarre was that?

They came back happy having enjoyed their night out, and the man took me home after paying me. They wondered if I was free to baby sit next week. Although they were a pleasant couple, I felt I was busy and graciously declined.

I can't believe my parents let me go to a place they knew nothing about. The age of twelve was too young not to know with whom I was going, or even where I was going, even if I wanted to.

I was taught a great life lesson because I seldom forgot to guard my eyes and mind. I have tried not to subject my mind to such a demoralizing place, either by what I read or watched on TV or at the movies. I have learned when I watch something distasteful or inappropriate, especially sexual scenes, they stay with me a long time. I do not know if others are like that, but I have learned what affects me deep within. Maybe because of the things that I have experienced in my past, it left a sensitive imprint on me.

The most important thing is what God can do with any situation, physical or mental. He has the answer, even if we are in an unexpected situation and not aware. Nothing is a surprise to God. I am so thankful that He was there with me and without a doubt, showed me an escape. God provided me with such a dramatic experience with the rat, that my mind was totally occupied with it. I am in awe when I think of how much God loves me, sees me, and helps me. He is so creative with his answers to our prayers.

24. Branching Out

It was an uneventful year, but I enjoyed my teacher Mr. Bodner. He instilled some self-confidence in me, by encouraging me to try out for the baseball team. I was so happy when I made it and proudly shared the news with my family. Quickly I was told, there would be no time for baseball, as there was too much to do at home. The angry feelings I had were suppressed and I obeyed. Continuously trying to do the things other girls did, I came up against a brick wall every time.

I also joined Girl Guides that year and loved it. We got together at the new Eastwood School, where I attended. It was located on Stewart Road near Lakeshore Road but shortly after I was forbidden to go to Guides. Betty Ann Jeffery and I decided to hitch hike down Stewart Road to Guides one evening. It wasn't long before an old, wreck of a car and taxi wanted to pick us up, and we said we had no money and were hitchhiking. He insisted on giving us a ride anyways and asked what in the world we were doing hitchhiking, out in the country by ourselves. He said we should call our parents for a ride home. We couldn't do that as we had no phone. We promised him that we would tell someone at Guides about not having a ride home. He seemed relieved when we told him it was a promise. I now thank God for this caring man who gave us a free ride and was so concerned about our safety.

At Guides we had a great time until the captain found out what we had done to get there. The captain took us home and told us never to repeat our actions again, and we agreed. The only problem was that we had no other way of getting to Guides. It was one of the last times I was able to get there.

I loved sports and entered all the running and running broad jumps that year. Doing well in all of them didn't matter as I missed all the field days. My mom took us out of school to work on the farm whenever possible. Field days were not deemed as important and necessary days to attend.

That summer, I worked on the farm making my own money and as it was for myself, I opened a bank account. I was so enthusiastic, and I valued working instead of remaining at our home. I don't know who babysat, but it could have been my brother George. I didn't really care as I was elated to be going to work every day. During that summer I earned enough money to purchase all my school clothes and supplies and it left me with a delightful sense of independence. My work consisted of picking strawberries, cherries, some peaches and of course still babysitting for others.

Most of the babysitting was done for a young couple that rented an apartment at the Schulz house. It was a very clean home, and the couple was a wonderful pair who cared about me. They had a little girl and a new baby boy. Mary had freshly made cherry pie in the fridge, and I had to restrain myself not to have the whole pie. It was recently baked and just too good. Cherry pie was a favorite of mine for many years into married life and cherry pie is usually served with a side of fond memories thanks to Mary, the lady of that house. Mary Wall had checked out my qualifications with my mother as to whether I would be able to handle her little newborn boy. I had already taken care of her little girl many times in the past. This couple appeared to be what a married couple should be like, and they were happy and went out at least a couple of times a month, but never later than eleven, dependably returning on time.

It was a highlight going there and the home was quiet and clean as I felt such peace in their space. Besides enjoying being at their home they paid me for coming to babysit those well-behaved children. The little girl was a sweet gentle spirit, tiny framed, and as cute as a button, and the little boy usually in bed for the night, was always easy to babysit.

Mrs. Wall sent me a card years later when I was married to the effect of doing my job maturely and wished God's blessing on both Harry and me. They had moved out of the country years later and so I had lost touch with them.

While I write this, I am amazed how little things have impacted me.

The past in my life has molded me to be who I am today. From cherry pie to how to relate to people. The early years of life have also molded the present aspects of life that I enjoy and that energize me daily. I remember thinking how wonderful it would be one day to have a family and a home of my own, like theirs.

Housework was never a favorite of mine. I felt inadequate about my housework since Mom was never happy with the job I did. Someday I would have my own home and do things the way I liked.

25. Short, But Powerful

Teach me to do your will, for you are my God!
Let your good spirit lead me on level ground!

Psalm 143:10

That summer a bunch of us kids got together weekly and walked to the show iindowntown St. Catharines on Saturdays. We always had an awesome time as it was away from home and housework. The chores were finished in the early morning if we hurried, and we were off. Once again, I was the only girl. It was fun until one of these movies had nudity in it. Although I only saw the back of the naked woman, the impact was great, and it bothered me. It was not the nakedness as much as the feeling it gave me. I felt compromised and with a short powerful nudge from God, I decided I would not go to the movies anymore and make these kinds of concessions in my life. I distinguished that it was not something God desired for me, but the others continued to enjoy their Saturday outings into town without me. They continued to interact as friends relating and sharing wonderful times together. It is indisputable that most of the movies were harmless, but I recognized when God spoke to me, and I had to listen. He had plans for me and would guide me as to the steps I should take. God knew what would impact me more than I did, and my creator knew how to steer me in the direction towards a life with freedom.

26. Choir

Mr. Bodner was also my teacher in grade seven. He was an awesome teacher, able to pull out talents and abilities that his students had buried deep within. They were just starting to become teens and develop their aptitudes. I can recall how he encouraged students in art classes and music as they developed their abilities. There was something different in a good way about him, but at that age I could not put my finger on it.

It was a year for making friends, as I had bonded with a few kids the year before. I became good friends with Elizabeth, as she was in my class. I was able to go to her house and she came to my place for dinner one evening when Mom wasn't home. She was an "A" student always doing her homework which was important to me. Visiting many times and developing a camaraderie, we spent a year together until she moved.

We had another male music teacher who led the choir and during practice one day, I had a challenging experience. I was in the first row beside all the talkative girls. I didn't say too much at school and above all nothing out of turn.

After addressing the choir with many stern warnings to be quiet, the teacher was ready to explode at the lack of obedience. I turned around to see what was happening behind me as someone poked me in the back. Wham! A hand hit me in the middle of my back, so hard that I couldn't catch my breath as my knees buckled. I didn't know what hit me as I bent over trying to breathe. I finally regained my composure, only to break out in tears. I was uncontrollably crying.

The kids were horrified, and silence fell on the choir participants. I was told by the teacher to go to the nurse's room if I couldn't stop crying. There I composed myself and although I could feel my back, it didn't hurt that much anymore. I can honestly say I have a weak spot in my spine in that same area and it hurts often. It has been manageable, needing a good adjustment now and again. There were no lasting injuries except that of a distasteful memory.

The choir students were so mortified that this could happen to one of them. That week I became popular at school, which I had never been before, but even so it was a horrendous week. The students and especially my classmates thought I should sue, and every time the teacher was outside on yard duty, the girls would follow him around, taunting and declaring he would be sued as they tried to scare him. Thinking about it now, he also must have had a week from hell. I didn't have enough courage and wisdom to tell my peers that we were not suing.

Finally, the principal, Mr. Palmer, called me into the office and in-quired about what we were going to do about the lawsuit. I had to admit that I hadn't even told my parents about the incident, and nothing was going to happen. The teacher must have been so relieved. His week from hell was over and so was mine. The girls were told to stop their taunting. The torture he endured must have been emotionally draining, and I can only imagine how that would take every bit of peace from your workday and your spirit.

I don't blame him, although his actions were unethical. We all make mistakes and mess up and wish we could erase some of those days from our minds and life. I know it has been that way in my life.

To my surprise, the subject came up about a month later at home when one of the kids told my parents we should have sued. Then they told the whole story as I listened in horror. I should have known that nothing more would be said about the matter. I didn't know if my parents thought I was in the wrong or if they thought I should have told them, or even what they were thinking. They said nothing, and it left me sadly wondering about the lack of communication between my parents and myself, as there was no encouragement to talk about anything. By this time, it was spring, and we were all looking forward to working again.

I worked at a nursery that summer, and it was interesting but hard labor as we grafted peach trees and the job meant I was bent over all day.

Although I wore a white long-sleeved shirt, I sunburned so badly that the back of my arms were blistered. My brother Mat seemed to enjoy the camaraderie with the boss and enjoyed his job too. Our mom also worked along with us that summer.

27. Church Camp

We have this as a sure and steadfast anchor of the soul, a hope that enters the inner place behind the curtain.

Hebrews 6:19

I was invited to Bethel Park by Herta and Mary, two girls from my neighborhood and church. They were at least three to four years older than I, but girls I looked up to because of their steadfast Christian walk. Being at church camp, we would spend a week together in one of the original rustic old cabins. Bethel Park is near Rodney Ontario on Lake Erie. The church services gave me a feeling of intimidation, but I was not sure why. It was so foreign to me and how I related to God, as our relationship was secretive and very personal. Maybe because I was like a fish out of water and not used to these surroundings. People prayed out loud and shared and it felt so strange although I could feel the presence of my God there.

One evening I walked down the aisle to the front of the church because I felt God tugging at my heart. I was used to God's nudging and teaching me how I should live my life. Everyone thought I was going for salvation, but I had already taken that step in Sunday school, in the Lutheran church. I knew I was saved although I needed to grow and mature in God and know how to express it.

God was calling me for another reason. I ended up in a corner by myself and there, with God beside me, I cried and cried. It was like a tap that didn't close, and I released my emotions and wept with God holding me tightly. That is how it felt to me. I remember after the service people congratulating me and I wondered for what. I was still crying and couldn't converse with them at this time. I didn't know what God was doing inside me.

The next evening, I went back to my corner. I loved the thought of getting together with my God all alone, just the two of us, as we have always done. As I knelt to pray, God did a different thing in me. For some reason He decided to take me to a new experience. It was the most wonderful, contented peaceful feeling I had ever known. After a while, I could hear people around me, but I didn't care to join them. I couldn't move even if I wanted to, and I didn't know for many years what God was doing at that time. I felt so close to God and so energized in Him when I became aware, as I had not known such peace, ever before, and it didn't matter that I did not know what was happening to me as I trusted God and he was becoming a trusted father to me. I learned many years later that I was "slain in the spirit" as it is called. God was healing something deep within me, and with my emotions out of the way, a healing began deep within the secret places of my soul, behind the curtain. There were more times when God did this for me. God's spirit ministered to mine about things I did not understand, and I liken it to a spiritual realm that you enter. If you have passed out and are coming to, will know a similar feeling. You are at peace and do not want to come back even though you hear your name being called. This is how it felt. I did not want to, nor could I have come back to consciousness until God was done helping my hurt.

It was a great week and I felt spiritually alive until I got home. I had learned many new songs and was singing often. One day doing dishes, my mother asked me not to sing those songs anymore. She said what I had experienced would not last, and after that I didn't sing or express my viewpoint in our home, but I knew God would remain my friend and had no doubts about that.

28. The Clouds Are Parting

"For I know the plans I have for you," declares the Lord, "plans to prosper you and not harm you, plans to give you hope and a future."

Jeremiah 29:11

I realized there was still a degree of disconnect within me as I still wanted to tell lies. The revelation was that I realized this and wanted to be free and live in truth. Wanting reality, I was asking God for an intervention in my life. Of course, God had never failed me through my young life, so I expected Him to be able to prevent me from thinking and expressing untruthful thoughts now and teach me to release accurate sincere expressions. I was learning that God intended to give me good things and a good future if I depended on Him. I could experience myself cultivating truth as it became triumphant as God's love developed His strength within me.

In grade eight I had Mr. Palmer as my teacher, and I benefited from the class immensely. I learned to become confident in myself and asserted myself even more than usual. One thing no teacher could dispute during my school years was that I worked hard and tried my best as my report cards all verify that fact. At one point I redid all my notes from beginning to end, on new paper. The notebook, printed in one-color ink, was very impressive and pristine looking. The pages looked so untouched that the teacher asked me what I did to keep my book from looking worn. I revealed to the vice principal that I had just newly recopied them the night before, and she was in awe. I can still see the little pictures in the top corners to illustrate their contents. This also enabled me to remember the material when I studied for a test as I could recall the page with the little drawings. They consisted of little cabins, rivers, flowers, soldiers and animals, and I sensed a feeling of gratification and great achievement.

I don't recall much in the way of my family that year, although I do remember one morning getting up but still feeling very tired. I went to school as usual and later that day found I had started my menstrual cycle. It was such a shock to me as no one had told me about this strange thing that was happening to me. The girls at school took me to the nurse's room and were very helpful in filling me in on what I needed to know. I cannot believe I was that naïve at the age of thirteen but had missed the health class concerning all these details as I had to be home that day babysitting. Pearl, my friend was much wiser and knowledgeable about these things even though her mother passed away many years before.

Pearl was a lot of fun and always had new clothes to wear. She purchased these at her favorite store, Towers, the new shopping store out our way, although it was still across the canal and not within walking distance. Pearl had a huge crush on a guy who drove a car and went to high school. As she told me all these things it took my nervousness away over what I was experiencing.

When I got home after school I told my dad about my period, and he suggested that I tell my mom. She set me up with all the uncomfortable supplies, a belt and pads. In those days nothing else was said, except that she had washed my bedding, which foretold the experiences of the day. Somehow, I had an intimate bond with my dad, and not with my mom. I couldn't understand why, as I was purposely distancing myself from my dad and had made up my mind not to ever kiss him. Mom still gave me the feeling like everything was my fault. I couldn't figure it out and just went on with my life. I was learning to have hope God would be with me and be there for me no matter what happened.

The summer was one of work and play. My new friend Jane had just moved into the neighborhood. She was the picture of beauty in my mind with her bouncy curly hair and tall slender frame. She kept busy because she was older and in high school and dating and I was quite plain compared to her and living a simple lifestyle. Jane and my brother liked each other until they realized they were not going for the same things in life. I later found out that the only reason she hung out with me was to see him. That came from her mouth and diary. She let me scrutinize it one night when she invited me for a sleep over. She also told me that she didn't feel that way anymore and that was why I could now read the diary. We became good friends and shared many thoughts, but differed on many more. I accepted that and went on with the friendship and took significant pleasure in her companionship.

The two of us were so different and our view of life and morality were on the opposite side of the scale. Many times, I could not understand her thoughts and actions. She was the first person I saw in a two-piece bathing suit. I had to figure out if it was a sin or was it a risky fashion statement for that time, depending on how much material was used. I concluded for myself, it to be the latter and figured out that one should always present themselves as if walking beside Jesus.

We drifted apart when she went to grade nine and had different attitudes and actions that I could not go along with. Her younger brother Bill was liked by everyone, and he had a wonderful sense of humor, and he could make anyone laugh.

Many years later Jane and I reconnected in a special way. We would get together occasionally, but after many years something changed. Janna as she now calls herself by her birth name, seemed to be a different person. She had become a Christian and married a great man of faith. After losing many productive years, Janna fostered children and loved them like her own. She was still a woman of passion, only now for Jesus.

A girl named Heidi moved into our neighborhood. She was a few years younger than I but mature in many ways. Her family was also German and was compatible with our close-knit community. We got along very well and spent numerous hours doing various activities together. We biked, walked and swam, and at times just hung out enjoying each other's company. We watched TV at her place since it was a quieter more peaceful house than mine. There was a lot of action at my home. Of course, I loved going to her place so I could get out of work as well as babysitting.

I admired her musical abilities as she could play whatever instrument she picked up. Heidi would play the piano, mandolin or flute. She would have played more instruments if she owned them. Her musical talent was so appreciated and admired. She had a brilliant mind as well, and it could have made me envious. Her much older brother Hans Jürgen was a quiet, stay at home type of guy, except for some weekends when he would hook up with his best friend.

The next summer the guys took us both to a house party. We were so nervous and elated to go with these two older, more mature guys. We were not their dates but went as friends. While there, I was asked to dance with this guy to a slow Elvis song, "Surrender." Wow, my first dance and thank goodness I knew how it was done.

Some kids at this supposedly grown-up party, were not so innocent. They took turns going into a closet to, "neck" as we called it. I thought it to be rather childish. The way they were broadcasting the fact so immaturely made me wonder how they regarded themselves. Heidi and I were elated about our first dance with an older guy, and we went home delighted about our new experiences in dancing and the fact that these two older guys took us along with them. My parents didn't know where I spent the evening, but that wasn't new to my life and I felt all was as it should be.

29. Tire Marks

But you, O Lord, are a shield about me, my glory, and the lifter of my head.
Psalm 3:3

I was supposed to babysit Willy, my youngest brother while Mom and Dad went grocery shopping. Babysitting elsewhere or at home would still be babysitting, wouldn't it? I placed Willy who was still very young, in my bike carrier. We had an amusing time and rode to the canal for something to do. After riding around with him for a while I became a little careless and he fell out of my carrier and knocked one of his baby teeth loose. We headed straight home where I cleaned up the blood and tried to put the tooth into place. I settled him down just in time for my parents to return from shopping. I can't remember if they were told, but I thought he was so brave for not making a fuss. Willy learned to roll with the punches as he was the youngest child in the family but reported on us often as he got older and was teased beyond his tolerance.

When he was even younger, just barely walking, our mother was giving him a bath on the kitchen table. She had the small white porcelain tub sitting on the table with the boiled warm water mixed with cold, to just the right temperature. (As an adult I still had this tub and gave it to Willy's son Jeremy). Willy was lying on the table being somewhat lethargic, but compliant while Mom took his clothes off for his bath.

Suddenly, we heard a loud command to us, *"Kinder kommt her!"* ("Children come here!") Looking directly at me, she scrutinized my every move. I was questioned and with trembling and fear in my voice declared, "I don't know what had happened to him!"

I was intently staring at his belly which had bruised tire marks from one side to the other. Still staring at the marks, I had no idea what had occurred while Mom immediately went on to interrogate my older brother. He confessed that they had been playing at the neighbors, the Plett property.

Willy was put inside the car to keep him safe. As they pushed the car down the yard Willy fell out and the car went over top of him. They got him up and he seemed fine. He was, until that evening when he started to vomit a substance which looked like feces. When the vomiting started in the evening Mom was concerned. That was when Mom was going to bathe him and found the tire marks.

He was taken to the hospital, and they examined his little body for broken bones and internal bleeding. He was declared well enough to go home if Mom and Dad kept a close eye on him.

What a miracle instead of a tragedy that it could have been. We had unconsciously witnessed a miracle. Not realizing at the time, God graciously had his angels working overtime in our family.

That summer I once again labored on the farm to generate enough money for high school. We had to buy our own books, binders, and school clothing. I enjoyed my summer working, swimming and getting to know the kids in the neighborhood as a young teen.

Heidi and I took long bike rides along the canal and swam at the Weir. That fall Heidi moved into town and it left a huge hole in my lonely life. She was now a city slicker. It is too bad, but in time we drifted apart. Only great memories remain, as we did not connect relationally again for a long time.

We met again quite by coincidence at the Club LaSalle for a function dinner, and she told me she was an author. I had just written and published my first book too, so we had a great deal to talk about. It appears your childhood friends are friends forever as you can pick up where you left off any time. We stay in touch to this day.

30. High School

And forgive us our debts, as we also have forgiven our debtors.

Matthew 6:12

At high school I found a new friend in an old acquaintance from Eastwood School, Susan. We got to know each other in grades six, seven and eight. When Susan was absent from school, I felt abandoned and didn't know how to achieve that sense of belonging during those lengthy lunch hours. I felt immensely isolated in a school with hundreds of young people. Functioning well at my schoolwork, including completing my homework without fail, I became a dependable commodity to many students who copied my work every morning, depending on the correct answers.

My brother Mat worked hard that summer and he did not like school. I wasn't tuned in enough to know why he never did homework. He copied mine when I was finished as we were both in grade nine, but in different classes.

I tolerated high school and worked diligently to complete my assignments. Home economics was a hands-on favorite of mine. We were able to use smooth-working, new sewing machines in our class, so unlike the old model we had at home. I loved sewing and fashioned myself a pair of yellow dress pants, and a multi-colored blouse to match. Mom even let me use her sewing machine after seeing my projects.

I restyled my pigtails before school and created a more fashionable ponytail, trying to fit in with the styles. Most girls were wearing large puffy hairdos all teased up. My ponytail didn't quite create the fashion statement I desired but it was one step towards it.

Looking forward to joining the band on Saturday mornings with my accordion generated excitement. This euphoria didn't last as my dad couldn't give me a ride into school on Saturdays. I was trying to step out of my comfort zone and hit a roadblock once again.

Before the ninth grade was over, I was getting together with some of the teens in our neighborhood. I had a little crush on a new guy. He, Billy, Betty, and I were out on a Sunday afternoon just having a splendid social time. We went to Bill's place and went to the barn to see his horse. It was every teen's dream to have their own horse. We ended up in the hayloft talking. As we sat there chatting, I leaned back and fell between two stacks of hay. The hay was piled very high so as to have enough food for the horse throughout the winter. The fellow I had a crush on squeezed in with me and kissed me.

A note to young people who might be reading this. Make up your mind what and how far you will go with the opposite sex right now. I did, and my limit was permitting myself to kiss, and that was it.

Bill's dad came up to the loft and broke up the party with accusations, so we left. As a parent I can totally understand what his suspicions must have been. As a teen I thought, what are you talking about, we did nothing except kiss.

The next day, school was uneventful, and I went home feeling at peace. When I got into the house, Mat informed me of the appalling and horrible rumors spreading throughout the school. The guy I was with had spread the rumors that I went all the way with him, and he was bragging about it. I was shocked and devastated as I cried throughout the night. After many hours of anguish, and unbearable pain I directed my thoughts towards God. I was too embarrassed and demeaned to know what to do. I just wanted to quit school and never go back. This was a transforming shift in a life changing attitude that God helped me to carve into my life.

Since I was used to talking to God regarding the confusing feelings, God was now my best friend and certainly came through for me that time. He spoke to me of being true, genuine and faithful to myself, and above all to Him. If you know the facts and are blameless, your innocence is not changed by what people say. I must answer to God and God alone. That night God took my shame away and became the lifter of my head, although my name still meant a good deal to me. It was an overwhelmingly difficult task to go to school with my head held high, even while leaning on my Strength. I didn't hold my head up high under the best of circumstances, so this became a challenge and converted into a corner stone to the building blocks of my life. It was torture going back to school with my peers but I leaned on God every step of the way; that is what I learned to do.

I also learned that I should be careful with whom I spend time and where I spend it. I learned not to put my reputation in jeopardy. I had been naïve and trusting and wondered if I could remember this in the future.

This time in my life left me wondering what my mom thought. She must have seen my eyes in the morning and was she concerned? Nothing was ever said about being concerned, or support, or asked if something was wrong. We learned to battle most situations ourselves and who ever we wanted to confide in. In my case it was a tangible God.

31. God Still Speaking

While I am writing this, I am once again confronted with that significantly powerful but quiet voice of God, who wants me to forgive this person for what he said about me. It never came to my mind previously, so I willed to forgive him. I would have thought I did that at some point after all these years, but when I thought about him, I just thought about the untruths that hurt me so much. I Could not honestly say the thought of forgiveness came to mind.

"I forgive you, forgive you for the hurt you caused me." By this time in my life, I know I must make it an act of the will to forgive, and God will release the feeling of pain. I believe what we release in this world; will also be released in the spiritual realm. Even though I don't know where he is now, I forgive because God forgives, and I will pray for his salvation from now on when I think of him.

God never ceases to surprise me. He is cleaning up our lives when we don't expect it and in places where we don't anticipate it. He is ever changing us for the better and I am so grateful.

32. A Great Summer

It was a summer in which I learned to take many freedoms, and I was succeeding at becoming a full-fledged qualified teen.

Growing up, personal hygiene developed into a continuous problem as we did not have an indoor bathroom, and it took great calculations for privacy as I took my many sponge baths. This was the reason I especially enjoyed my swims at the canal, recalling it was so refreshing to immerse your whole body in the water. I would go for a swim by myself and take a bar of soap and towel for my bath. Many in our little neighborhood did the same thing, especially after their prolonged, challenging days at work.

I cherished the time spent attending my church and I continuously made it a priority, even when the other kids were outside running and playing. The church was right next to our house, and it had the little portable screens in the windows for some ventilation. I would have enjoyed playing with the other kids many times hearing them as they delighted themselves in the outdoors, but it never entered my mind to skip a service. I received something at church that I desperately desired and needed as God was filling a void that no one else or nothing else could satisfy before.

One of the girls, almost four years older than I, was kind to me and even befriended me for a time. She compared herself to the other two girls her age in the church and didn't feel like she measured up. The other two girls were together often and had developed a deep friendship. They had the respect of others in the congregation as being strong Christians. My older friend played the piano with ease and her skill in serving the church in this way should have given her so much to feel good about but didn't. I noticed that how we see ourselves is how we project ourselves to others and it affects our attitudes and actions. Seeing this unfold before me did not give me the confidence or insight to change this in my life at that time. Sometimes, it takes years to figure this out, but with God's help we do.

The fashions that all three girls wore were enough to make a young, needy teen envious. It appeared as if every Sunday the three would have contemporary outfits. I must say my older friend's outfits were the most sensational and dramatic. Everything from cowhide vests to cashmere. The shoes always matched as well as the handbags. I could only dream of clothes like this. Getting a job and buying new clothes sure sounded like the lifestyle I wanted.

I was gifted some beautiful outfits in mint condition, from Mrs. Erisman. She was always thoughtful to me and on this occasion, gave me a few gently used outfits that her daughter Erna was not wearing anymore. I loved those outfits as they were so stylish and fit so well, realizing I could never have afforded to buy them myself. I wore them often with satisfaction and pride and above all, they improved my self-esteem.

One of the girls, Herta, became a missionary with her husband in Brazil, South America, where they raised their family. The other was Harry's cousin Mary. We ended up having many things in common in our married lives. Mary was an unassuming gentle and kind spirit who continually had her eyes on God. They were both people who never disappointed me as far as living for the Lord. My other friend moved to another town, we lost contact, and sadly she has now passed away, but she left this world ready to meet her savior and friend.

I was finding myself having to distinguish between rules of the church and rules of God. Makeup, earrings, and shaving my legs were considered a sin by the church. The Christians I knew said dancing was also a sin. I had grown enough in God to have confidence that He would nudge me in the right direction. I was learning from God and without much outward conflict I just learned to do what I thought was right.

By the time summer concluded, I had earned enough money to buy my modest but limited school wardrobe as well as necessary supplies. I was allowed to go to school with my hair fashioned into a ponytail and I even cut my bangs to make my hair a little looser and fluffier around my face. In grade ten the secretarial subjects I chose were not very interesting to me. I enjoyed the typing and practiced diligently after buying myself a typewriter. That year, English was also a preferred subject of mine. Bookkeeping was not my favorite but later in life I used those skills often, giving our business an edge.

One of my teachers, Mr. Hancock, had a thing he did with his lips as he pushed his glasses up his nose with the two fingers. His front lower lip protruded beyond his upper lip as he adjusted his glasses. I enjoyed his English class and the way he presented the material. He kept me engaged and was a distinguished teacher who seemed to be a teacher forever.

One day my son came home from the Collegiate in St. Catharines in grade twelve and told me about one teacher's odd habit. I said, "That is Mr. Hancock." He couldn't believe he had the same teacher that his mother had in high school. Mr. Hancock had not only stood the test of time, but of generations. The best part was that kids still took pleasure in experiencing his class after all those years. He was still a remarkable, illustrious teacher, engaging his students.

Going back to my teen years, on many Sunday afternoons we would pile into Ed's car and go for rides. He was a friend from our neighborhood a little older than I. The group was made up of one girl and four guys. There was a good deal of entertainment as we drove to the canal and viewed the locks, all just friends and enjoying each other's company.

One time after a rainy week, we took the grape road between Highway 8 and Niagara Stone Road. I don't know if it was a road at all. Well, you guessed it, the car got stuck in a foot of mud and after a lot of pushing by the guys and spinning the tires, the car was in even deeper. It was close enough to walk home, so I did.

My parents, of course, did not know where I was and would not have been happy about me joy-riding in someone's car; or would they care? I wonder what the other siblings were doing on those Sunday afternoons when they were locked out of the house. Everyone was happy, Mom and Dad had their quiet afternoon snooze, and we had our freedom.

‡

It was a good year as I finally learned how to study and retain information. I had a terrible time reading and comprehending and now learned how to compensate.

This year left me forever grateful to the librarian who noticed my slow snail's pace at reading. Mr. Bramble took me aside to teach me how to read more efficiently, coaching me to use a ruler under the lines and look at a group of words, all at the same time instead of each one individually. It took discipline and practice on my part, but I persisted until it became normal. This compassionate teacher will never know how many times I think of him with gratitude. He revolutionized my reading skills and for the first time I read a novel. This has left me with a never-ending appreciation for teachers, especially for Mr. Bramble who cared enough to make a change!

My marks were better than they had ever been. I was known in my class as, "The Brain of 10E," far from the truth. This nickname was probably because I was the only one in the class that did their homework without fail. Their interpretation was such a switch for me, but it made me feel good about who I was as I was learning to have confidence in myself.

I joined the decorating committee for the prom and loved going to the meetings for the preparations. I was also put in charge of guarding the punch table at the prom, as kids would spike it without a watchdog present.

It was fun being there and watching all the girls with their extravagant dresses and elaborate hairdos, which had the effect of making them look ten years older. Some teen girls already had left school at noon to manage their beauty appointments, including hair, manicures, pedicures and make-up.

I recall some of the popular girls as they all paused for their photos, presenting themselves as important, while posing with the special, notable man of their dreams. They danced all night, reveling in the music, and it was the most significant night of their lives. You could sense the surrender of the girls to their princes who held them tenderly in their arms. Of course, that was only for the slow romantic dances. "The Twist" by Chubby Checker paved the way for the release of energy, twisting and even breaking out in a sweat. What a night! I watched in amazement at the mood swings before my eyes and it caught my attention how the music dictated the mood.

Interesting to look back now and realize that every one of us had dreams for the future. Some of them came to pass and others vanished into a fog, forever to disappear.

That year there were so many underlying feuds going on in our class of girls. At one point two girls got into a cat fight and it was wild. After they had passed notes back and forth, they jumped out of their seats and grabbed each other, yelling and screaming as only girls can do. They yanked at each other's hair and it came out by the clumps. They scratched and clawed at each other until a teacher came in to interrupt them. Afterward I was told the brawl was about one girl going after the other one's boyfriend, but that was just hearsay. I thought it really seemed out of character for girls, but one never understood what young love could trigger.

33. Lesson Redo

And let our people learn to be devoted themselves to good works, to help cases
of urgent need, and not be unfruitful.

Titus 3:14

It was this year that I had a crush on a guy from our neighborhood. He even gave me a going steady ring. Wow, that was like getting engaged in my mom's eyes. She was so angry with me and talked about me marrying a Catholic boy. I took the ring so matter-of-factly and thought no, I do not want to marry this boy either, Catholic or not. So, what is the big deal as I was just dating him. In those days, Protestants, even though they were not practicing Christianity, did not look favorably on marrying a Catholic. This made no sense to me as my most favorite couple in the world were Catholic, and my parents loved them too. I was told to give the ring back or I would be sorry, and the arguing went on and on for a couple of days.

My grade ten class party was that weekend, and I was pleased that I had someone who I was fond of, to attend with. It is peculiar because I don't think my parents even realized where I was going, and remember not disclosing to them because it was assumed that I wasn't supposed to see him. I got a ride with my classmate and her boyfriend. We all met at the beach party, including my date, who showed up with his own vehicle.

I was kissed or French kissed as we called it and I thought to myself, this does not feel pleasant and what makes people do this. The perplexing thing is that I did not stop him from kissing me this way, but I continued while listening to other conversations at the same time. I unmistakably see now; I was not prepared or ready for kissing at the time and especially not taken up with passion at all. I knew, "This was not love," but had chosen and decided to experience life, just a little, limiting that experience to merely kissing, nothing else.

What was that lesson I learned just a year ago about being in the wrong place at the wrong time and my reputation? I didn't even consider that. What was I thinking? "I wasn't!"

On the way home my date parked the truck in a place unfamiliar to me, and it was so dark and black with no light in sight. We were in the middle of nowhere. This time his hands wandered around my back. My arms immediately clamped down and I pulled away. I had made up my mind long before this, that I would not do more than kiss. What was he thinking?

There were just a few short words like, "take me home!" Nothing more was said. In defense of this fellow knowing what I know today, it was not fair to let him kiss, in what he thought was a passionate way. It could have been misleading but it was not permission to go further. He also could have heard at school that I was easy, and by kissing him this way might have confirmed that in his mind.

Those were my mistakes and I take full responsibility for them. Again, in his defense, he started the truck and we departed for home as soon as I voiced the words. So appreciative that he honored my request immediately without question. I breathed a sigh of relief as I had no idea where I was or how to get home from there. Can you imagine being with someone who forced themselves on you and you did not know where you were? It could have been a different scene and I thank God it was not.

The next day a bunch of us were sitting in my dad's car in the driveway. It was just me and two guys from the neighborhood. Being a common pastime to sit in the stationary cars to chat, I told them of how I felt, relaying I was afraid to hurt this guy if I broke up with him. Without saying what happened the night before, I asked for their opinion. I was part of this group of guys, and the only girl, so I could often get the male perspective or viewpoint even at times when I didn't want it.

I was very upset because I thought I would hurt my date's feelings. My friends thought I should not worry about that. The emotion of hurting someone on my part was a good level of maturity, although this is too common amongst teen girls, who aim to please to be liked. As I ponder, I am overwhelmed with thankfulness as to my limits on how far I would please, just to be liked. Of course, most kids back then as now, called it to be loved. I always knew better than that and knew it was only a temporary feeling that would disappear. I had an underlying mistrust of most guys. Knowing that trust would not be given easily, I would have to feel true love before I would give way to my emotions.

My male friends both encouraged me to quit being so stupid about my feelings and of course break up if I wanted to. A short while later I spotted my date from the night before, looking for me. He found me chatting with the guys, which he felt not appropriate. He didn't understand that these were my friends too, people I spent some time with, not boyfriends. Together, my date and I walked down the pathway towards all the shacks.

When out of sight, we stopped to talk and I gave him his ring back while announcing I had to break up with him. He said he figured I would because of his behavior at the class party and afterwards. It was done. Having no regrets except that of having to hurt someone, I was feeling good about my decision.

Knowing I had totally disregarded the painful lesson of the past year. "Watch where you go, and with whom, and what you do." I was learning about bearing good Christian fruit in the way of obedience, as well as my failures, taking note of my lessons learned once more. Learning this I would make a decisive, determined resolution to overcome the next test when it came along expecting God's guidance.

I was so pleased that we were still friends and socially hung out together when in our group. He even introduced his new girlfriend to our neighborhood company. She was very pretty with dark, natural curly hair, and I liked her.

The neighborhood teens played football every day after supper, and I valued the interaction. One of the guys was Harry, who had moved back to the neighborhood, and we were all good friends. It was energizing to get together with teens and I looked forward to it daily.

I stood under the two homemade poles with a bar across them as Harry pole-vaulted over the top of me. All the other guys deliberated that I was foolish and crazy to do such a radically dangerous thing. Especially one of them who would always natter at me about it. I wasn't dating him or anything, so I do not know why he was telling me what to do all the time.

Here in our unique community, there was opportunity to disregard God's protecting guidance, but I loved God and He was a faithful best friend, giving me all the love and protection that I needed. He was starting to fill this deep chasm within me, even though I did not understand that profound pain, or know why it was there.

Life is a long journey, but I recall a few girls that stay vivid in my mind forever. These girls made impressions on me when I was young and continue to as an adult. It is so wonderful to have the connection of youth that grows into one of maturity, even to old age.

One of course is Jane, (now called Janna) a close friend at that time, even though we were on two different planets most of our young lives. We now share our faith and I have seen the miracle of a life radically changed into one of victory.

Sue's poise and stature remain constant from high school to this day. It was what made me notice her. She has conquered many obstacles and has flourished as a Christian mother, wife and motivational speaker writing many books. She has inspired me as well as others to conquer our own limitations. Something I needed to work on in my life.

Heidi's brilliant mind and talents have spurned me on to do better and do things for the love of doing them. She continues to be an active wife, grandparent and writer, expressing herself with many talents. Heidi is always trying new things and ready to learn as she travels through life.

Ruth is another one of those special people. We played many times as children enjoying birthday parties and the old neighborhood. She continues to be kind and personable and has thrived in her profession. Her faith has grown into one directed by God. We still enjoy our times together chatting about the good old days and the present as well as those of our future years. We can see how God carried us from our Little Germany to the present day.

Going back to my High School days; during the time of our last set of exams for the year, I would study outside on a blanket. It was deliberate positioning on my part, as I was waiting for Harry to show his face.

He locked himself in a little office, studying for his exams. Occasionally he would come out for some fresh air, and I looked forward to getting a glimpse of him.

He moved back to our neighborhood but still went to Lakeport High School to finish up grade twelve. I didn't know him personally except for seeing him at church where he was never without a Bible in his hands. He faithfully wore his blackish-brown suit, as in those days you only owned one, if you could afford that. I thought of him as a super Christian and was attracted to his strong discipline in attending church. Occasionally he would see me and I would be able to wave across the two yards between us. We even exchanged some words once when he came over to speak to me about his studying and how he didn't enjoy school.

He was going to look for a job in a factory as soon as possible. His dad was a bricklayer and very efficiently ran his own business, but Harry did not relish the thoughts of the brick laying occupation.

He alleged he could give me a ride into town if I needed one, as he was going to apply for some jobs. I replied that I planned on applying at the Career School of Hairdressing and intended on starting in the fall.

He was one of those guys that continuously gave people rides with his car and with his own gas money. Many people in the neighborhood had him chauffeur them many times, and he never complained.

Harry was tall being six feet two inches, with a strong but lean build. I can still see him in his tight semi dress pants, as that was the style of the time. Jeans weren't worn by anyone that we knew of in those days. The styles were such that you wore a dressier pant everywhere. The old ones were worn for work and new ones for dress.

He had a baby face with rounded cheeks and rounded chin even though he was thin. His hair was in an Elvis look with just enough wave to style well. He drove this unique turquoise blue 1953 Ford and the pine scent from the air fresheners he hung in the vehicle signified Harry. I can't say it suited my taste but was enjoyed because it represented Harry and his car.

My parents were quite happy to find me looking for a job to secure my future. I wanted to go into hair dressing, as my dream to be a stewardess was deflated because of my flat feet, or so I was told. I dreamed of flying all over the world while making money doing what I loved. It represented many unknown corners of the world to see as well as hidden experiences.

Nevertheless, currently, my exciting trip was going downtown with Harry in his '53 Ford. He was going to Thompson Products and I was going to the Career School of Hairdressing, and I can still remember what I wore.

It was a white pleated skirt, a multicolored blue and white flowered blouse and a light turquoise blue sweater. I felt so grown up as I got into the front seat of his car. I remember feeling awkward as far as conversation and of course indebted to his generosity. My social skills were unpracticed and primitive as my world was small, being confined to our family home and our little neighborhood.

It was decided with Mom and Dad that I would start the Career School of Hairdressing on Queen Street, at the Dominion Building in September, and I would work diligently to make the money to pay for school during the summer. It was working out well as I found a job at Boese Foods, a canning factory. I disliked this job so much but persevered to eventually do something I would love. The bus came to the end of our street at five in the morning, when it was still dark and dreary before the sun came up.

The days working at Boese Foods were long and lonely. Most girls had friends to eat lunch with, all the while chatting. Asserting myself near the end of the summer, I met Trudy and her friend. I remember seeing them at school with their steady boyfriends. They had been a couple for a few years as they were a few years older than I and getting married the next year. It was interesting to hear them talk of their dreams for marriage and their plans with their future husbands. I know now life had a few surprises for them, but with God they experienced good times and had accomplished marriages. They were successful and spent many years serving God.

A memorable night was one where all of us from the neighborhood got together. There were no girls to hang out with as Lorraine couldn't go that night and Jane and her fiancé Hans were making plans to get married.

We all sat at the corner of Niagara Stone Road and Stewart Road talking as we witnessed cars going around the curve hitting a deep pothole. As the cars jumped in and out of the potholes, we laughed. The harder the cars hit the harder we laughed. Why, I don't know, but it was funny then? After dark we walked to Avondale Dairy just talking and having great fellowship. We walked along the canal road and then we went to Avondale Dairy. Everyone got their special treat, and I had my first soda ever. Harry bought it for me after much protest on my part. I wasn't used to taking from people and didn't know how to handle that.

Stewart Road was a more direct way for that time of night and that is how we walked home. Laughing and chatting all the way back, I just hated to go back into our house. I still loved the freedom of the outdoors whenever I could experience it.

It was the last time the neighborhood gang spent quality time together before we all went our own way. Many quit school that year as I did and our lives took many directions away from this, our supposedly safe and unique environment. Whenever I saw one of the guys after this, it just wasn't the same. They felt like strangers with only a few similarities recognizable as the people I knew well. They also moved in directions I did not understand. I couldn't relate anymore as the time and the direction we took severed our close relationships. You never think you would ever be without those special childhood friends in your life.

Even stranger is the fact that these people come back into your life later, and you can reconnect because of your rich childhood memories together. You are never strangers ever again, connection only being a hello away. That is how it has been with so many people from the little neighborhood. Reconnecting with some on totally different levels. Whoever they are and wherever they fit into the past, there will always be a special place for them in my life and future.

Reconnection works when you have been able to live your life without regrets. Many years later, it will enable you to look someone in the eyes without embarrassment, or any love lost between you both. Then re-acquaintance becomes a new chapter in your life and not reliving an old one. This has happened with so many of my past friends who are now again friends of the present.

34. God's Voice

"Then you will call upon me and come and pray to me, and I will listen to you. You will seek me and find me when you seek me with all your heart."
Jeremiah 29:12-13

It was September and time to go to hair dressing school. Harry was on the day shift and volunteered to drive Mary, his cousin, and myself into town the first week. He was kind enough to drop me at career school, and then dropped Mary off at work. The ride helped to ease the stress of starting something new and the nervousness of hairdressing school. With excitement and anticipation, he began his new job at Foster Wheeler. Mary was an awesome person to spend these commutes with. She continued her job at the bakery and seemed to take pleasure in it. When we didn't have a ride, we walked to catch the bus at the Rainbow Inn early in the mornings. We teamed up to go back home on the bus in the evening. I got to school an hour early as the bus had a limited schedule.

Harry asked me on a date shortly after and we went out after the evening church service. It was to my dismay, that for a change I asked my parents for permission. Of course Dad said nothing, but Mom said too much, and with a great deal of debate they let me go if I was back by ten that evening. I ultimately stated that this was not possible because church services were long in those days and ended after nine.

War broke out and I walked out saying they could beat me upon my return, but I was staying out until eleven. It was my first date, and Harry asked me out to go somewhere with him alone! He was a nice guy, it was a big deal, and why did it have to be diminished with so much criticism and lack of understanding. Above all they knew Harry, his family and the kind of person he was. This of course was from my perspective. After all, I was an emotional teen girl who thought she knew character. I knew Harry would never hurt me or put me in danger; he wasn't Catholic, as Mom protested in the past, but he was a Christian! I was never to find out my mom's reason for the roadblock, as we just did not talk about anything much in those days. I knew it would take some time to get to Ontario Street and back, especially if the bridge was up.

We left after church and talked as we drove. Harry said he didn't agree with kissing on the first date. The pressure was off, although I must say I would have been disappointed if he would have tried. He took me to a drive-in restaurant called McMurry's Drive-In on Ontario Street. It was an awesome place to experience my first delicious hamburger and thick cold vanilla milk shake. I had never even had home-made hamburgers up to that day, and as far as a milk shake, I didn't quite know what to expect. They were so delicious and the first of a long list of burgers and drinks we tried in the future. Harry was such a gentleman as he made me feel very special and he cared what I thought. We drove through downtown St. Catharines, as that is what you did in those days. It was the first of many times we would drive down St. Paul Street in his turquoise '53 Ford.

As we got to my place, I had no idea what time it was, but imagined we were there before eleven as Harry was known to be punctual, and I had told him about my dramatic exit earlier.

We sat in the driveway and talked about dating many people because we were both too young to be tied down. I totally agreed, as I had no intention of being serious with anyone just yet. Our thoughts were in sync, and it was easy to express them because we understood each other.

My thoughts of Harry were that he was next to God and I thought he never sinned or came close to it. I was not very emotionally mature and not realistic but nevertheless, that is how I perceived him. We said good night with only words, and I left to go in the house.

I was overwhelmed with the excitement of my first real date while walking down the driveway to the back of the house. I wasn't even afraid of what my parents might do.

Reaching and turning the corner at the back of the house, I suddenly heard God speak to me. It was so powerful; a moment of life changing trust was imparted to me forever. God said I would marry Harry; it would be all right and I could trust him. I argued internally with God, "This cannot be, we both want to date other people." I almost felt guilty betraying Harry as we both decided we would date many people. As it was an odd and unusual experience for me at that time, I put what God said deep within my heart and kept it safe there. It gave me confidence and trust towards a person of the opposite sex, that I didn't have before.

Of course, I confided in no one, not even Harry. Some things are better left unsaid until God releases them to be freed and spoken. The message was not for Harry, but for me. I needed to know that I could be vulnerable in the presence of this man. My only Friend and Guide knew Harry and God put the stamp of approval on him. He was a Friend who I confided in and trusted in all things. I would trust Him now, even with this unusual confirmation, as I always had before.

Career School of Hairdressing was very gratifying, and I would get good grades all the way through. The haircuts seemed easy to learn and to project from my creative mind onto a client. This excited me and outwardly I also gained experiences for living and hopes grew for my future. In the past we were not allowed to become adult people with our own ideas and thoughts, never mind speaking of them. Now I could relate to people at school as needed. Meeting the new students with their unique personalities was also an eye opener, as well as rewarding.

My favorite person was Alice who was a slim figured Dutch blonde girl with many of the same principles I had. She felt you should be true to your boyfriend, a not so common trait in our present surroundings. She was easy to get along with and was kind. Those were my first impressions as I got to know her, and we became good friends and hung out a lot.

Harry and I had gotten to know each other more on those rides to work and he asked me out again, on a Sunday afternoon. We went driving along the Niagara River Parkway and Harry parked the car. As I pass by this spot now, it is impossible not to remember this moment with a smile. I was not a great conversationalist, although there were many words imprisoned somewhere inside of me. Harry suddenly pulled me over to him away from the passenger door, which I was glued to. Then came the unthinkable, a kiss! We were both disappointed, Harry, because I didn't respond and I, because I froze. I blushed as I moved back to my side of the seat. Upon looking at me, Harry asked if I could refrain from blushing when we saw each other at church. I said I would try but couldn't promise as blushing was a part of who I was and I did it well and often. In those days we would go to church with no acknowledgment of dating. You didn't sit with a guy unless you were engaged, and you were never caught holding hands.

After months of school and many rides with Harry, he visited me often on lunch hours. Excited and delighted to see him, I sat right beside him as the car had bench seats.

It took effort and maneuvering to make sure not to get a customer that extended into the lunch hour. I could not do a tint, perm, or even a comb out at that time. Alice, my dependable friend, would take over if I did get one. There were no cell phones or texting to say you were busy. I don't know if my parents were aware of our daily visits at lunchtime and it wouldn't have occurred to me to tell them. We got to know each other well as we spent so much time together.

We hung out with Alice and Wally, her boyfriend, and our weekends were exciting, spending many days in Wally's boat enjoying the fresh air, waves and each other's company. We explored the Skylon Tower, went to the flower gardens and drove around sight-seeing. Those days added so much to my life outside the home. They were such a wonderful couple as were Wally's parents who had roast beef dinner every Sunday, and we were so kindly invited. Of course, we enjoyed the offer, except that we had to rush off to go to church every Sunday evening. They lived in Port Colborne, and it was a rush at times, especially since you would always have to change into your Sunday best before going to church. I don't know how we did it, but we did. It would have been better to take the time and speak to our friends of how much the Lord meant to us, and His purpose in our lives, rather than rush off. We were so immature this way and lived by the rules, "Be at church, in your Sunday best, on time, no matter what." I wasn't raised with these rules, but they were important to Harry, so I accepted them into my life thinking that they were not harmful. I later discovered we missed the will of God many times, following those rules because they were man's rules, not God's rules.

My life at home was not pleasant as Mom and I fought often as well as Mom and Dad. Mom was putting roadblocks in the way of everything I wanted to do. I slept in the living room as Dad had added a new kitchen and living room. As I said before, it became tiring to wait until everyone would leave the room so I could drag in my mattress and bedding. Sometimes I would have to make my bed up late and I was so tired. Why did I have to sleep here? Everyone else could sleep in their bedroom.

Harry gave me a camera for my birthday which I cherished and used every chance I got. My mother would take pictures out of my albums and send them to Germany, and it made me so angry. I retorted with angry words and cried all the time. Although very upset, I never swore at my mother or called her down as it just wasn't a part of who I was. She just didn't seem to care about how I felt, and this went on until l got married.

I loved taking pictures and since money was not plentiful and each penny was represented by hard work, getting them developed was sacrificial for myself. I loved putting them in my brown album with black pages and black corners to hold the pictures. Naturally, they were black and white in those days, but they captured and fed my memories.

The phone we didn't have also created a war in our home. Mother said it wasn't necessary, but I insisted that my boss could not reach me for work, if we had no phone. I had secured a job after school, working as a shampoo girl on Thursday and Friday evening as well as Saturdays, but was called in when they got busy.

Finally, a decision was made, and I could order the phone if I paid for it. I picked the color; it was powder blue as I loved blue and still do.

Years later the phone sat in my room at the cottage, and now is in my family room. I enjoy seeing the original numbers displayed on the rotary dial telephone. Even though it was a party line, and you never knew who was listening, it was access to my place of work. I had a job at Kunselman's and appreciated the experience as well as loved working and it energized me while I learned so much from the girls that worked there.

I worked at the beauty salon on King Street as a shampoo girl the whole time I was training, and my job was much more exciting than going to school. After school I was able to walk down to the beauty parlor and work until closing time at nine. Saturdays I would work from eight until four in the afternoon. The group of hairdressers Larry the owner had working were, Mini, Kay, Louise, Angie, Jenny and Helen. They were a great bunch of girls and I learned so many work skills from them. Angie and I hit it off and I learned by watching her skills as a creative hairdresser. She was fabulous and I gravitated to her style of doing long hair, cutting and coloring hair. Beside this, she was exceptionally kind to everyone and would give you the shirt off her back, if you know what I mean. What an impact she made on me as a mentor for that time in my life.

One night I worked with Angie, and we closed the shop late after my bus left. She hid the money in the dark creepy basement as directed by Larry and said I could leave as she locked up. My dad or brother couldn't pick me up, so I decided to take the city bus to the Victoria Lawn Cemetery. It was a city bus that had a good schedule to that end of town. I did these trips many times before and knew it would be quite a long walk home, but it wasn't too cold.

The ride was soothing, and my tired body relaxed while my feet needing the break, were put on the seat, being ever so mindful of my skirted uniform. There was no one else on the bus, as it was now past nine. I wondered if the bridge would be up, as I would have to stand there and wait. Leaving the bus, I noticed it was dark along the sidewalk of the cemetery and so my steps were hurried. As I neared the bridge it was brighter, and I sighed with relief as the bridge was down. What a break as I hurried across the canal and walked on the shoulder of the road as there were no sidewalks.

The Rainbow Inn was a familiar landmark, thinking it was so good to be that far. I crossed Niagara Stone Road, to the Rainbow Inn side, because the other side along the canal was so dark, as it was densely treed and ran along the canal mud hole.

As I got to Louis Garage just past the Rainbow Inn, I noticed the lights darkened. He was closing the garage for the night. Just then a car pulled up very close beside me. He had his window down and asked me questions while stretching close to the window on my side. Then he insisted

I take a ride with him as I got uncomfortable because my body was squeezed between the car and the deep drop-off ditch in front of Louis Garage. No one had seat belts and he was leaning drastically near the window towards me. As quickly as I could say," No," he grabbed my coat sleeve and started to yank me against the car, holding on to me. Instinct took over as my body hurled itself the other way and I fell into the deep ditch. That was a blessing! After climbing out on the other side of the ditch, I went running towards the dark garage. Pounding on the door with all my might I saw the light go on slowly. Instantly a screeching of tires preceded the car's departure. I was so relieved as Louis asked what the problem was as I begged him if I could use the phone. Of course, he let me call after carefully looking around for the car. My dad came to pick me up after pleading with him on the phone. I told him I would never walk this stretch at this time of night again.

When I told Harry what had happened, he made it his priority to pick me up whenever I was finished work. I was not only grateful for the ride, but it was another chance to get to see him. I think I was becoming addicted and dependent on him. The reason I call it that, is I loved being with him and when I wasn't, I was thinking about him. Since I would have missed supper, as I worked late, Harry introduced me to all the drive -through places on Ontario Street, and I cannot believe how much I ate and didn't gain an ounce on my thin body.

I drifted so far away from my family and what was going on in their lives. My brother came home late and sometimes slept in his car until the morning. Many mornings I checked to make sure his car was there. He also started smoking, and there were many arguments about this, although my dad was a chain smoker, he protested about his children doing the same.

One thing was certain; Mat always took his job seriously and worked hard as a laborer. He even took correspondence courses and much later got his degrees and more. He made up for the angry times as a teen. We all went through stuff on our own, working through emotions and feelings, not understanding them or where they came from. The amazing thing was that Mat was determined to make something of himself, despite his sur-roundings, just like his other siblings.

I don't know what the other siblings were doing at that time. My brother George tells me that he remembers the terrible fighting between Mom and myself. I think I came out of the house upset every time Harry picked me up. How did he ever put up with me and the drama of my home?

35. Be Faithful to God

Know therefore that the Lord your God is God, the faithful God who keeps covenant and stead-
fast love with those who love him and keep his commandments, to a thousand generations.

Deuteronomy 7:9

Early on in Harry's and my relationship, I noticed another friend of mine was not attending church as often. The word was that it was my fault. That is a heavy thought to have to live with and I guess a little of my character came out at the time. I needed to confront that lie that it was my fault. I saw him on the church steps as I was waiting for Harry to pick me up. I went to talk to him regarding this.

I spoke to him that it was not my fault that I had no romantic feelings for him, but I wished him well. I also told him that I knew God wanted Harry in my life. I relayed that God expected us to follow Him no matter who we were going with or what we were doing. I reminded him he should follow God and His plan for his life as well. We parted as friends, and I pray he decided to make good choices for his life as well as go with God. I learned never to take ownership of something you are not responsible for. You are responsible for the decisions you make and not those of others. Be faithful to the faithful One.

This was a truth that I did not come by easily. I have learned through hard lessons and failures. I learned that failures of mine helped me to understand not to lean on myself but rather on the One who created and loved me, God the faithful.

I was grateful that I went with God's choice for my life, a strong Christian man who would serve God no matter what. Not that another person would have been the wrong choice if God was in it.

wouldn't make it. The bus came and we boarded. I just got to my seat when I felt like throwing up, and I dumped my lunch bag and put the bag to my mouth but only managed a few heaves. Thinking about it now, she must have thought I was pregnant. I knew I couldn't be, so it never entered my mind back then, but it sure looked different to others.

To this day if I put my body through drastic change or kick-start too quickly in the mornings, I will react the same way and feel faint and even get sick or pass out. I don't exert myself first thing in the morning and this has worked well for me.

One evening after working late I wasn't feeling well. Harry helped me drag my mattress into the living room and helped make up the bed. I lay right in front of the living room couch, where he kept me company. It was late, about eleven when I started to heave. There was nowhere to go but outside or to the kitchen sink. The living room fold away doors were flung open, and I headed for the sink.

Barely finishing, I yelled, "Fire!" Harry could see the smoke, so we ran to the back bedrooms where the other siblings slept. There was my brother Mat lying in bed with his mattress smoldering. He wouldn't wake up, so we rolled him out of bed onto the floor. Of course, Mom and Dad hearing the commotion were there as well as the younger siblings who slept in the same room. Harry and Dad carried the mattress to the kitchen door where it was tossed into the yard. Mat didn't totally come to his senses until after the ordeal was over. He fell asleep in bed while smoking a cigarette. Dad and Mat smoked everywhere so it was not uncommon to smoke in bed, until that night.

I was grateful to have gotten sick when I did and thankful for the family to be safe. I sometimes wondered if God used the sickness to warn the family of danger. In any case the timing of being sick was perfect.

Harry and I made friends with a couple, Ernie and Cookie. Cookie was a nickname given to her by Ernie and it stuck. We met when she started attending our little church with Ernie when they started dating and we became good friends. It was nice relating on a Christian level with another couple who had the same views.

We experienced horseback riding, All Night Sings, skating, bowling, hockey games and more. Heidi, Cookie's sister, and her boyfriend Ray also became good friends. It was a great time in my life enjoying the fellowship of young couples. We were blessed to know wonderful young couples who appreciated our values and loved hanging out.

By the next Christmas, I had saved some money and bought everyone in my family a Christmas gift. Mom got a wall mirror with two wall cherub candleholders, and Dad a penguin clothes brush that I still have. It was so much fun giving gifts and I have never lost the joy of giving gifts since that time. I got Harry a blue sweater from Warren Woolens. They had a reputation of having the best quality knits. The next year was one of finding my groove in life and living it.

We went to the German Church Camp, Bethel Park together. The church band was invited to play in front of the parliament buildings, so we went to Ottawa. Harry played the trumpet and Ernie the saxophone. We drove with Cookie and Ernie, and it was so much fun. The girls got new outfits for the occasion and each of the guys, of course, wore his one and only suits. The band played well under the direction of Mr. Reschke. Art and Liz were also dating, and we three couples did a lot together.

I broke off with Harry only once. I waffled with the thought that I wasn't good enough for him even though he never made me feel that way. Never lose sight of what you know to be true. God said I would marry Harry and it would be okay. I thought of Harry as such a spiritual guy and myself as so unspiritual and not good enough. He carried a Bible, and I didn't even own one. He prayed out loud at church and I didn't even know how to pray, I just talked to God quietly. He was raised in a Christian home, and I grew up in a place of confusion. He seemed so strong, and I was always needing God's help. Sunday, after the evening church service I gave the going steady ring back to him. It broke my heart and it pained me. All I could think of was Harry and what was he thinking.

After church I went home, but when Harry arrived at his home, he called me and asked if we could talk and could I come over. As I neared his house two doors down from ours, I saw Walter and Gertrude's car and felt embarrassed. Harry was waiting at the door, and we went downstairs to the basement to talk. Of course, Harry was always logical and made me realize

I wasn't bad for him, and I agreed I wanted him in my life.

The two of us went through some tough times as I was very guarded and inward as far as communicating. I would not and could not easily say what was on my mind, as years of suppressing my feelings, thoughts and words had created a hiding place for myself. It was a safe place or so I thought, until I wanted out, then it became my prison.

Harry spent hours forcing me to say words instead of cry. I would cry first and then be forced to use words. It was such a struggle for me, and this battle took many years to overcome, continually realizing Harry's patience was more than enough.

Many times, in more recent years, Harry has wished for that compliant, quiet Marg to return to him. This is only because he has forgotten the difficulty we had in releasing me from my prison. Naturally, he would not have totally understood the pain in my life, as even I didn't back then. I would never want to go back to that prison after finding my freedom in God.

Every Sunday evening the four or six of us would get together after church. Cookie, Ernie, Art and Liz continually heard that Harry hated the thoughts of going to work the next day, on Monday. He was so disillusioned with his job and so totally bored all day. They just didn't give him enough work or stimulation. He would ask for more jobs from his foreman, but it took hours before he came with some. It used to be a standing joke with us that every weekend he would complain about his job.

It was some time that year that our church had a baptism. Baptisms didn't happen as often as now as it was a small church membership. It was an exciting event in my life, stepping into the unknown. The service was held in Port Colborne at the Pentecostal Church as it had an indoor baptismal tank. Ernie, Ruth, Art and I got baptized at the same time. Ruth and I got baptized one after another and afterwards, we were so elated that we uncontrollably laughed rejoicing with each other over the step we had just taken with God. From outside the change room, we were told to be quiet as people thought we were being disrespectful. That was not the situation; it was just a case of total elation.

After the long service of which I don't remember much, we were brought into membership, and had communion. You had to be baptized to become a member and had to be a member to take communion. I was puzzled about that. Since then, I have come to realize these commands all have separate purposes in our life as Christians, one not depending on another. It was these church rules that made these steps towards God so difficult for me.

In the evening service at our little church in St. Catharines, the congregation prayed for the new members, and everyone had their parents and relatives there to pray with them and I felt so alone. I scanned the congregation in hopes of getting a glimpse of my dad or mom, after all they just lived next door. So disappointed at not seeing them, I held my tears only until after the service was over. I cried as I felt so hurt and abandoned. Didn't they care or didn't they love me? I felt loved by Harry, and he had to listen as I dealt with my emotions about disappointments.

Harry and I were getting engaged on my birthday that spring and I didn't know that it was a requirement to keep it a secret. I told Cookie of our plans and later found out it was unconventional to tell anyone before the fact. In any case, Harry and I made our plans and Harry shopped for a ring while I was working. It had to be within our budget, but of course just the right ring. He took me shopping on Saturday after work but had already picked one out. He wanted to see if I would like it. As I scanned the ring counter at Jacks Jewelers, my eyes spotted the most beautiful ring I ever saw. I didn't know about looking for the size of diamond, clarity, or anything else but it had to be something that appealed to me. It was the exact one he had picked out and we were delighted. I never thought of having a diamond that large and especially one that cost so much. Mom just wore a wedding band, as did most women I knew.

My ring was white gold, very popular at that time, with one large diamond in the center and two smaller on either side. The band was in the shape of an oval, made up of two swirls going in opposite directions. The wedding band had three small diamonds and fit snuggly around the swirl of the engagement ring. To complete the set, Harry surprised me with another ring to fit on the opposite side for our first anniversary.

We looked for a man's wedding band and found just the right one.

It was cut white gold with three star-like, polished starbursts around each diamond. We decided what we wanted engraved, and we were done. It was a great sense of accomplishment to buy the rings. We would pay for our own wedding as my parents couldn't afford to and watching our pennies was a must.

My birthday came, and we got engaged. The strange thing is that I have forgotten most of that special celebration. Forgetting the details for the most important moments would be a pattern for the future.

Mom made an engagement party and invited Harry's family and ours, as was our tradition. There was a lovely meal and gifts were brought. I still have and use the roly-poly glasses with the silver platinum rims from Gert and Walt. I loved them then and love them now. Mom got us bedding and I don't know what else we received. You don't know how exciting it was to receive these gifts and dream of using them in our place in the future.

Our family home was small, and I didn't know where we put the gifts. Where did Mom put all the people? Our home was modest, and Mom was not used to entertaining in this way. I took it for granted at the time, but now appreciate the effort she put forth for me. I would be the first to marry in our family and Harry was the fourth in his.

My parents did not attend the little church next door and were intimidated, feeling they never measured up to the others that regularly did. Most of the neighborhood attended this German church, so my parents believed that everyone looked down on them, and their marital problems failed to give them confidence. Of course, in those days, mental illness came with many unspoken attitudes from others. My dad had a history of problems in the past as well as present. He was forever accusing our mom of cheating on him. He had huge blowups about nothing or so I thought, and it put the house in a very tense state. Mom and Dad lived according to their feelings and couldn't grow past them. Needless to say; they put their feelings aside as they asserted themselves and did a wonderful job on our engagement party. I can appreciate this as I think back on it now.

I learned so much from Cockie, as she was well versed in social protocol. I was learning the dos and don'ts of entertaining. I also learned what should make the list of what needed to be done for our future wedding.

Harry and I never needed expensive china and good silver on our list. In fact, there was no list. Harry was just starting to save money, as was I, so every penny would be saved for the wedding. We wanted to be debt free when we got married. That included our wedding costs, most of the furniture and honeymoon. I think we still owed for our couch, which I paid off every month for a while.

Harry switched from a boiler maker to a plumbing apprentice and his pay was cut in half. The steady day shift was a great benefit to Harry's new job. Ernie had a managerial position at Canadian Tire and Cookie was a legal secretary. One thing the four of us had in common was our dreams for the future, meaning marriage and happiness with God at the center.

It was a stressful but exciting year as we worked to secure the photographer, and our hall, as well as every detail that made our wedding a success. Our church was planning on buying another building in town and I was not sure of the timeline.

We decided to rent Westminster United Church on Queenston Street. We ordered flowers and invitations for the wedding. The furniture was bought in order of importance, the bedroom set was first and then the living room couch, chair, end tables, and coffee table, as well as an inexpensive kitchen set but it lasted for many years. Our style was very traditional except for the bedroom; it had straight lines, black in color with high mirrors on both side tables and on the dresser. I wish we still had it, as it would be so in style with its straight lines and modern look. I paid a small amount weekly on the vacuum cleaner we ordered. It took quite a while to pay it off, but I was only making twenty-nine dollars a week.

Harry and I got engaged first and the other two couples got engaged within a few months, but they both got married before we did. Cookie and Ernie got married that winter and Art and Liz that spring. We were married May 6, 1967, and jokingly referred to the wedding as our centennial project.

Harry had changed jobs in October the year before we were married. He went to Sheldon Plumbing repeatedly asking for an apprenticeship and finally, one day they said yes, they would accept his application. Harry's dad thought he was out of his mind to leave a factory job for one of hard labor, but Harry was filled with anticipation to start his new career. He was going to be a plumber and the apprenticeship would take four years as he got one year credit for his training at Foster Wheeler. His pay was cut, so we had to redo the budget to pay for our wedding; recalculating again, there just wasn't much money. I remember not having much but we had happiness and contentment, and it didn't really matter if we got material things, as I was in love. I was never used to having much as I was from a poor home, realizing I already had more now than I ever had before, and it was filling my emptiness. My focus was on my relationship with someone that loved me, and next to God knew me, and what was important to me.

That Christmas Harry gave me a cedar chest, as in those days it was a tradition. It was a beautiful piece of furniture, as well as the only piece we bought from the highly esteemed Critelli Furniture store. This chest held all my treasured items until the wedding. It had a key, and I could lock everything up and keep it safe.

I purchased a Maple Leaf Tartan plaid sports jacket for Harry. He cherished it and wore it often, alternating with his only suit. He looked so handsome wearing that vibrant jacket, so fashionable at the time.

Harry was taking great pleasure in his job and acquiring plumbing skills quickly. We didn't have to listen to his complaints about work but rather listening about the interesting happenings while on the job site. He appreciated working with the guys at Sheldon and John Hajcman was one that he benefited working with the most. He took Harry under his wing and taught him well as he was speedy doing his job efficiently, and Harry learned to give him a run for his money. He was also very particular about how things were done, and so Harry learned to be extremely competent at doing the job well. He and Harry got along and became exceptionally compatible.

The wedding was nearing, and our bridesmaids' dresses had to be altered for the last fitting. My sister Helen and Harry's sister Erika being only twelve, both special to Harry and me, were an important part of our wedding party, our junior bridesmaids. Their dresses were made to match the style of the other bridesmaids' dresses. As we were getting ready to leave, my mother decided Helen would not go, and I wondered what she was thinking. I do not know as she never explained, and I didn't enjoy the arguing that I had to do to get Helen out of the house for the fitting. This kind of thing happened so often as I walked out of the house crying more times than I care to remember, but always tried to go on with the wedding preparations as best as we could.

The other attendants were Heidi and Ray, Alice and Wally, and matron of honor and best man Cookie and Ernie. Donny Ledwez was our ring bearer and Patty Schild along with Laurie Hildebrandt were flower girls. Donny was only three, but so well behaved. He did everything he was told, and I still had the pillow he carried the rings on. Over twenty-five years ago I gave it to our son Shawn and Nerissa, when Donny's son, Alex was ring bearer for their wedding. The flower girls had an enjoyable time together. Laurie lived in British Columbia and she and Patty got to know each other.

There were two weddings the year before ours and we were in Harry's cousin Mary and Eric's wedding party. We were so green and inexperienced regarding what needed to be done. Saying that, we enjoyed being a part of their special day as they were a Christian couple who you could look up to and learn from by watching their lifestyle. Herta's wedding was also that year, leaving memories of a hot sticky day with everyone looking for a slight breeze that never arrived. I think God was preparing Herta and Waldy for the warm weather they would experience during their time in South America as missionaries for years to come.

We were in Cookie and Ernie's wedding party, and I had never been so involved in a wedding before. It was a great experience in learning a lot of the protocol required for a wedding. Cookie had showers as well as a bridal tea. I learned how tables should be set and the kind of foods that were served at showers. She knew what she wanted and needed to have things done as perfectly as possible. Her attention to detail gave her a lot of stress.

I felt I had more than I ever had in my life, and I loved things the way I wanted but had not raised my expectations to an unreachable level for myself. There was one obsession I had that Harry reminds me of even to this day.

This was to have Harry build this little church for the top of our car with a bride and groom in it. Why I made the poor guy do such a thing I don't know, other than it symbolized the importance that church played in my life, as I yearned for us to have a Christian marriage, being a desired dream of mine. I cannot think of a good reason why I had him work on such a project otherwise. He was so kind and worked at it although he found no importance in it. The only significance was that I thought it was necessary and he was pleasing his wife to be. Can I say again how kind he was, and the first person that I ever felt so connected to and trusted with my emotions, thoughts and wants.

In those days there were a lot of Tupperware parties and showers. I decided to have a Tupperware shower for Cookie as we all loved Tupperware. Gertrude (my sister-in-law), being so generous with her time and home, hosted the shower that I made for Cookie. She and Walter (Harry's brother) were married six years prior. We all looked up to them; they knew everything there was to know about marriage, or so we thought. It is so good for young couples to have more senior Christian mentors to pattern their marriage after. They never disappointed either of us couples in all the years to follow.

Gert was a great cook and baker, and that challenged me to duplicate some of her creations that I had never tasted before. Mom provided very well for us on a shoestring budget. Her baking skills were limited to a few varieties and her cooking was very simple but delicious, making exception to her mentally numbered canning jars which lined the fruit cellar walls. Naturally, later, when they were financially more stable, she too branched out to expand her culinary skills. By that time, I wasn't around much.

The Tupperware shower for Cookie was a success and it gave the host an opportunity to choose different items from a gift list as well as more Tupperware. It still embarrasses me to think that I received all the extras, as they should have gone to Cookie who the shower was for. This might be a small thing to some people, but it was a big thing to me. Not everything we do is valued the same to everyone. You must judge and deal with things in truth as they come along, and in honesty see them for how they affect you. I have found in life, trying to learn from these situations is my responsibility and reaction. Like I said before, ask God to forgive you, forgive yourself, learn from it, and go on.

Stress was revealed in the form of tears, which was probably a good thing. I never thought about it, but my tears flowed so often in those days that I probably didn't let emotion build. Unfortunately, Harry got the full dump of tears many times.

The engagement period of our lives was memorable as we had so many good times. We looked forward to our future lives together.

The morning of our wedding I went to Harry's house, two doors down and had a bath. We had no inside plumbing yet and the canal just wouldn't do for this May wedding day. I went into town and got my hair done by Angie, who had become a dependable friend.

The photographer came and took pictures at my house. I remember disliking the picture that was taken with my dad putting my garter on my leg. I had not kissed my dad for years and was aware that the smell of his aftershave mixed with the odor of tobacco was enough to turn my stomach. I was so aware of this that I stayed away from him without much attention given to the matter. It was like an internal decision or a line I drew years before. I don't remember when, or why, I made such a radical decision, but it felt good to have that barrier and I needed that control. I decided that morning I would let Dad kiss me one more time, for a picture, as I would not have to kiss him ever again after this day, not ever and I didn't consider why I felt this way. You must understand there was no hate or animosity towards my dad as we were closer than my mother and myself. I enjoyed his quiet personality most times, and knew he worked hard to support his family, as well as enjoyed having fun with them. My limitations were just a feeling of distance I needed at that time in my life. To have to kiss him would cause much anxiety and fear to surface. I told myself the combination of cigarette tobacco and aftershave that almost made me sick was the reason for the distancing.

I can't remember the wedding rehearsal and we did not have a rehearsal dinner or even snacks. Afterwards, at the apartment, Harry gave me a precious gift, and I was apologetic because I didn't know a husband and wife-to-be should get gifts for each other. It was the most beautiful brush and comb set with little trinket jars and picture frames. Each piece was engraved with my new initials, MEL. It was the most beautiful, unexpected gift. The little jars sat on our dresser and held precious little items. Later they held our children's baby teeth for years until well into their adulthood. I made a Christmas ornament, which included our son Shawn's teeth many years later when he already had children.

Getting married was the best day of my life. Harry and I walked down the aisle together, as was tradition in our German church. It suited me just fine as I didn't have dreams of my dad walking me down the aisle. I don't know how Dad felt about that and it didn't even dawn on me to discuss it.

I know when our girls got married, we would have been devastated not to have given them away. Harry was so honored as he walked them down the aisle to their new partners for life. We were proud of who they had become and the choices they made.

Reverend Miller directed our wedding ceremony. I know it was a big moment as I blocked out the whole service. Coming back to reality afterwards, only to realize that Harry and I didn't kiss during the ceremony. Every bride and groom kissed at the alter, didn't they? In my mind they did, and I missed out on what I thought was important in a marriage ceremony and of course afterwards, asked why. Apparently, it was not allowed in our legalistic type of church, and I couldn't believe I didn't know that.

The wedding reception was the usual for that time and had musical specials, poems and songs. Dinner was never my favorite with my family as I felt picked on and I didn't want to start crying at our reception meal. I held it together as Mat my brother yelled out something to embarrass me.

I can't remember what Harry said, but he said something to me too and I just about let my tears loose. He remembers my face and he felt bad afterwards. It was probably nothing, but my fragile emotions were waiting for that usual crash.

I was also shocked as the legalism carried over to the wedding reception. The first time the glasses were clanged the pastor got up and announced that the bride and groom wished there to be no clanging of glasses or kissing, and I was shocked. Harry and I had no idea! These were quite the eye openers of rules that did not make sense to me.

The evening was over, and we couldn't wait to leave our reception. I went home to my parent's house to change into my going away outfit, a brocade blue, with white fur on cuffs, and a large, flowered hat. The long white gloves I wore were the only ones I owned beside the black gloves from Cookie's wedding. My new brocaded white shoes and purse matched. They were the first pair of shoes that genuinely fit my flat feet well. I remember them caressing my feet with comfort and pondered why I had not had shoes that fit so perfectly before, not realizing shoes could feel this way.

Harry's dad let him use his car, as ours was a Volkswagen. The drive away was so freeing. We were on our way to our honeymoon suite in Buffalo.

37. Our Honeymoon

We were heading for the Poconos in Pennsylvania for our honeymoon, so we stayed in Buffalo for the night. I was so embarrassed to go into the Hotel as a new bride. I think at that time I was sexually immature, not wanting to talk about sex or acknowledge that it even happened. I felt everyone in the hotel knew what we were going to do. Of course, we were going to celebrate our new freedom found in marriage, including sex.

Our attractive suite was so beautiful with a grand mural above the large bed. It was done in my favorite blue colors and made me feel comfortable at first glance. This bed would be mine to share with Harry all night and I would not have to pick it up in the morning, or even make it! I took in my surroundings as they revealed their luxury to me, and I felt at peace. Even though I have never remembered the most intimate portion of our first night, Harry assures me it happened, and it was great. My life was a fog most of the time and I could only remember small portions of our honeymoon and nothing to do with sex.

It was like a picturesque dream arriving at the resort. We never stayed anywhere for a week especially a place as lovely as this one. Our meals would be prepared and served in ways so different to our lifestyle. Of course, after years of enjoying different foods, we now know about presentation of the finest cuisine.

Our cabin was beside a rippling brook and sounded tranquil as we drove up to it. As you entered the front door there was a sitting room with a fireplace. It was cozy with a bedroom and a bathroom off that. I wish I could, but I don't even recall one moment sleeping in the bed, never mind anything else. My spirit would have soared to wake up in the morning with the love of my life still there beside me.

We met other couples and socialized with them, even though being shy. Some honeymooners had heart shaped tubs and raised beds in their rooms as well as fireplaces. Their room was luxurious just like the bridal magazines displayed in the Poconos Honeymoon Resorts brochures.

About thirty years later, Harry and I went back to see if we could find our cabin. We set out on one of our little getaway holidays and decided this would be one of our destinations. With anticipation we arrived, only to be disappointed. It had been neglected and looked shabby to say the least. The exterior had a weathered appearance, and the smell of mold was prominent. We forgot about all else for a minute and held our breath. The door was open, and we walked inside.

Putting the foul odor aside we tried going back in time and spoke of our first days as man and wife. We remembered Harry sitting at the little desk and our little fireplace. The bedroom had diminished in size as our minds remembered a larger room. Even the interior, locked in a time warp, had aged beyond its life. The wallpaper still looked the same, only now had that aged darker look bearing many years of dirt and grime taking it back decades in design. The grounds were overgrown. The bushes were disfigured beyond repair and the flowerbeds overrun with weeds. We decided that our marriage had weathered time in a more graceful manner as we not only looked well, but our marriage was still looking to the future, and we were still growing relationally. We were not stuck in the past, tired and just waiting to die, as this property seemed to be.

We had no idea what awaited us in life as we enjoyed the security of this little cottage, so many years earlier. We knew we loved each other and were totally devoted to one another also having great confidence in God to help us, no matter what situation we were in.

I was not going to be like my parents who were not happy. Determined that I would do everything in my power to have an extremely successful marriage, no matter how much work it took.

There was something deep within me and I knew I would not stay with a man that abused me. It was how I interpreted the feelings that haunted me. What else would give me that feeling of helplessness and crippling fear? I did not know why I felt this way, but I verbalized it to Harry many times, trying to figure out why I felt so strongly about this.

Acknowledging a difference in our opinions wasn't difficult at that time, as I didn't have too many opinions that I dared to voice. Not that Harry didn't let me, I just couldn't zero in on what they were. I didn't have too many of my own wants and thoughts. I had not developed emotionally enough to accept that I had a right or deserved my own desires.

Girls have such a romantic outlook on life and men have a sexual image of marriage. It was one of the first differences that I remember learning.

Harry told me he was so disappointed in the negligee. He expected a sheer exposing little number, that revealed everything he could have imagined and ever dreamed of laying his eyes and hands on. Instead, my negligee had not only two, but three layers and a layered coat over top. It wasn't what he expected, but it made me feel so beautiful. The blue lace empire waist bodice and sheer flowing layers of the skirt made me feel desirable and glamorous. The layers were set-off with those wonderful, white-feathered slippers, popular at the time. They fulfilled a dream I had since I saw them in a movie years earlier. I wouldn't have thought in a thousand years that he would not feel the same as I did. Of course, he didn't tell me this at that moment, but sometime later. We were both immature as well as naïve.

Speaking with other couples, the guys all had the same complaints about the negligees. I guess we were not the only ones with that deflated reality.

As we left this private unrealistic world, we plunged into thoughts of home. The drive home was more solemn than the ride to a place never to be duplicated ever again. The sexual freedom met expectations we had waited for so long, so I was told. Spending a week together never saying goodbye for the night but being able to fall asleep in your lover's arms, was the best feeling. No late-night good-byes, longing for your partner to stay.

Our honeymoon was behind us, and for the first time a feeling that I was really wanted and belonged to someone who loved me. We enjoyed our time together so much, as I didn't give much thought to the fact until years later, that I could not remember the most intimate parts. Of course, at that time it didn't ever enter our minds and I didn't even know that I should remember more, as I was oblivious to being in and out of reality.

When going to my safe place mentally, it enabled me to function in those times. Normally I would not be able to. Even though being unaware of the blocking, it was helpful to be able to start a new marriage and all the physical aspects that come into play.

We decided to take Harry's dad's car back first and saw that Walter and Gert were visiting with their two children, Don, and Ken. I felt so awkward and shy about going in, especially thinking that they knew what we had done. I really don't know how many brides were like me or was I in a small group of the ill adjusted.

After taking the car back, we visited a while and went home to our apartment. It was satisfying to be home amongst all those new things we had purchased for our life together. The gifts we received were there to unpack and we were enthusiastic and eager.

We went for groceries and the cost was astounding, as we needed all the basics, as well as the weekly items. It was liberating to be able to buy anything we wanted. I purchased a large package of pork sausages and proceeded to fry them up for dinner that night.

My portion at home growing up used to be one and a half sausages, and now I would enjoy as many as I desired. The first three were so delicious. The next few somehow lost their flavor and by the last mouth full, I disliked them. I ate until I couldn't eat any more. My overindulgence totally quenched my deprived taste for breakfast sausages. It cured me of ever craving another one.

Half a banana was our treat every week after our parents came home from grocery shopping. Naturally I bought many over the years and still love a whole banana to myself, even to this day. It makes me feel special and indulging to have a whole banana even though they have a lot of calories and sugar. Half of a banana reminds me of being rationed. I am so thankful that I didn't ruin my love for bananas the same way I did for pork sausages!

Harry became my true knight in shining armor. He was compassionate and kind, loving me unconditionally no matter what. After I cooked our first formal meal and we sat down to enjoy it, I became overwhelmed with tears. What was happening? I left Harry sitting at the table quietly eating as I ran to the bedroom crying. I wasn't in touch with my feelings, so

I couldn't interpret the situation. Not able to express my feelings, I released tears and it was not an effective way to communicate. Even words have been known to be wrongly interpreted, never mind irrational tears.

Harry showed his love and patience and sat there eating quietly as I wept. He tried to have me tell him what the problem was, but I couldn't find the words to say what I felt. Dinnertime was such a painful time for me growing up that I crashed emotionally in the fear of it happening again in my own home. It took me some time to keep myself from sabotaging events before they happened as I thought they would be hurtful or not turn out. That took years to realize, never mind work on. In this case I got better at it every meal that we ate together. Realizing I was in a safe place with Harry, we were able to sit and have good meals as well as good conversations.

My work at Kunselman's was enjoyable, but I didn't get home until four thirty on Saturdays. Harry would clean the house and wax and polish the hardwood floors with our new polisher. When he picked me up after work, we had the rest of the evening to visit with friends. In the summer months we would go to Jones Beach, near Port Weller and we pulled our boat with the Volkswagen Beetle, what a team! The duo demanded much attention from bystanders as the boat pushed the vehicle along the road, or so it seemed.

The boat was often loaded full of camping gear as Cookie and Ernie would venture out camping with us. We would never have gotten everything into a car. We used Ernie's vehicle to pull the boat ,which prompted Harry and Ernie to work almost all night before many of these outings, getting the vehicles ready.

We spent so much time together and became very close friends. We got to know some of the bad and good about one another. We were friends that accepted all the inadequacies and wonderful traits about each other. Good friends know that people are not perfect but love them, despite this.

We knew exactly how we were going to raise our children, and exactly how they would behave as well as when we would decide to have them. It makes me chuckle as I recall the conversations, and how much life has taught us all.

We were very involved in our church and were eager for God to move in our lives and use us. Harry was in the band and was the church choir director for a while. I taught the youngest children's class in Sunday school as my German wasn't as fluent as most of the parishioners. Harry and I spoke English in our home and didn't think our German was developed enough to use regularly.

38. Emotions Crash

Every Sunday before our church service we all seemed to gravitate to our regular pews. I sat beside Cookie as Ernie played in the band. Harry was sitting at the front with the band too, as he usually did for the first part of the service.

I was totally immobilized by a terrifying experience. A person, who was always gentle and kind to everyone, sat behind us. It was a quiet peaceful atmosphere and one of complete safety. I relished the services even though many of the words to the hymns escaped my bilingual comprehension, and just remained a lovely tune. Suddenly, a shrill scream penetrated my soul, along with a powerful hit over the head with a hymnal. The scream was much worse than being walloped over the head. Instinct made me turn towards the commotion and I saw her glaring eyes penetrate my being as well as hearing her words. I was frozen. Cookie did what I should have done and ducked forward away from the action. I turned and embraced the action, and I was struck to my core. An explosion of action and words followed from her. We all knew this person and she was usually a loving quiet personality with some emotional issues. Why did this trigger such deep anxiety in me?

There was something horrifying that the shock related to, but I didn't know what. It woke feelings of pain and torment although nothing was that fearful in the past, or was it? It left me scared, and I became overwhelmed with fear that was buried deep within me, and I could not expose it, to help myself. By the next day I was terrified to be alone and couldn't function. I was trying to tell Harry what I was feeling, but I didn't know myself what I was grappling with.

We were staying at Gert and Walter's, house sitting, but I couldn't stay. I thought I was having a breakdown, and I needed to go to our place. The shock of this experience had unleashed a fear in me, and I didn't know why or what to do with it. Harry had to go to a meeting that evening and I cowered in the corner on the couch and remained there all evening. It took so long for Harry to arrive home that night, as my fear and anxiety grew every second he was gone. The next day I went to work, and it felt so good to know things were normal again. Harry was going to go to choir that evening, and I was alone once more. I took my place in the corner of my couch where I spotted something very strange. I stared and stared, and I couldn't believe it. Closing my eyes for a long while, I refocused after opening them. What was I seeing? It looked like a face, but I couldn't make out the features. I looked away but had to look back again. Yes, it appeared again. I had no idea what it meant, but I was terrified, and Harry arrived home just in time. I told him what I saw, and of course he thought I was seeing the face of the girl at church, but I knew it wasn't. I hated being alone and couldn't shake it. It was a troublesome week, and my evenings were long and fear provoking. I felt so bewildered and did not know how to suppress this fear that had seized my mind.

We managed to get ready for our long weekend trip and I was looking forward to unbroken companionship as I was so fearful of being alone. The change was good for me. One second, then one minute, then one hour, then one day, and then finally, I forgot about the incident and the face that plagued me from the previous week. Life became normal again and I didn't see that face until many years later, when it tormented me in my nightmares, until it became all too clear to me.

How did Harry have the patience for this mad behavior? I was living the puzzle of life with Harry, and we were trying to find and place all the pieces that would show us a beautiful picture of the wonderful marriage that we expected.

The first time we had my family down for a meal, Harry thought I was insane. I had made a roaster full of dozens of chicken pieces, a large pot of potatoes, lots of vegetables, bread, and dessert. He said we would have too much left over as there were only six coming for dinner. I had lived with them long enough to know there would be enough but not many leftovers.

As usual, my family did not disappoint me and proved me to be right.

It was a great experience having them to our home, where I was in charge and was the respected hostess of the dinner table. The conversation was light, and we had a good time. It was the first meal of many to follow where we had good fellowship around a table of food. My brothers enjoyed their food so much, that it was an honor to watch them eat. Every mouthful was discussed and critiqued as how good it tasted continuing until every morsel was gone. This has not changed, even to this day.

One thing you might take note of in case you dine with them, they do not share their food or drinks and your life is on the line if you try to sample from their plates. For years I had a difficult time sharing my food, and it took until in my late fifties and longer to realize that tomorrow is another day, and there will be more food. My first instinct is to hoard my food but given a second thought, of course, I would share. Although I still love a whole banana, I really don't mind sharing.

One Saturday after work, I decided to do a facial with egg whites. Someone at work said it was a great facial, but don't talk while it is drying. I put the thick layer of slimy egg whites on my face, while my hair was in rollers, as it kept the hair back from getting egg whites on it. The white slime had dried nicely when the doorbell rang. While looking through the peephole, I saw the paperboy and before opening the door, I gathered my money from the kitchen table. It was only the paperboy, so I opened the door, and as I said hello my face cracked into a million pieces. I gave the money to him and thanked him as he was fixated on my every move. I closed the door with him still standing frozen and staring at me.

After a few minutes it was time to clean my face and I did my hair. I felt like a new person my face cleansed, and my hair was freshly done.

The doorbell rang again. I peeked through the peephole once more, and it was the paperboy. Thinking that maybe I had short-changed him, I opened the door and saw he was accompanied by a friend. Both were hugging the opposite wall with their backs and arms but focusing on our door. They watched in horror as I unlocked the door expecting to see Frankenstein. He brought his friend to see a horror show and then I realized, oh no, that was me! I asked if I could help him, and they ran away. Why did I answer the door with that egg white on my face? He was probably so relieved when Harry took over, paying him again.

Every day I realized there was a great void deep within me. There were so many needs and feelings that were unanswered and left me wondering. I had no idea where they came from, or what should be done with them. I longed to have a baby and fulfill another need to love. I knew Harry loved me and he showed it constantly, but I couldn't explain why I felt I needed more. I didn't know what that more was yet.

During our first year of marriage, we were free to do and go wherever, having had many good times, we camped a lot and boating was one of our favorite past times. Although we only tented, and roughed it most of the time, we made lasting memories to build on. Boating gave us more activities than we would have imagined. You could fish, water ski, swim or just enjoy looking at new surroundings. We were comfortable in our apartment as our contented life was satisfying, and I felt for the first time, like I was a real person living a genuine life. I was overwhelmed, in a good way with my freedom.

Our first Christmas Harry went way overboard on gifts for me. I got casual boots, dress boots and more. I was embarrassed at getting so much as we were opening our gifts with his mom and dad at their place. I had never been so spoiled. I saved my pennies and bought Harry the best sound system I could afford, and it was a portable record player with two speakers attached and could be carried as one unit. Harry enjoyed and appreciated music and I knew he would love it, and I was right as Harry delighted in playing the records and harmonizing with them.

39. The Bus

But He said to me, "My grace is sufficient for you, for my power is made perfect in weakness."
Therefore, I will boast more gladly about my weakness, so that Christ's power may rest on me.

2 Corinthians 12:9

It was some time that summer when everything was going so perfectly that I found myself in great difficulty. Our apartment was on Linwell Road, beside the fire hall, and I had to walk to the corner at Geneva to catch my bus for work and never minded the exercise but rather appreciated it, realizing it was much better than walking to the Victoria Lawn Cemetery from my parents' house. I was on the same schedule for work that week, I would see the same bus driver for a couple of days. Since the bus only had a couple of passengers on it, the driver and I often talked about a variety of things. One day I wore a short wig and the driver commented that he liked my hair. I didn't know his name and he did not know mine. The problem was that my mind took off in a direction far from reality. I started to dress in the morning to see him and thought of him constantly. He took over my mind all day long. Harry didn't know about these thoughts, as it was one of those quick things that happens to a person before they realize it. After a couple of days of mental torment, I felt guilt and I realized what I was letting my mind do. I was not thinking anything sexual but was giving an importance that did not belong to this person. I recognized I had sinned and betrayed Harry even if only in my mind. It was the first time while being married or dating Harry that this had happened. God directed me as I deliberately prayed for forgiveness, and courage to change my circumstance and thoughts. I remember weeping on my knees at the side of my bed, pleading with God to clear my mind of all those thoughts not approving of

Him. God was so gracious all my life and taught me lessons in such overwhelming but real ways.

God spoke to me, not audibly, but I knew the answer came from Him. He impressed upon me that, "I should not feel exempt from falling into sin and I should keep watch, guarding my heart." I needed to remember to guard my mind and heart, as God had taught me in past years, and be aware of the lies of the devil. Living my happy life, I lost track and had forgotten. He also affirmed that He loved me, and I was forgiven. This was a few days after it all started. Many people fall into these innocent situations and let their minds play with their thought life, until it becomes a huge barrier in their marriage. God has been so gracious to me and brought to light His will in my life and I am so grateful, knowing that all sin begins in the mind.

The personal battles I fought were the most life changing and positive, causing spiritual growth in my life. What God told me that day, is all backed up with the Bible. I was not that familiar with the Bible yet and I am in awe of how I was so wonderfully taught the same principles.

Harry was not home as I was off work on Mondays because the hair dressing shop was closed. It was great timing to become aware of this mind game I had going on, and be able to talk to God privately, and take the time to release it. Sometimes we need to take intervals from life and deal with things within us and regain a new perspective. Once again, harnessing my mind, was an imperative discipline for me as I could not go where I had no control and let lies take hold. Truth had to take first place. The reality of the situation was that the bus driver was just a nice guy who liked conversation while doing his job. It was a boring and slow route in those days. It was really like having a casual coffee with someone at Tim Hortons by today's standard. My mind ran wild and out of control as I let down my guard. You might be wondering if it was instant release from my mind games, or did it take time and what did I do.

First, I worked through it without telling Harry at that time. I willed myself not to dwell on those thoughts anymore. I changed my bus schedule, although inconvenient at many times. I was so shocked that this could happen to me because I was deliriously and totally in love with my husband.

I lived in a rose-colored bubble, which for the first time had been burst. I was so grateful that God loved catching me when my bubble burst, as He was always there ready to teach and help me. Harry was told of this crazy thing that I had worked through and didn't think it as serious as I did. He said he thought most people played mind games, but I knew for myself it was an area that I could not indulge in.

40. My Secret Prayers

The Lord is close to the brokenhearted and saves those who are crushed in spirit.

Psalm 34:18

In the weeks to follow the mind battle was no more, and I lived once more a realistic and happy life. Since church was a continuous part of our expression of faith, we attended at least two or three times a week. I would weep by myself at the altar. I stayed for as long as it was open and did so quietly while I spoke to God. I wanted a child. No, I wanted twins. I felt like I needed a child and pleaded for twins.

We had decided that we would wait a few years as our finances were not yet stable. This was a good decision for us both, but I also knew that I could tell God my secret wants and desires. I did this all the time.

Harry's cousin Mary just had twins and I knew it would be the greatest blessing, as they considered their twins to be so. I also knew, God would have to convince Harry that the time was right and therefore I was pleading with God.

I stopped taking the birth control pills six months into our marriage as they didn't agree with me. Of course, Harry and I made that decision together. I tried two different kinds of pills. We used every kind of contraceptive to prevent a pregnancy and were both very diligent about trying not to get pregnant.

Harry didn't know what I was praying for but asked me if all was going well. He decided others might think we were having marriage problems if I kept weeping at the altar. I wasn't so concerned about what people thought and believed, I just needed to be true to God and if He knew my heart, that is all that mattered.

There was a particular evening service that I received total peace from God regarding wanting children, and I never asked again. It is just awesome how God can bring about such surrender to His will if we just ask. It was like I knew God heard me and I found total peace in knowing His will was mine. I was content to know he heard me and that I would be happy to live according to His plan for me. I had total contentment and rest in my Lord.

I realized there was a big difference between Harry and me. He lived a lot for how it looked to others, and I did things because God had taught me to do them, in a very personal way. Harry was raised in the church by Christian parents and there was a level of respect, and awareness of what was expected from those in the congregation. I on the other hand, heeded no rules in the church, but lived by God's rules, of course not without failing many times.

Up to this point, I thought our intimacy was as it should be. Harry and I were learning together, and we both enjoyed the process. I had no idea when we were dating the battles I would have after marriage. There were experiences that I was fighting constantly but they had nothing to do with what Harry did or didn't do, but rather with my emotions. I could not stop triggers that produced overwhelming negative reactions. The longer we were married, the more I was plagued with triggers. I constantly fought all the harder within myself to overcome every fear that raised its ugly head. I had to fight these battles over and over, always being on guard.

The scent and sight of semen and everything about it made me feel ill and provoked such uneasy feelings somewhere deep inside me. Who could explain it? I had a terrible time seeing the male genitals, especially if his hands were in the same frame. This took many years to overcome. It also sent me into another zone, somewhere my conscious mind couldn't go. I was sent into a state of desperation. The feelings inside me raged like that of a violent sea where I was drowning. I did everything I could to suppress those feelings, as I didn't know where or what they were, and just thought I should not have them, so fighting to get rid of them was ongoing. Assuming I must be very strange and odd and would have to work on myself, which was done with diligence. Harry was oblivious to what was going on within me and why not; even I didn't know how to articulate that.

He thought everything was great and I was just learning how to enjoy this newfound freedom of ours. I became very efficient at suppressing things when I wanted to. I could do a great job neglecting and hiding my feelings in such a way that Harry wouldn't even realize most times. I was so angry, condemning myself for feeling the way I did. It took many years before Harry, or I would know what the underlying problem was. Harry was more than patient and I realized it even back then.

God certainly provided the right man for me. All the right feelings were there to want this person I loved intimately, longing to be together in each other's arms without fear. I could not figure out why these times of fear, sickness and repulsion happened. If you would have asked me at that time, I would have said sex was great. It was, but it was just me that had these problems that I continually had to deal with.

If you have any of these triggers or others as I had many more, please don't assume you are gender confused or have problems with the opposite sex. There can be causes for this that are still hidden from you. Ask God to reveal them to you. It may take time, but with God's leading you can become free from your fears.

41. Ouija Board

It is God who arms me with strength and keeps my way secure.

Psalms 18:32

I had changed job locations and went to work for Angie as she had opened her own shop, the Flamingo. The shop was located on Court Street across from the St. Catharines Bus Terminal.

Our supplier came in to show us some new products and was talking to Angie in the back room. I was working on a client and when finished went to the back to use the washroom. They were using a Ouija Board and asking it questions and it was giving them the right answers. I had not seen one before and stood and watched thinking it was so silly, and as I stood there, it stopped working. I went to the washroom and watched again when I came out. They told me to leave, as the board did not work when I was standing there. I found that strange and went to get my customer out from the dryer. Later when I learned more about this kind of thing, I was in awe of how God protects you even when you do not know the danger around you. God knew I should not be entangled in these kinds of things as I already had a spiritual battle that I was not aware of.

42. God Answers My Cry

Evening, morning, and noon I cry out in distress, and he hears my voice.

Psalm 32:6

I was working on a long hairdo, I opened the bobby pin with my teeth as I usually did, and I uncharacteristically gagged. Since it was a regular procedure for me to open a hairpin in this way, I thought this strange. I even told Angie to watch as I could repeat my reaction as we laughed at the strangeness of this. At home while getting the lunch meats for sandwiches, I started to gag and feel nauseated. The next morning when my eyes opened, I could hardly make it to the bathroom. Could this be what we think it was? I would never try to get pregnant or do anything except pray to make it happen, as we were trying not to have a child at this time. This would be an answer to prayer. God was such a good friend and He cared so deeply for me to bring this pregnancy into my life.

It was some time before Christmas when I started getting nauseated. We tried to keep it a secret, but the constant heaving made it so difficult. I was pregnant and consequently I was sick at home, sick at the bus stop, and sick at work when I got there. I was dragging myself but once ten o'clock rolled around, I felt a little better and my stomach settled somewhat. I ate lots of tomato soup and toast, morning, noon, and night. At first, I lost a lot of weight and after a couple of months the doctor told me I had to drink milk and follow the Canada food rules. I didn't ever drink milk and didn't like butter too much. This was difficult while feeling ill, but after three months were up, they worked well as a guide.

In those days we wore heavy girdles to hold up our nylons so you can imagine how uncomfortable that was. It was during a Sunday morning just after I sang in the choir, I felt the largest kick, and it was the first time I felt life within me. My thoughts were overwhelmed with the reality of what I felt. It was strange, as I felt movement in three different areas at one time and I could visualize my baby with both feet as well as elbow poking its mother. I had never been pregnant before so did not know how this was supposed to feel.

After four months we told our parents and asked them not to tell anyone yet. My mother granted our wish but put all kinds of baby outfits on the clothesline for the neighborhood to see. So much for secrecy!

I was ecstatic about the thought of having a baby, but Harry was panicked, and he became the ultra-dedicated provider for our family. The boat was sold, and we looked for another place to live. The apartment was too small with one bedroom, and we needed to save more money. Harry's parents had a little cottage beside their home, and we decided to rent that. It was very tiny, much smaller than the apartment but had direct access to the outside. We would once again be in our old neighborhood.

Harry moved us a week early from our apartment to the cottage on a Saturday while I was working. He wanted to make life easier for me, but I was mortified as I don't even think the place was all packed up yet. I know I didn't have an ounce of energy to spare after work and appreciated his efforts. I can still recall how tired I felt and the waves of nausea. My hormones were going crazy and if you got the idea that I cried a lot before, you should have seen me then.

We were invited to Cookie and Ernie's new home for dinner one Saturday evening. They built a lovely home on the property they received from Cookie's parents, and the setting beside a brook was exceptional. Her table was beautifully set, and the dinner was delicious. We were having great conversation when I excused myself to go to the washroom. When I didn't return, Harry came to see what was happening and found me crying. He asked why I was sad, and I answered I didn't know, all I knew was that I couldn't stop.

That is what makes good friends so valuable. You can have these uncontrollable displays of emotion and they try to understand, or at least accept this as part of who you are. The four of us anticipated starting our families together. My pregnancy was only one of many plans that became reality, in ways other than what we planned.

I was getting so big, and everyone would say are you having twins. I responded that I was not and accepted the fact that I was bigger than normal. When I was about six months, we were having Easter dinner at Harry's parents in the basement, and I was carrying some food down the stairs, I tripped and fell about four steps and slid on my tummy. That evening I felt the baby drop and a lot of pressure on my lower abdomen. Not worried at all and too naïve to be concerned, I went on with life. At my regular checkup the doctor questioned me as to when I got pregnant because he thought I was further along than I thought. The doctor announced I would have a very large baby according to what he could feel. There were no convenient ultrasounds in those days, and I got so huge I thought maybe I would stop work after my seventh month. It was difficult to reach my clients while shampooing. My legs were very swollen every evening, and I was so tired by the time Harry picked me up from work nightly, as I didn't have my driver's license and appreciated the ride so very much.

It was my last Saturday at work, and it felt great to be finished this segment of my life for a little while. Sunday passed quickly and I was looking forward to Monday, my first real day off. Monday was an exceptional day as I cleaned the little cottage and did laundry. By two o'clock I got ready and walk all the way downtown for my doctor's appointment. I didn't even waver at the thought of that being too much exercise. What was I thinking? My doctor's appointment went well, and I patiently waited for Harry at the corner of King and Queen Street after he got off work. We had dinner and relaxed that evening. I had committed to babysit Donny and Ken for Walter and Gert the next evening as they were going out for their anniversary on June 17. She was expecting but was due in July, one month before me. My due date was Aug 17.

My sleep was restless and after getting up often to go to the bathroom, I started to get cramps. By six in the morning Harry wondered what I was doing, and I relayed that I felt rather strange and had small pains. He timed them and announced they were ten minutes apart. We decided to call the doctor who said we should come to the hospital.

We hoped it wasn't a false alarm, not even thinking that it was way too early and so much could go wrong. At the hospital I was still comfortable when the doctor said I would have my baby today and he would have to break my water. After the painful examination of many interns, he broke my water. They all jumped back as the bed and floor flooded and they declared they had never seen so much water!

The doctor knew when my water broke at the last minute he would have to help my babies, as they were too small to make it on their own. He couldn't tell this until he broke my water and realized there were two, although he never told me there were two.

All I heard throughout my pregnancy was that I would have a large baby and now everyone was excitedly saying I was going to have a very small baby. I didn't grasp the reality of having any baby until my pains became unbearable. Shortly after twelve noon, I was rolled into the delivery room.

Harry was told he could not be with me although he attended those prenatal classes faithfully. All those preparations and nothing was going as it was planned. We didn't even have the nursery ready as we had two months until my due date.

It was a relief to push instinctively. To experience the miracle of how God has programmed our bodies so naturally to deliver a child is an amazing experience. Another big push and I had a baby. It was so overwhelming, and we had a little girl. They didn't put the baby on my tummy, but the doctor said push again. I had learned in prenatal classes that this would be the afterbirth. I didn't know it would take such a lot of work. I pushed hard when told to and to my surprise it was another baby!

43. A Specific Answer

Delight yourself in the Lord and he will give you the desires of your heart.

Psalm 37:4

We had two girls, identical twins, born 2 minutes apart. You should have heard me thanking the doctor as if he was handing babies out and I got first prize. The doctor just said push again and I totally flipped out saying, "Another one, how nice! Thank you! Thank you!" They all laughed and said this was the afterbirth. The first twin was born at 1:25 and weighed 2 lb. 12 oz., and the next 1:27 weighing 2lb 14 oz., and I was immediately reminded of my days weeping before God, pleading for twins. I thanked God for his answer to my prayers. God was and is so faithful and so specific! He hears every word and thought that comes from the heart.

The nurse rolled the incubator out into the hall to where Harry was nervously waiting. Smiling she told him to come and have a look. He peeked into the isolette and said, "Oh so small." After chuckling again, she said, "No, have another look." He got closer again and looked right into the glass encasement from the top. He had a good look and was totally confused! We were told repeatedly, it would be a large baby and now we not only had one, but two very small babies. He was stunned and in shock. He was the proud father of two baby girls. We were so inexperienced and didn't know much about a lot of things, especially twins.

We only had one name picked out for a girl and one for a boy as we thought we would have only one child. They both remained nameless for two days, as we felt bad naming one without the other. Their bracelets called them baby A and baby B.

The name Tammy was a more modern name, and our parents didn't really relate to it, never mind pronounce it properly. We decided to pick the name Teresa for the other twin as our parents were familiar with this traditional name. I had already decided back then that I would call her Terry. Baby A first born was named Teresa Marie and Baby B, was named Tammy Lynn.

Shortly after the girls were born, Cookie and Ernie arrived. I was still in such an excited euphoric state. We had a short but good visit. Harry called friends and family to let them know we had twins and told the guys at Sheldon he had Siamese twins and they asked where they were attached. He said, "No, they just look alike." They told him that he meant identical twins and we have laughed about that many times since then.

Harry sent a beautiful flower arrangement to the hospital, and it was done in pink with a stork holding a baby cuddled in a blanket hanging from its long beak. I think I still have it in my box of old memorabilia. We didn't get many flower arrangements in those days, and it was so special to receive something arranged so beautifully. I kept it for many years in the nursery on my little girls' dresser.

It was such a happy time, but one of the most difficult and painfully emotional times I experienced. Unless you are a mother, you have no idea how attached you become as soon as your child is born. We stood at the glass just staring at our children as my heart ached to touch them. Terry lost so much weight and ended up weighing under two pounds. The doctor told Harry we shouldn't expect too much as they were very small and weak, but I never worried about them as I knew God answered my prayer and why would He take them from me now. I was learning to have confidence in God, when He said something, He came through with the answer, I was trusting that if He said it, it would happen.

Longing with everything within me, I stood at the glass gazing at my undersized babies. This is where my heart-to-heart talks with my sweet little girls began, I figured hearts can communicate without words and spent hours talking to them through the glass, as I stared into their incubators and then isolettes. We engaged in many conversations, although we were always separated by the glass wall and no audible words were spoken.

It was difficult going home without my children, as all I wanted to do was go to the hospital to stand at the glass window and have my heart-to-heart with them. It is so different now as parents are allowed to hold their children no matter what size and situation. The human touch was important, and I prayed my babies would not lack because I could not touch them, but I decided to give that worry to God as I could not change the situation and He could intervene.

I felt great even in the hospital and my weight dropped off and I had time to recuperate physically. Within a week I was back to normal although my breasts were so engorged, and it was very painful. I am sure it would have been easier to nurse. They never even encouraged me to pump, and I certainly didn't know if that was possible. I was continually leaking and finally had to bind myself for a week to get control of the lactating.

After I returned home to our little cottage, we wallpapered and made the little nursery, into our little girls' retreat. We borrowed a crib from Rosa Fry as she was finished using it for both of her girls, but it was in excellent shape. We thought the girls could sleep in the same crib, one on each end for a while. The only new purchase for the nursery was a white dresser and a little lamp that I valued as just the right piece to finish off the room. Their bedroom would be a partitioned space in our bedroom. With the pink and blue wallpaper and a window, it looked quite bright.

Cookie and Ernie invited us up to a cottage they had rented. Harry thought it might make me less depressed to go for a holiday instead of standing at the nursery windows of the hospital. Against my better judgment, I agreed to go, but what a mistake that was! All I could do was think of my girls and what was happening to them, and I cried constantly and just wanted to go home. That time was so dramatic that I suppressed most of it. Harry agreed to take me home and I was so relieved to be standing at the glass peering intently at my children.

The nurses fed them with tubes, as they were too weak to eat, and the doctor said this would sustain them. They just wore little diapers for the longest time and one day when we came in, they were wearing clothes. They were both so annoyed to wear clothes, as they weren't used to them. Terry cried so hard and fussed so much, that she kicked her foot through the isolette hand access and popped the cover right off. This was one step closer to getting home and the nurses were delighted at the spunk she displayed.

There was a beautiful nurse on duty throughout the girls' stay in the hospital and she seemed very attentive and did her duties joyfully. She was touching my precious girls, so I took special note of her, as she was often moving her mouth and singing or talking. Later, I was reacquainted with her at Central Church, where she attended, and I learned she was a Christian. I was so relieved that someone that loved God was touching my children regularly and even praying for them while working on them. This was important to me as I couldn't touch them myself.

Mrs. Balthazar was known to pray with all the babies she cared for. It was her ministry. I thanked God for the answer to prayer when I found this out many years later at her funeral. She worked with these newborn babies for many years and left a legacy of prayer, lovingly handling them, giving each one deserved attention. I was so grateful to her and thankful to God for answering my prayer in that way. He showed He cared about little aspects of life, and we were so privileged to know this God in a personal way.

44. Children and Farm Life

It was over two months of this routine, and I finally was able to hold and feed my children. That next week, Tammy was able to come home, as she was five pounds six ounces. We brought her home in a very little sweater set made just for her when Mrs. Jeffrey found out I had two very small girls. She was a neighbor who had knit a beautiful boy's sweater for me and asked if she could make two new ones for our little girls. I was delighted. They were so soft and pink.

It took some time to find the tiny little dresses I purchased for my sweet little girls. They were doll size, but the girls still got lost in them. For her trip home Tammy wore her little white with pink trim dress, bubble patterned sweater, hat, little white socks and satin shoes. She was so adorable and looked like a little doll. The neat thing was, taking Tammy home was like taking home an over two-month-old baby, just in super small size. Tammy looked right at us, and we felt like we could relate to her, and she understood us. We told her about going home, and she was quiet and didn't cry which made us very relieved and relaxed. I couldn't be tense about taking her home, as I was just too excited to have one of my children with me. Saying this, it was difficult to leave Terry at the hospital and we were torn. Three of us left and we had to leave her there, and it felt like I was leaving part of my heart behind. We hoped she would be able to come home soon but Terry didn't weigh enough yet but was gaining well.

Tammy was put in the little plastic car seat, which according to today's standard, would be a doll seat. We had a red XL Ford Galaxy and she fit nicely on my lap in her seat. All the care and feeding orders were given to us and Tammy had to be fed every two hours and we needed a lot of formula.

Walking into our small humble cottage, we felt so blessed to have one child home with us. I put Tammy in her crib, and she looked so lost and alone. I longed for her to stay awake, but instead, she just had a long nap.

The next morning, we received the call that they would let Terry come home. What excitement, as we dressed Tammy, and away we went to pick up her twin. At the hospital, I dressed Terry in her white and pink dress with her little bubble knit sweater set, her little white lace socks and satin shoes, just like I did with her sister. She looked so sweet and so tiny, while Tammy lay on the bed next to her waiting for her sister. Now we had two little girls to care for, just as it should be. Our little preemies lay there so content making my job so easy, as it seemed like they knew they were going home together. I was deliriously happy, and Harry was a bundle of nerves.

Tammy was placed between Harry and I on the front console, and Terry was on my lap, both in their own flimsy plastic seat. It was a good ride home and having both girls at home was the most fulfilling feeling and my life felt complete.

It was a full day of feeding every two hours also bathing and changing my half-pints. Their navels healed while in the hospital, so I didn't have to worry about being careful with them. The girls were over two and a half months old and so they weren't like newborn babies, only small. We had a double baby buggy that also served as a travelling bed. We would put it into the back seat and lay the girls in it as we drove. They would sleep and relax during the car rides. This is very different than nowadays, when a child must be in an inspected up-to-date car seat. Harry oversaw the making of all the formula, boiling it and steaming the bottles. We had such a difficult time feeding our new babies.

They were lazy feeders, as their mouth muscles didn't get the practice of a regular baby. At the hospital they used a feeding tube for such a long time, they were too weak to suck on the nipple of a bottle. Harry finally took a heated needle and made the hole in the nipples larger so they would feed without falling asleep. We had to make sure they drank a certain amount every feeding.

The first Sunday, we took them to church, and Harry said his stomach did somersaults. The girls were good, but he knew he would have to take one if they were both fussy and crying. He was busy during the service in the band and choir. Our sleep was at a premium in those days, but I never minded mothering our children.

One night, Harry caught me sitting in bed sleeping while holding a bottle in each child's mouth on either side of me. He had to work the next day and I did not want to bother him. He took the bottles and told me to go to sleep. He finished feeding them as well as burping which took a long time. Getting into a routine, we knew life was at its best, appreciating all our new experiences as we learned to handle them.

We purchased a clothes washer, which Harry put in the bathroom, but couldn't afford a dryer at this time. I didn't use disposables, but washed diapers daily. Diapers were hung outside in summer and all over the cottage when the weather got cold. I would go into the laundromat to make it a little easier, while Harry went to choir. I did not drive so he would have to drop me off and pick me up again afterwards. We were very fortunate to have Mom around to babysit on those nights.

It was an excellent autumn with our new family except for the three hours every night. The girls cried every evening for these hours. It was from about eight to eleven. I didn't know whether it was because Mom and Dad came down every night and held the girls. Did they want to be held after my parents left or did they just not like going to sleep? I never did figure it out.

Harry worked overtime every night for a long time trying to be a responsible dad as he provided for the financial needs of his family. He would come home about eleven when all the commotion was over.

As I said our bedroom had a low dividing wall built to make it two rooms, and it was not very private. When we would go to bed, the girls would cry whenever they heard the lamp switch click. Harry got smart after a while and just unscrewed our light bulb. No more crying. The thing was they were little but so aware of their surroundings and older in awareness than they appeared.

To celebrate our first Christmas when they were six months, we took a picture of them on the couch. I loved dressing my little girls every day. They had different outfits on, socks and shoes to match and sweaters complimenting their style for the day For these photos there were outfits given to them by Angie and looked so adorable. We propped them up leaning them against each other. The pictures were made into Christmas cards with them wearing the next size dresses. It was a big deal to graduate to the next size as they were so far behind other babies in size. Larry (their cousin) was born in July and looked like a monster in size in comparison.

The first winter the girls had measles, chicken pox and croup. I remember one stretch I couldn't attend church or any other function for over two months. They both took turns having croup, then one got the measles and after a week the next one got the measles. The chicken pox added another month of sickness. Not realizing at the time how tough the year was, we just did whatever we had to do to make it no matter how tired we were. They grew and we grew a little wiser with them.

The Jolly Jumper hanging in the doorway provided many hours of fun for all of us. We also got two walkers and a playpen from my parents. They were so taken up with their grandchildren and their generosity was well appreciated. Our small living room held a couch, end table, television, as well as one large size play pen. It just stayed up as we could put the girls in it, in their seats or lay them down. We would put one in the walker and one in the Jolly Jumper. The one in the walker would always go to the jumper and they kept each other busy. After a while we would change them into the alternate mobile.

We had an exposed oil stove in our kitchen for heat and had to be careful they didn't touch it. We also borrowed two highchairs, which came in very handy for feeding. I usually fed them at the same time, meaning one spoon for one and the next for the other and so on, not liking one to have to wait until the other was finished. They ate well as we tried many varieties of food.

I loved the adorable miniature beds we borrowed from the church nursery. They were beside each other and each had their own secondhand mobile. One day I went in to get them after their nap and they were both in one crib. I can't even tell you which one did the climbing. They weren't even walking yet, just standing up against furniture.

We noticed that Tammy got a tooth one day and Terry the next.

Tammy crawled one day and Terry the next. Tammy held her bottle one day and Terry the next. Tammy stood by herself one day and Terry the next. It seemed like Terry knew how to do everything but watched first and then acted. She was more cautious than her sister. We found this so interesting. It seemed almost like an inner clock. You don't plan cutting teeth on a certain day, and the sequence even pertained to that.

Harry worked long and demanding hours so we could afford to buy a home in the future. I worked for Angie while she was on her honeymoon in Italy but found it very difficult as I needed a ride into town and home again. I also missed my girls and when they got sick at Mom's I could hardly stay at work. There was no one else working with me so I had to stay and do the customers. I knew I was not the kind of person to leave my family and work outside the home every day.

Terry and Tammy's first birthdays were special, and we had small cakes for each of them to smush. They sat in their highchairs to do the demolition. I made them each a small chocolate and cherry, "Tortenboden." They were about five inches in diameter. This was a German fruit flan. They first eyed their two cakes and then got a taste. After that it was all hands-on deck, and it became a mess. I was pleased that they enjoyed their cakes and it looked like they were going to be dessert girls.

There was a kid's party in the afternoon that warm lovely day. I put the small pool outside and filled it with warm water. We invited some of their friends, Scott, Heidi and Larry. Larry was also going to be a year old, on July 17th. He was much taller and looked much older. My half-pints were still very tiny, but after that first winter of a plethora of illnesses they were very healthy. They didn't walk yet but were very close to it. The twins were doing very well, and we were so pleased with our little family. As they got older, we had such valuable times and life became so much easier. I loved and appreciated motherhood and took pleasure in being home with my children.

There was a change happening within me. I was living in the moment, and I could recall almost any moment I wished. I could recall raising my children, Terry and Tammy as well as recalling times of intimacy since their birth. I still struggled with triggers, but life became living color for me. I enjoyed every bit of it as well as being a vital part of it. It seemed that having children awakened something in me to enable me to live in the present. I didn't get transported to a far-away unknown place. I was a mother now, and it was important to be always present, with my children.

We decided to look for a new place to live. After talking to the bank, we realized we needed a larger down payment and Harry's dad lent us the money for a second mortgage for one year. We got our first mortgage approved and looked for a home. People from our church were in the process of selling their farm. Harry wanted to buy a farm and thought it would be a wonderful way of life. I agreed, and we purchased the farm for nineteen thousand dollars. We stripped all the hard wood floors and had them refinished. Painted every room and had the kitchen updated by putting trim on the kitchen cupboard doors and a side panel down the side of the fridge. I antiqued them in a trendy olive green. I loved sewing so I made my curtains, dressing all the windows on a tight budget.

The kitchen was a good size and with two large windows it had lots of light. The great thing about this farmhouse was the room right off the kitchen. We put all the kids' toys and a small pullout couch and television in it. It was a wonderful place for them to play and the gate in the doorway kept them out of trouble most of the time. We had a toy box made by Reverend Wentland who was very handy with woodwork. It was a replica of a house and the roof flipped up to retrieve the toys. It kept the room tidy when it needed to be.

Terry and Tammy had many bladder infections when they were very young. After too many of them the specialist suggested for them to have a cystoscopy. They were booked to have them the same day and would have to stay in the hospital for a couple of days. I hated not driving and after Harry got home from work, we were so anxious and excited to see them. Upon arriving at their room in the hospital, we saw that they had nets over their cribs. I didn't like that and asked why they did that? I was informed that they would climb out of their cribs into each other's cribs continually. The nurses were afraid they would fall on the hard floor and hurt themselves. I could understand that completely as this was the girl's daily ritual, and I also worried about the same thing. I recall fighting my tears as I walked out of the hospital, leaving my most precious little children there alone. The next day I was called, and they were released to once again make our home complete with their presence.

Afternoon naps were such an ordeal. The girls would climb out of their beds every day and empty their dresser drawers. Were they trying to tell me that they loved clothes? There were clothes all over the room every time I entered after their nap.

There were no childproof drawer closures back then, and I would try to catch them as soon as they woke up, but upon entering the room they were both in their cribs and the room was a mess. I tried watching before they went to sleep, but they were quiet, and I never caught them. I never got angry, just weary of cleaning up their clothes.

In the evening for bedtime, they would rock in their cribs, and you could hear them from downstairs as the cribs moved across the floor. Once Harry had to force the door open as the crib was right in front of it. I never thought of this back then but maybe they wanted to be next to each other and that was why they rocked their cribs. Thank goodness that also ended one day.

I was home with the girls one Sunday morning as they had the croup. It was Christmas time, and we had our tree nicely decorated in the front living room, where the door was usually closed. My brothers and sister visited as they were skipping out of church. The living room door remained open after they left.

Both girls ran in, and each quickly took an ornament from the tree and put them in their mouths at the same time. I went crazy, as I knew they were glass balls, grabbing the closest one, and carefully extracted it out of her mouth and ran for to other. I had screamed for her not to bite it and she stood frozen knowing she had done something wrong. I don't even know who was closest to me as it didn't matter, I needed to get to both before they got hurt. The ornament came out but in two pieces, thankfully not accompanied with blood. I couldn't believe it, and it was such a relief to know they were safe. Why would they both put an ornament in their mouths? Carefully piecing the ornament together, I could finally relax about the ordeal. There were no pieces missing as one came out whole. Harry wondered why I was so wrung out by the time he got home from church, as it should have been a very easy relaxed Sunday morning for me. After relaying our experiences of the morning, I still don't think he realized the stress of it.

A surveyor came to the outside tap to get a drink. They were surveying our property as we were going to sell the farm in the future. The girls were outside playing, and they started to yell intently at him, "No don't touch, dirty," repeatedly. I ran outside to see what the commotion was, and found a black man frozen in his tracks, beside the outside tap wanting to get a drink. The girls thought he was dirty and should not touch the tap. How embarrassing, and I apologized to him for the girls' reaction and took them inside.

I got him a drink and explained they had never had the experience of meeting a darker skinned person before. He understood and was very nice about it. We talked a while, and he had no ill feeling of racism. I must say, there is something to be said for living in a multicultural community as your children develop a sense of understanding and safety while being with people of different color.

On another occasion, after a weekend of the girls having a slight temperature, I found them in their room, out of their beds, and on the dresser. They were in the diaper bag and had baby aspirins in their hands. I had used them the day before to make sure their temperature didn't get out of control. They were both chewing on something that looked like aspirins and I didn't know how many they consumed. I didn't have my license and couldn't drive to take them to the hospital, so I called someone to take us there to have them checked out. There they gave the girls something to make them sick to their stomachs, and I felt so bad for them as they threw up. These were the days before what I call, child proof containers. I was also feeling so inadequate as a parent as how could I not have thought of the medication in their diaper bag. The main point was that they were fine, and I learned to empty my diaper bag of everything and above all, not to leave it in their room. They were busy little children and did things so quickly as they were more than efficient climbers. I am surprised they did not take up rock climbing as adults as they certainly had a natural ability for it.

They were up to so much during naptime that I think they weren't tired enough to sleep. They unquestionably seemed tired after lunch, but their actions proved otherwise. They were not the type of kids that would cry to nap or get overtired. They would just keep on going until they were put to bed. I must say their good nature made the responsibility of having twins an easy task, but their inquisitive nature presented it to be a demanding one.

I was pregnant again and thrilled that we would have a baby near the end of February. It was a hard summer on the farm, but I felt well. Terry and Tammy were put into a small picket fence play area. It had a pear tree for shade and many toys. I cleaned and picked strawberries, picked plums, pears and loaded grape bushels onto a tractor trailer.

I remember for our anniversary; we had no extra money to go out for dinner to celebrate. In those days you didn't go out when you could not afford it, so we didn't. We stayed home and I made good use of the evening picking strawberries. They needed to be harvested and I took great pleasure in doing just that.

We would celebrate our anniversary in a quiet way when our little family was safely put to bed.

I harvested the fruit and packed it during the day, and Harry would rush home after working all day, and take the fruit to the co-op before it closed. I still didn't have my driver's license, and it wouldn't have helped as I would have had to use a truck and take the girls, which would have been too difficult.

What a busy summer. Our garden was at least an acre, and the soil was so enjoyable to work in as we grew our vegetables. We ate nothing but fresh fruits and vegetables and what we couldn't use we canned and put in the freezer. Harry would set up the tomato juicer outside and turn the tomatoes into juice for me, with the girls help of course. I can still see them on a warm fall evening, Harry sitting on a stool with the machine set up in front of him, and the girls throwing tomatoes into the funnel while Harry turned the handle to separate the pulp from the juice. Terry and Tammy had exceptional times aiding us in all that we did and became our dependable helpers. The juice would be cooked to make tomato juice, and some of it would be reduced even more to make pasta sauce. I was becoming my mother in that my fruit cellar was lined row by row with peaches, pears, sauces, and every different juice we could make. We made bushels of grape juice and grape jelly.

My mom and mother-in-law came down to help me on the farm a lot that summer. Thank goodness for their help or I never would have made it as that fall I was five months pregnant, and it was still a secret. I loaded the full bushels of grapes by myself, onto the trailer and drove the tractor as these special ladies harvested the grapes. It was such heavy work, but somehow, I didn't think that I would injure the baby or myself. We were so grateful to our moms who were cutting the fruit bundles, and it helped so much as I could not do it all myself. Thinking about it now, I wouldn't know how to start a tractor, never mind drive one. How did I do it all?

During these days harvesting our fruit, the girls spent time near the farmhouse in a little white picket fence. It contained a sandbox, toys, and a very important pear tree. Terry and Tammy were often commanded to stay in the shade of the pear tree for shelter from the sun. I couldn't imagine leaving my children so far out of my sight now as the farm went a distance and I worked near the back of it at times.

I was the leader for Missionettes, a girl's group at our church. I accompanied the girls on a twenty-five-mile walkathon. It started at our church on Carlton and Currie Street and ended on our farm in Niagara-on-the-Lake. I made it as far as East West Line and River Road when my lower back seized up, and I couldn't walk any more. The same thing used to happen when I was pregnant with our girls. Sometimes I couldn't even get out of a car or out of a bathtub. I think we decided to tell everyone that I was expecting, for fear of being stuck somewhere and not being able to move. This way there wouldn't be too many explanations needed.

There was a big barn on our farm with a huge loft. When we moved in, Harry cut a small opening in the front and created a door for our pet. Our dog Sandy was a beautiful large well-natured dog. She looked much like a Golden Retriever and was the color of sand. The girls enjoyed her companionship. Sandy had five fluffy little puppies in the spring, and they were their entertainment for a few months. Terry and Tammy would take them and put them into their doll carriages and give them rides up and down the bumpy gravel driveway. As they were careful not to let the puppies jump out, Sandy just walked along side of them, while keeping a mindful watch over her young.

I was running in the direction of one of the girls, trying to stop her from running towards the busy road. Sandy ran up to her, placing herself between the road and her body. The dog pushed her back until she sat on her behind. I was so surprised that the dog would do this, and realized what a great dog she was, especially for protecting the children.

Puttering in the front yard, I let the girls play outside, but not in their fence. When I came to the back yard I panicked, I called, but no one answered. I knew they had not gone to the road as that is where I was working. After checking the house, I ran towards the back of our farm where there was a shallow creek with a wooden bridge over it. No one was there so I ran across the field to the neighbors, where Jackie and Francis lived. The girls played with them at times, and I thought maybe they cut across the yard to their house without me seeing them. I was frantic as they were not there. Full of panic, I ran back home and looked through the house one more time and then the barn. Calling for them the whole time, I ran up the stairs to the loft of the very large barn, but the heavy gigantic trap door was down. I knew they couldn't be up there but had no recourse but to look there as I had exhausted everywhere else. It was heavy but I lifted it about six inches, enough to let my eyes search and scan the loft. There they were, standing frozen in their tracks, in the middle of the loft, and staring at me. I was so relieved and so angry and so happy and so upset. How did they get that door down without hurting themselves? It was a very huge trap door, at least four feet by six feet and very heavy. I was so thankful to find them, as they stood there so quietly while I was lifting the door to get up to the large loft. I surmised that they must have gotten in through the dog door from outside, climbed the stairs, and then looked around the loft. I never found out how they achieved maneuvering the door back into its place and figured it must have fallen by itself. I was grateful that God protected them as so much could have gone wrong: that door could have pinned them down or fallen on them.

Sewing for the girls kept me busy that winter and I appreciated the sewing machine that Harry purchased for me with those handy zigzag stitches. My small sewing room above the stairs was changed to a little nursery and painted a light blue in hopes of and getting ready for a little boy. We prepared ourselves for another girl of course but knowing no matter where we went, the girls got so much attention being twins, and we thought it would be difficult for the next one, especially if it was a girl. Cookie and Ernie had a boy, Scott, on May 17th so a boy would have been perfect.

It was such a long pregnancy as it took not only nine months, but the baby was two weeks overdue. I felt so much bigger than when pregnant with the girls and I had no reason to think I would not lose the weight just as quickly as before. I was certain this was only one baby as I could feel movement and kicking in a very different way. I also carried totally different this time, not so much at the front, but I carried more rounded.

We went to church on Sunday morning, and I made it to the end of the service. I had such an uncomfortable feeling and very slight contractions. We realized it was time to go the hospital, so we dropped the girls off at my mom's, and asked her to babysit, saying we were looking at houses. We didn't want to see more baby clothes on the line again. Mom had told me how she was sick to her stomach when she had the boys, and this did not happen with her girls. That was interesting, but right now we had to hurry to get to the hospital, cutting all conversation short.

We were intending on moving from the farm as soon as we could and were seriously looking at houses. I think we had enough of farming, and it would have been too much work with the three kids. It was hard enough keeping track of my girls, never mind another one as I had to leave them in their little fenced area or napping while I worked the farm. This practice is not acceptable nowadays, but they were different times and with that came different rules.

We didn't have time to stop for something to eat on the way to the hospital, so Harry stopped to buy me a chocolate bar as my labor pains were getting closer and I seemed to be in business.

The labor was different as I was sick to my stomach. I threw up the chocolate that Harry had bought for quick energy for the task ahead, and it didn't end well.

As a matter of fact, the labor took all afternoon until suppertime. My labor stopped just before the baby crowned and I was forced to push, not with instinct, but sheer determination. It was brutal and took every ounce of energy that I could muster.

Finally! Our baby boy was born! Although it was a tough time, it wasn't enough to have stopped me from trying for another. It was a boy, and we were blessed! He was over seven pounds two ounces, and I could hold him all I wanted. I can still remember his blonde peach fuzz and strong appearance. I wasn't used to having such a large baby, although he really wasn't that large.

We couldn't afford much, and I was so grateful as Hildegard Wolff (my Sunday school teacher as a child) came to visit at the hospital and gave me some of her gently used boy's baby clothes. It was so kind of her to make that trip in to see me and bring me the appreciated gift.

I cherished being in the hospital with Shawn as I could hold him every feeding and have my heart-to-heart talks with him. Hearts always understand each other even though words are not used. I learned this when I had my precious girls, and I know because I didn't have the time to hold them, it was even more treasured, and valued. Shawn fed well and finished his bottle in no time. Then I could snuggle with him until he burped, and they came to snatch him out of my arms and took him to the nursery.

When we brought Shawn home, he wore a little blue outfit with a bib attached. He wore the little blue sweater, a gift from Hildegard. We still used one of those flimsy car seats but were so happy to take our little man home with us, not having to wait for months. Shawn would meet his big sisters Terry and Tammy, and we could not wait to see their reactions.

We got home and the girls arrived home shortly after, as they were at my mom and dads for the duration of my hospital stay. Terry and Tammy were so excited about their little brother coming home and as I laid him on my bed, we couldn't even get them to leave him long enough to get their coats off. They were just over two and a half years, and it was a lot to take in. Shawn not only had one mom, but two little mothers to cater to his every need. I could see he would be well taken care of by his big sisters.

Continuing to demand feed Shawn, he loved to eat, so he gained too much weight. The doctor suggested I put him on water for the night hours and that worked very well, and he even started sleeping through the night!

I quickly sewed a couple of little outfits for him. We didn't have hospital pictures done so we took Shawn for his 6-week photos. He wore one of the outfits I made for him of course. The baby blue color went so well with his blue eyes.

Shawn fit into our lives quite naturally and was kept busy by having his personal entertainment directors. No matter where he was, in the house or outside, he was accompanied by his dedicated care team.

One day I was getting supper ready at the kitchen sink and looked out of the large window. Shawn was in the buggy right outside the window so I could keep an eye on him. It was chilly but he was warmly bundled in a little snow suit, and the girls had their winter hat and coats on. I would say it was sometime in May on a nippy day.

Suddenly, I noticed the empty buggy! I immediately ran outside to see what happened to Shawn. Looking around in a panic, I saw a bundle lying inside the little white fence. It was between the house and barn. I ran over not knowing what to expect! He was lying under a pear tree as happy as could be.

How did those little recreation directors get him out of his buggy? Did they drop him when they carried him over to the fence? How did they get him over the fence? It was taller than they were! I couldn't believe my eyes! He couldn't have been hurt as he was so happy, and I would have heard him cry. I questioned the girls and they just said he should stay in the shade under the pear tree and play with them. I had to find the humor in it and just warned them never to do that again. There were so many opportunities to be thankful as the children grew up and it kept your mind on the goodness of God.

Of course, I checked him over and there was no mark or bruise on him. I was so grateful for his protective snowsuit that covered him from head to toe with only a small part of his little face exposed. The children's guardian angels were kept busy, and I was kept on my toes, even though I wasn't a ballerina and didn't have the proper equipment.

On another occasion, I was making dinner. Terry and Tammy were playing in the kitchen just behind me. Shawn was in his little plastic chair on the floor being entertained as usual by his sibling duo. When I turned around to look at them the girls were feeding him dog food, out of the dog dish! To my surprise, he was enjoying his cuisine immensely. I yelled and said, "No!!!" They looked terrified and froze in their usual stance, as they looked at me. I gained my composure and explained this is not good for humans to eat and they shouldn't feed their brother, unless I said it was good for him. Nodding they agreed as I cleaned up their brother and made sure there was nothing more in his mouth. Shawn had nothing left to take out as he ate that dog food as soon as it entered his mouth, he loved to eat. Even so he was too young for solid food although he proved he could manage it just fine.

I recall that Mother's Day as being a solemn one. We were not raised to bless our moms or dads on their special days. I realized that I wanted more from special days not just Mother's Day but Father's Day and so on. Since my ideals were to be passed down to my family, I felt a compulsion and desired to start traditions.

Harry was not cooperating at all, and he was tired, wanting to nap and rightfully so. He worked many hours to support his family and I understood that.

I had sewn the girls' little polka-dot dresses. The dresses were white with navy polka-dots, trimmed with a navy zig-zag border around the neck, puffy sleeves and full skirted bottom. The girls just looked like spring, so fresh like the blossoms on our fruit trees that were so perfect this Mother's Day Sunday. I just wanted some help in getting a picture of the kids sitting in the tree with white blossoms all around them. Terry and Tammy looked so sweet and pretty in their new dresses. I remember taking pictures of the girls by myself being afraid that they would fall from the branches. I was so angry at Harry for not extending himself for us for just a few minutes.

I was keen to start new traditions that were meaningful and honoring. We were a team and we needed to be together in our expectations. I expected to be honored by doing something together as a family, so we could make memories together for the future. It fulfilled me as a new mother to spend time with my family.

This day made memories, but not good ones. We talked about it later, but the day was gone. It was a lesson to be learned for our future. I don't remember one special day that Harry has forgotten, or not made special since. Even though it is not his job, he has more than fulfilled my dreams and hopes of all those special days in our lives. I hope it wasn't too much pressure for him. From my point of view, he over succeeded for the rest of our lives. We truly have the best memories of so many family occasions as we celebrated with joy and appreciation of those events.

Having children didn't only wake me intimately, but also emotionally. By this I mean I knew I was living in the moment and could remember what I was doing as well as how I was feeling. This was a revelation in my life. Before I would tune out often, not willingly but as a way of protection, but now I could remember our intimate times, as well as being fully present as a mom, while raising my children.

I started to speak my thoughts and wishes after much prodding from Harry to do so. I still, to this day, remember the hours he spent coaxing me to speak instead of cry. I had such a difficult time being able to express my feelings, but I was getting so much better at it, as expression was a challenge. Our time on the farm was a segment of our lives that Harry and I found very fulfilling, spiritually, physically and mentally.

We entertained our friends and started to know who we were as a couple. I learned to be more confident with cooking; crying at the supper table was a thing of the distant past. We worked hard, and didn't have extra money, but saved what we had. We dreamed big, loved lots, and appreciated our family. We grew in the Lord and worked hard in the church and that included loving our pastor.

Our pastors were Rev. and Mrs. Wentland. What a change they made in our lives. They gave us space to grow and became real people to count on as well as good friends, as we felt loved by them and their family. The Wentlands wanted nothing more than to grow the church and mature its people in the Lord. They had two children, Joyce was in my Missionette group, and so I got to know her and her talents. I am sure she is still using her talents in many areas.

When Shawn was dedicated, he wore the little suit I made for him, and he looked like a little gentleman, with a little pocket and handkerchief in it. He was the absolute cutest little guy with his white, iridescent hair. My little man was so handsome like his dad.

That spring we put our farm up for sale and bought four acres on Garner Road, Niagara Falls, between Mountain and Thorold Stone Road as Harry thought it was a wonderful spot to build our home. I thought it to be too flat and boring. It ended up being the best place to raise our family and his instincts were right on.

The farm didn't take long to sell, as it was in pristine condition and the house was clean and nicely decorated.

We started building our home after the plans were drawn up. Peter Wall was the builder we chose; Peter was the same man I babysat for as a teen when they rented from Joe Schulz.

Our home would be a raised bi-level, although I preferred a side split. My tastes were starting to develop enough to know what I liked, but not strong enough to make them a reality. Harry and I made all decisions for our new home together and discovered we enjoyed the process immensely. It was an opportunity to pick carpets, tiles, woodwork, cupboards, and you name it. Of course, we budgeted as much as possible, and I think everything cost us about twenty-five thousand with the property. By the fall we were ready to move in. It was a busy time with a young family.

45. Moving to Garner Road

The move was overwhelming but very exciting as the build went as planned, and we had finished building our first of many homes. We could move our belongings at our leisure, but you know that did not happen. Harry wanted to get it all in, all at one time. We found the house provided so much room to spread out in. Tammy and Terry shared a room at the end of the hall, but Shawn had his own room as it was the smaller one. We all revered and appreciated our new home and larger surroundings.

Talk about surroundings; the mud around the house stayed until the following spring and it… was…so… muddy! The girls got stuck in it so many times and Terry even lost her boot. On another occasion we heard our son screaming for help in the front yard. He was over his knees in the mud with his boots suctioned deep into it and couldn't move. Harry became super dad, and retrieved him out of the mud, boots and all.

These were busy years working on the house and yard. We got to know our neighbors and found two boys exactly Shawn's age and a girl, "the twins age." I say the twins because from there on they were called the twins even if there was only one being spoken to. Of course, the neighbors as well as relatives couldn't distinguish one from the other except for Tammy's birthmark. It was a mark that she developed in the isolette when she was only a month old. The specialist told me it would be gone by the time she went to kindergarten, and they were right as it was very minimal by that time. David, Billy, Troy and Heather were their best friends.

Terry and Tammy's room had a pink shag carpet and their spindled bunk beds painted white were a nice contrast. We got the bunk beds from Lenora. Their multi-shades of pink floral print curtains and bedspread added that pop of color.

Shawn had a short blue shag carpet and a smaller room, as he was the only one in his room. For this exact reason he fell asleep nightly, with his head sticking out into the hall as he wanted to be with the rest of the family. He said, Harry and I shared a room, Terry and Tammy shared a room and he had no one to share with, and this makes me sad to think of.

He would often sneak to our room and quietly whisper to me, "Mom, move over." As Harry watched one night, he said I just turned and moved over without really waking. I woke up wondering why the bed was so squishy and put a stop to his joining us. Then he started lying on the floor beside our bed. He needed a brother or sister, but things don't always turn out like we want, but they do turn out like they should be, out of our control, but in God's. I believe if we live our lives honoring God it will be as it should be.

Our little man liked the boy toys from the time he was young. Even before he was a year, he took a hair clip and drove it like a car, accompanied by a *bruuuuuum*....... sound. We thought it was time to get him a car instead of the dolls that took priority all over our house.

Shawn had a beautiful black eye for his second birthday, and it was the most unusual but cutest thing to have for a memory of this special day. He was inclined to get hurt more than the usual child, as his very existence portrayed action.

When he was about nine months old, he was sitting in his highchair. Secondhand or new, highchairs in those days did not have all the safety straps that they have nowadays. They were roomy and I remember I used to measure myself by being able to sit in it.

I was right beside him and I turned to reach for his lunch from the counter behind me. In one second, he flung himself out of his chair and landed on the back of his head on a heating vent. I bent to pick up his lifeless body. He had turned white; his eyes were rolled back, and it seemed like he was not breathing. I thought he was dying, and with him in my arms, I frantically called the doctor while I was pleading for God to intervene. There was no 911 in those days and I was overcome with fear as I waited for the secretary to answer. Shawn's color came back while lying in my arms, and his eyes started to roll into place and focus. The secretary said I should take him to the hospital for an examination and to see if he had a concussion. I did not drive yet and called John Schild, my brother in-law to give us a ride to the hospital. Shawn ended up being fine after a checkup and we were able to go home after the long wait. I was so terrified when that happened and thought I had lost him. I cannot tell you how it feels to hold your child in your arms, being so helpless, and think that he is dying, while you cannot save him.

Harry finished building the family room and I set up my hair dressing business in the laundry room downstairs. My customers came from Niagara-on-the-Lake, and more were added from the neighborhood as well as our church. I became very busy, but didn't work Friday evenings, or Saturdays unless a client was getting married. Our children had a playroom downstairs, so their toys were never strewn throughout the house. My customers brought their children, and they hung out in the playroom too. This was not a plus as the room became a mess from one end to the other.

It is around this time in my life that Harry taught me how to drive. The three children were taken with us on our driving lessons. I thought I was doing well and went for my license. Harry was a methodical and impressive teacher making sure I knew every step to being a careful and safe driver. I developed my lead foot years later perfecting it on my own, as it was not part of my training. I left with my driving-test instructor and did very well even in parking our car. Then he asked me if that was all I had to do. I answered yes when he asked me to put the hand brakes on. I was shocked and did not know how to do that and where they were. He showed me how to use them and I thought I failed for sure. When we got back, I found out I had passed and was overwhelmed with gratitude. I was calm even though I had missed the emergency brakes and it helped to know I could function under pressure.

Ann and George babysat the kids for us one Saturday. Shawn was around two and a half, and Terry and Tammy five. They were playing outside in her yard and before she knew it, they were gone. These children of mine were very quick and knew how to do the disappearing act as they had practiced their moves well. She called their names and looked everywhere. They lived on Keswick Street near a deep gully. The kids were nowhere to be found and she wondered how she would tell us she not only lost one child but three children.

Finally, after a long while of calling and running around searching, she saw one, two, and then three, blonde heads in the tall grass. They were coming up from the deep ravine very close to their house. Our children were so used to wandering as we lived in the country, and they enjoyed the freedom of their large acreage. Shawn was so little; I wonder how he made that hill. Ann reported that she was so angry and so relieved at the same time, and she will never forget her fear.

Another time Ann babysat, and Shawn was a little younger but almost two years old. She put him to bed, and he became very upset. He said with a commanding voice, "Socky off, socky off." Ann did not know what was happening and trusted that we were not using vulgar language with our children. Shawn became very frustrated, lifted his foot in the air and pointed to his sock while repeating, "Socky off." She was so relieved to know what he meant and took his socks off. My kids, as myself, did not like to have socks on, never mind sleep with them, as that would not do at all. We had a good laugh about that when she told us about her ordeal and misunderstanding with Shawn. We appreciated them babysitting for us and knew the kids were always well taken care of and loved by them.

Just after we moved in, Harry had gone out on a Saturday, and I was doing some wash when the tap blew off and water was spraying everywhere causing a flood in the basement. I didn't know where the water shut off was and ran to the neighbors soaking wet. Bruce came over and found the shut off after a few minutes of searching. What a relief that was! During this time of upheaval, Shawn was having his nap in his crib upstairs, but where was Tammy and Terry? I called and no one answered. I searched the house and found no one and ran outside to find them at the end of our driveway. They assumed something terrible was happening and they had better get out of the house. What a day! You should always know where your water shut off is as well as your children! Do you know where your water shut off is right now, and do you know where your children are?

Harry finished the bathroom downstairs; it contained a tile shower, toilet and vanity. This was a terrific country home to raise our family in, and I was able to be home with the kids, even though I was working a good deal of the time. The children learned to be somewhat independent. They matured quickly as far as getting their own drinks, snacks and making decisions for themselves in and around the house. If they were not good decisions, I would hear about them from one or another.

That first Christmas was celebrated in our new recreation room. In the far corner was a big potbelly tumbled brick fireplace, very modern at the time as well as being quite the deluxe model. We spent many memorable hours as a family, indulging ourselves in this newly developed space. We celebrated, ate snacks, watched TV, played games and just hung out in this marvelous room.

The next spring, we put in a ten-foot by ten-foot section of sod, where our patio would be put in sometime soon. We added the old picket fence from the farm around it and the kids had a play area. It wasn't soon enough as Shawn, Tammy and Terry were running in the mud and often covered from head to toe. Only Shawn's eyes could be seen peering from under his little mud-covered body. The three looked so hilarious I just had to take a picture before I cleaned them up. It remains to be a happy memory as it was one that fed my joy of homelife with family.

46. Not Too Young for Salvation

I am the light of the world. Whoever follows me will never walk in darkness but will have the light of life.

John 8:12

One evening, since Harry was working late, we had a quiet macaroni dinner. Sitting around our kitchen table with our youngest in his highchair on my left and the girls beside him, I received an impression from God. I felt I should ask Terry and Tammy if they wanted to ask Jesus into their hearts. My first thought was that they were too young. They were only three but had a keen sense of God. After listening to my explanation, they both said yes, and we prayed. It was a prayer that stayed with them for the rest of their lives, and they say they can remember it too. Of course, my prayer was that my children should have the advantage of knowing more about God than I did. I had always prayed that God reveal himself to my children and He did. This was an answer to my prayers for them and the girls remember that their commitment at that time of only three years old, changed their lives. My beautiful daughters, inside and out, have had a keen sense of who God was to them all their lives, and lived according to what God meant to them. I appreciated how God led and molded them at an early age to honor Him.

47. Snippets of Life on Garner Road

Harry had chickens and enjoyed tending to them every day. We nurtured baby chicks in a box in the laundry room and let the children each name and keep one for a pet. I do not remember any of them except for one called Larry. He was Shawn's pet, and he carried this chicken around continuously, never putting it down, until it escaped his clutches. Shawn loved his older cousin Larry as he became one of his favorite people growing up, so he called his pet Larry in honor of him. Larry the chicken, became like a watchdog and he pecked at the kids if they came on the yard, and it even climbed up the slide to clear it of the children. I think it disliked children as it lost its freedom every time they were around. The children in the neighborhood had the highest respect for Larry and feared his aggressive nature.

Every day the farm fresh eggs provided a healthy, natural lifestyle but the soil was clay, and the garden was terrible. We decided to buy our vegetables and fruits from the farms for canning and freezing instead of toiling needlessly. We purchased bushels of vegetables and put sand on them in the garage, as that would keep them fresh until spring.

Willy, my youngest brother, babysat for us often and we exceedingly appreciated the hours he spent with our children. The kids loved him too, as he made them feel special, and played with them giving them undivided attention, becoming their favorite babysitter. He was truly a special part of their young lives.

The first day Terry and Tammy went to school was unwittingly sad for me, as I loved having them home, and was energized by sharing my space with them. Shawn and his friends were very lonely, so the moms decided to send them to nursery school. I got to know so many new people who became my clients through the nursery school. Shawn disliked the structured life of nursery school, and I decided that the next year he would not go. The other moms did the same, and the boys played for another year in our interesting neighborhood.

Our children had a great childhood. Harry made them a skating rink with a large streetlight, and we put it up ourselves. He had the pond dug out about two feet deep and then dug a hole for the light post. The city workers were taking a hydro pole down and dropped it off at our place. We hoisted it with ropes and pulled until it was upright. Not without fear on my part of course.

The neighborhood kids would skate on it even when we were not home, and other evenings they knocked on our door to ask if we could turn the light on for them. Later, we had youth parties and many other activities there.

The kids often went out on the snowmobile, getting stuck more times than not—especially Shawn, who was a little more daring and ready to exceed his parameters. He would get the snowmobile stuck somewhere out there and couldn't manage to free it by himself. He would run across the fields to the road where he would flag down his dad on the way home. The two would then go off to who knows where and retrieve it; sometimes an old basement foundation, sometimes a huge snow bank. They seemed to enjoy the camaraderie and the stories that resulted from their excursions together.

Terry, Tammy and I would often do crafts and spent many hours creating. We made furniture for their miniature dollhouse and were careful to make everything to scale. We made Christmas ornaments and even got the cooperation of Shawn to join us making some of them. To make it feasible for him I promised that we would make a boy ornament and I helped him create an ornament made with shells in the form of a cowboy. It worked out very well and we were both happy with it, and Shawn still has it on his tree to this day. He bucked many other crafts we tried to get him to participate in. The girls were very artistic and enjoyed working on so many more crafts throughout the years. I also started a tradition of giving one gift on the Sunday before Christmas—we called it "ornament Sunday." The kids got an ornament on ornament Sunday for years, and took them with them when they got married. This is a tradition that is now passed down, not only to my children, but my grandchildren too. I started Lily, my first great-grandchild, on her ornament for her first Christmas. It is on my Christmas tree, every year, and I am hoping to point it out every year until she wants to take it home, which of course she will, as it is hers. Haidyn, our next great-granddaughter, will also have one on our tree this year too. It will be hers to take when she wants it. I am happy to report that we are also expecting our first great-grandson in August, and there will be an ornament on our tree for him this year (2022).

The year 1977 was a time for boundless snowmobiling resulting from the "Blizzard of 77." The school called to say the kids would be coming home early by bus. I waited and no one came home, so I called the school back. Bert Warkentin, the principal, said they should be home by now. As I looked out of my front window, I became frantic. You couldn't see anything, not even the road. The children had to walk a distance from the turnaround, so I thought I would go and see what happened. I couldn't see anything and literally felt the snowbank all the way down the road to what I thought was the turnaround. No tracks, no bus! I felt my way back home and called the school again. No one had cell phones back then and no one knew where the bus was, but I was assured it was safe.

Harry was coming home from Fort Erie early after he listened to the weather reports. The weather was always worse in Fort Erie, and he did not want to get snowed-in at a construction site. He was sitting in his truck on Thorold Stone Road, where all the traffic had come to a halt because of the snowdrifts. The blowing snow cleared for a second and he thought he got glimpses of a school bus ahead and decided to check it out, finding our children sitting on the bus with the others from the neighborhood. Since the bus was stopped right in front of the corner store, he told them to go and stay inside the store while he went to get the snowmobile. He walked home in the blizzard, and it was at least two miles. After telling me what he was doing, Harry dressed warmly to rescue the children, and I was so relieved to hear the children were safe. I called the school and the parents of the children he was bringing home, as I knew they would be relieved too. The snowmobiles sure came in handy, not only for our kids, but the whole neighborhood. They all made it home thanks to Harry! He attached a Ski-boose to the snowmobile and was able to retrieve more kids at one time.

Harry went out many times as people were sitting in their cars covered with snowdrifts, waiting to be rescued. Some only had sweaters and slippers on as they were just going to pick up their kids from school or do very small errands. It taught many people a lesson: to dress according to the weather forecast no matter how small a trip or how the weather looked at that time.

The snowmobiles went over top of cars not seeing them buried in the snow. The snow drifted up to the eaves of buildings and there was nothing nicer than being in your warm house with your family safe beside you. We were fortunate to have food in our freezer, but many people needed groceries, supplies and medications. Harry kept busy with people and neighbors calling for this and that. Our road was not cleared for five days. No one came in and no one went out, except for the snowmobile.

People would drive down from St. Catharines, just to see what the hype was all about. When they got past Sand Plant Hill, they would get stuck while veering off the highway onto Mountain Road where the blizzard bordered. For us it was a good memory helping and assisting others, as well as a "stay-cation" for the family and a tremendous diversion from everyday life in this winter.

For Harry's birthday that year I bought a book, "The White Death" about the blizzard of 1977. In it I had placed a couple of tickets to the Dominican Republic for a surprise get-away. We were going to travel with friends Ann and Harry. This was a big step for me as I made this decision without Harry. I was ready to accept all the responsibility for my daring actions. He loved the surprise, and it was the first of many holidays travelling to foreign countries. Since then, Harry has had many surprises and not all to do with travel, as I was becoming a more confident person.

The teachers split the girls up into different classes, as they assumed they were copying each other's work. Their marks were too close for it to be a continual coincidence. I told them I was certain they worked independently but they could split them up if they wanted to. They still ended with marks only decimals apart. It was notable to prove the teachers wrong and confirm that Terry and Tammy did not cheat. Next year they shared the same room again. I thought it was an awesome test in how close my two girls really were in most things. In grade eight Tammy got an award and Bert the principal, told me it was difficult, as they had to break it down to decimals for her to win. I felt bad for Terry being so close behind, but Tammy was first. They both worked very hard for their marks, and both deserved them. There was never a word of disappointment from Terry or gloating from Tammy. I think they would have been accepting of the fact that they were tied. In any case, we were so proud of both Terry and Tammy as they worked diligently and deserved their marks.

Our son did not like school. Shawn never studied and still got respectable marks. I regularly repeated to him, "You can do anything, and just imagine what you could do if you would study." I knew he could be anything he wanted to be.

Shawn's life consisted of playing hockey and being with his friends. He also entered BMX racing, and soccer. Everything he did was made into a family outing and his sisters were more than willing to cheer him on as he collected his trophies. His mountain bike became like a lucky charm. Others had very expensive bikes but he rode with a natural skill and continuously won. He purchased his bike on our way back from our trip to the east coast.

The kids also bought their own roller skates. They couldn't wait to use them and there happened to be a poured cement pad near our campsite. It became a great testing area.

While roller skating in the camper, the door slammed on Shawn's finger. We opened it not knowing what we would find. His finger was still attached and to our amazement he just bruised and lost his nail. I can still feel the panic thinking about it and seeing his finger tightly wedged in between the door of the camper. We took him to the nearby hospital, and they wrapped it and said it was not broken making us once again, thankful.

On another occasion while camping, Tammy was running around playing with some children. She tripped and fell into the fire pit. There was no fire, but the coals were hot from the night before. Her hand went flat into the middle of the coals. Immediately a huge blister formed on the whole palm of her hand, and she screamed uncontrollably. We had to speak harshly to her to make her listen to us so we could help her. I thought she was going into shock, and it must have been so painful as the whole palm of her hand was burned.

She quieted down and we medicated and gently wrapped her hand. As quickly as possible we made a trip to the hospital where they just changed her dressing and warned us to keep it clean. It certainly didn't take long before Tammy was playing with the other kids and forgot about her hand, and we were pleased how well it healed.

For school the kids made their own lunches as they would never finish the ones I provided. Their lunch lady was a ruthless woman. She would retrieve the bags from the garbage and made kids finish their lunch, no matter what. Tammy stuffed her sandwich into her pencil case one time and another into her thermos. Shawn had bananas rotting in his school bag. Not "backpack," no one carried those at that time. Of course, I did not find out about all this until many years later. As far as I know Terry never participated in these shenanigans, or did she?

We had a motorbike, and everyone tried to ride it except for Terry. She did not feel ready, but Harry insisted she ride it and she ended up going towards the road and dumped the motorized bike. She was upset that he forced her to ride it and I think she needed more time to get used to it, and then Terry would have enjoyed the ride.

We were in the back yard watching the kids ride when Shawn passed us and was heading for the road at top speed like he couldn't stop. We ran to the front to see where he was, he was sitting at the end of the yard with the bike off. Harry asked how he shut it off. He said he remembered his dad telling him to pull off the spark plug wire in an emergency. Shawn was always very closely watching his dad, and apparently learned well. Harry was a good father and teacher always instructing.

Sometime later I felt nauseated and pregnant for a couple of weeks and knew something was not right. After a while I had a pregnancy test that came back negative. I guess that was because there were already complications. I wanted another child and was happy, but Harry was not. Shortly after my test I had a miscarriage.

When I miscarried, I went into a whirlwind of wild emotions promoted by unsettled hormones. Subconsciously I blamed Harry as he did not want another child and therefore blamed him. I was depressed and my hormones were going crazy. I thought I was going out of my mind and know now this reaction was mostly because of hormones but wish I would have known that then. I had a terrible time being near Harry because of the scent of his aftershave. It was again proven how I could hide my feelings, as Harry had no idea what I was going through at this time. Just like many times before, I would work through this by myself and not tell anyone of my sensitivity, until the implications made sense to me. Hormones can change your attitudes and mindset without you realizing what is going on, and I worked diligently to regain my moods.

This is what I have always done in the past and I realized this time, I was not blocking or tuning out my feeling of pain, as I was feeling everything. God helped me and I prayed continually that I would get over my feelings. God was faithful again and healed me from my loss. I wanted a dozen children and Harry did not want many. He was rather anxious when we had two to start with. I do believe that Shawn could have used a buddy while he was feeling alone in the family, but I would have to leave all those questions for God to answer.

Shawn's sisters were so close to one another, as it should be. They had such a tight bond being of one opinion in most things. Their likes and dislikes were the same. Even though this was true, our daughters, Terry and Tammy included Shawn in so many activities and he lived larger because of it. Naturally he was not aware of this and so could not appreciate it fully as he didn't know any different.

The kids spent a lot of time playing outdoors in the neighborhood. They made many forts, and one was in the cutters. We never knew until they were adults why they called the woods, "the cutters." It was because there was an old grass cutter that needed to be pulled by a tractor, laying abandoned in the woods.

Another fort was at their friend Martha's house. The kids came home one Sunday afternoon and asked if we would come and give it our approval. They spent hours upon hours over there so we thought it would be nice to look at it.

We had no idea until we got there! We stood in front of a massive haystack about fifteen feet high and just as wide. Getting down on our hands and knees we followed them, tailing them all the while crawling along zigzagging narrow, low, tunnels that led us to a trap door. It was a secret trap door that was undetectable unless you knew where it was. Going up one level through this door we were amazed with the layout and job the kids did with this fort. When we got through all the rooms and tunnels and were able to straighten our cramped backs, reality hit us. They would never have gotten out if it collapsed or if it caught on fire. We made them promise not to ever have fire anywhere near it. It was soon after that Mr. Miller used the hay, and the fort was gone. I must say although I wanted to give my children room to be independent, I was very relieved when that fort was gone.

The neighborhood kids almost lived at our place and swam in our above-ground pool. I tried to do all my customers in the morning and did gardening, or chores in the afternoon so I could be outside with them. I would have some customers between four and five mostly for haircuts. Supper was prepared early to be ready at five or five-thirty when Harry came home.

Harry and I were in the kitchen, and we could hear the kids swimming through the open back bedroom window. We heard Shawn saying he was going to do a back flip and then heard a huge thud on the wood deck. We both ran and bolted towards the pool. Upon arriving we saw he was alive and moving. He hit the deck with his back but was okay. I have no idea how he grew up in one piece.

We got Shawn a train set for Christmas one year and he loved it. We thought since he loved it, we would get him a huge, N scale set. Well, Harry and I loved it, but Shawn not so much. He enjoyed running the trains and all the scenery we created, but it wasn't that special train set. We spent hours in the basement working on grass, trees, rock formations, towns, and bridges, and I was elated to let my creativity lose and worked diligently at it. The problem was it wasn't simple to use, and it was not Shawn's first train set. I never knew he loved it so much, and we would never have exchanged it for another one if we would have realized this fact.

I learned that you should not upgrade your children's toys or get them something that they do not have a desire for. It is good for their want to grow first and their desires to linger a while, it makes the gift much more valuable in their eyes.

We babysat Aaron, Ann and George's son. He came to our house daily for a summer and loved catching frogs in the pond and swimming with the kids. My kids enjoyed him so much and loved teasing him. I would hear, "Auntie Marg, Auntie Marg," when the kids were throwing him into the pool.

One day at our place he decided he would shave like his dad. His dad gave him a razor that had no blade in it. Before I could get to him, he took the shaver from our bathroom and cut his chin leaving me feeling bad for him. We bandaged him up and he was good to go. We have so many good memories of Aaron and enjoyed him like a little brother.

In those days we visited with many friends and relatives as well as entertaining a lot and enjoyed our home. Shawn was hurt so many times either at our house or when we were visiting hitting his head too often and needing stitches. The hospital questioned us on one of these times insinuating that maybe we were abusing him. I appreciated them asking and realized he had stitches in his head too often. We could verify that it was not even us who hurt him, but he was thrown in the air by a relative and hit his head on the ceiling light in the hall. Last time it was hitting his head on their fireplace while rough housing with his cousins. Next time it was falling on the ice and then it was getting a huge sliver that had to be removed at the hospital and so on. He kept us busy with emergencies, and lots of good activities, but he grew up mostly unscathed and left us grateful for that.

My sister Helen had such a loud Volkswagen, and she would come by after work late at night and I would hear the car coming down the street. She would have problems because she was too trusting having a need to help everyone who wanted help and desired advice. Helen just happened to be a lovely, kind and very compassionate person. Now her family is blessed to have her as their wife, mom, and grandmother.

Her brothers know how kind she is. She took over my job as waitress, cleaning lady and cook, when I left the house at the age of eighteen and my brothers had it made. I don't remember much about Helen until she became a teen but as an adult, she proved herself to become a devoted Christian and she erred on the side of compassion, even when it meant breaking the rules.

48. Nights Praying

To you, Lord, I call: you are my rock, do not turn a deaf ear to me. For if you remain silent, I will be like those who go down to the pit. Hear my cry for mercy as I call to you for help, as I lift my hands towards your most Holy Place.

Psalm 28:1-2

There was still such a hole in my emotions, although I couldn't figure out why, or what could be done about it. Instead of speaking about my feelings, I would go to God in prayer usually at about two in the morning. I started to ask God to show me why I felt this way. I spoke to God since I was a little girl and even now God was still my best friend and comforted me. I would start with telling God the desperation I felt, and I thought that Harry would be better off without me, and he deserved someone far better and more capable. Forever trying, but never measuring up, I never contemplated killing myself, but just felt the world would be better off without me. Especially my family, they deserved the best and I wanted the best for them.

I didn't take criticism well as it made me feel even more worthless. The counsel Harry gave me was helpful, but I couldn't receive it. If I could have figured out why criticism made me feel so degraded, it would have spared me many, many anxious hours back then. There was a deep longing to be good enough for someone. I knew Jesus was a special comfort and friend to me but why did every critical word leave me feeling like a helpless child back in my parents' home once more? Mom and Dad belittled me, but both in different ways. Mom's words were hard and cut to the core. Would that ever change? Dad, well his mark was left in other ways that at that time I had no idea how. Always as honest as I knew how to be before God, I told Him just how devastated I felt. It was a feeling of hopeless despair. After telling God what I was thinking, He would tell me He loved me and always, without fail, impart this wonderful feeling of being loved and fill me with hope. The reality of being loved by God was so overwhelming as He was so faithful from my childhood until the present. He gave me strength and commitment for change. He made me feel worthy and was growing a longing in me to be whole.

I never left my place of prayer or talking to Him before I felt hopeful, and was renewed in my spirit to go on, and certainly not before I received that special hug from God giving me the power I needed. This happened in the living room, on my knees at the couch, in the dark, by myself, except for my best friend and comforter God. It was time I joined Harry, who was sleeping or so I hoped.

I wonder if the kids ever heard me cry. I wouldn't have wanted to upset them. I remember too well what it was like hearing my Mom weep at night. That is not what I wanted for my children. I realized that I wanted to fix all the wrongs that I experienced as a child and be a better parent than I experienced.

Harry didn't realize the depth of my hurt, but he gave me support and showed me strength when I needed it and when I confided in him. He was like a life coach who was on call 24/7.

Encouraging me to express myself in word and deed was an endless job on his part. I appreciate so much that he didn't give up on me. I wanted to be the best mom that I knew how to be, as well as the best wife ever. Even saying all that about my short-comings, these were the best years of my life – raising our family. It took diligent, deliberate work and I sensed and was delighted in myself for becoming stronger. I was able to care in a more mature and emotional way for my family. Harry and I had built a nice life for our children and felt secure in our love for each other and our marriage.

Some of our favorite times were when we played hide and seek in the house. Harry would cover his eyes and count as the kids would hide. They would frantically run into the kitchen and I assisted in hiding them by clearing out the cereal cupboard or pantry. Harry and Shanty, our dog, would hunt for the kids and Harry would say to the dog, "Get them, vicious," as the children squirmed and squealed in the cupboard, until Harry finally opened the doors and put them out of their misery. The broom closet was one of their favorite spots to hide, as it fit two at a time. What fun you can have as a family with no expense!

Shawn also had a little cat that followed him around everywhere. One day he was going into the garage and the cat followed. The automatic door closer was quicker than the kitten and it caught it's tail and cut it three quarters of the way through. We did not know what to do as Harry was working so we took the kitten to our neighbor. Gordy took sheet metal cutters and snipped it in the spot where it was almost severed. We put cream and a bandage on it but that only stayed on for a very short time. It healed up fine and the kitten survived.

One day Shawn, my little sidekick, and I were going to city hall in Niagara Falls to get plumbing permits for the business. After parking our car and feeding the meter, I noticed a little kitten that looked just like ours on the street. It couldn't be but it had a short tail like ours with the same coloring. This was Shawn's kitten, so we picked it up, put it in the car and then took it home with us. It must have been hiding under the hood of the car and was fortunate not to get killed while hiding there. Shawn was so relieved to have rescued his kitten.

The girls loved playing in the neighborhood with their good friend. They developed a tradition of having a Christmas tea, with fancy dishes and sweets, at which time they exchanged little gifts. They made delightful memories and had some meaningful times.

As good as their friend was, I felt she played one against the other by making verbal unfounded comparisons. I did not find it to be fair, but she was only a child and not mature in that way. My children sensed it and were affected by it, although they soon grew out of those feelings. It is not what life throws at you but how you deal with it that counts and Terry and Tammy were successful in how they dealt with most things in their lives.

We enjoyed our new church being an English speaking one and were very involved in many facets of it. We taught Sunday school, Harry sang in the choir, we did bus ministry and enjoyed drama in church as a family.

We would have up to one hundred and fifty kids in our Sunday school class at a time and taught both A and B Sunday schools. On the

Saturday before, we would pass out roadrunners to all the kids on our bus route. We started the route in Niagara Falls because of a contest that the kids participated in at Central Sunday school. Our kids recruited about twenty-some kids for the contest. This grew to fill a bus. Their friends loved coming to church with us and we even took them to McDonalds after a special Sunday morning.

I would take time to call each child in our Sunday school class that Saturday. The names were all placed in binders by Vicki, our super-efficient Sunday school secretary, who processed every child. She kept the names in little black binders with pink cards for girls and blue for the boys. These were exciting days and I believe our children enjoyed them and never lacked because of them. During the week we did not do much after school, except for going to Bible study and the kids went to "youth" when they were older.

49. God Heals

"But blessed is the man who trusts in the Lord, whose confidence is in him."

Jeremiah 17: 7

Terry developed an excruciating stomach ache just before church ended one evening. She couldn't straighten up and her pain was constant, so I decided to drop the family off at home and take her to the hospital to get some help.

Terry was admitted and they started some tests and blood work. The ward-like room was overfilled, containing six occupied beds, as well all the family members accompanying the patients. They drew all the curtains for privacy, except the ones facing the middle aisle, for the medical staff's easy access to the sick. At the far end, beside the window, a mom was holding a baby screaming so hard, that everyone already seemed tense in the room, and with the medical staff not appearing for what seemed an eternity, made it even worse. The insufferable, unbearable screaming didn't stop for a second, and I couldn't figure out why no one came in to help the mother or baby. I am sure the baby became a priority on everyone's minds. I peeked down the aisle to see the mother clutching her infant while pacing in her small space. As she became more anxious, everyone in the room became more nervous and uptight. Terry was just fine now, and she was as soon as we checked in, although, I must say, not relaxing, as the screams were overwhelming. We couldn't leave as not one medical staff came back into the room to check on anyone. God started to prompt me to step out and pray for the baby. I fought God for over an hour until I came to the realization that I wasn't doing anything, but God could. God always did what needed to be done, as I couldn't do anything, but merely pray. I was working up enough courage to step out from behind the curtain when Terry said, "Mom you should go and pray for that baby. I said, "Yes, I know and think so too." That was a great confirmation from God and what more did I need.

I stepped out from behind my curtain into the aisle. The strained faces all looked at me as I passed by them. When they realized I wasn't a nurse or doctor, they wondered where I was going and what I was doing from behind my curtain. I felt many eyes on me but didn't care as I knew what to do.

I followed that crying sound calling out to me to the far end of the room near the window. Everyone was waiting for a small measure of relief from the baby's endless screaming.

As I approached the dark-haired mother holding the baby, she appeared to have such fear in her eyes as she was trying to comfort her child. She looked like she was beside herself. Jerking her body and the baby up and down, holding it tightly to her body, she looked pleadingly at me. Looking directly into her eyes I asked if I could pray for her baby. She seemed like she was not well versed in English, but she nodded yes. I laid hands on the baby's head and prayed. As the room's eyes were on us, I don't remember what I said, and it doesn't matter but it was something to the effect of God healing and stopping the baby from crying and giving the mother peace. The baby became instantly quiet and restful! No more crying and the room had a noticeable transformation into a peaceful, calm, and quiet space. With all eyes in the room watching me, I quickly proceeded to my hiding place behind the curtain with Terry. My heart beat out of my chest as I became more aware of the quiet, as well as everyone still staring in our direction. The nurse came in immediately after and told us that Terry was fine, and we could leave. We knew as soon as Terry was admitted that she would be fine, as we heard the crying, and God was starting to prod me to pray for the baby. I was in a little bit of a daze having fought God for so long and then seeing Him do this healing for this baby in such an instant miraculous way. Terry got up and we walked out quickly. As we walked down the hall I said to Terry, "I hope the baby doesn't cry before we get out of here." Oh, ye of little faith. That was me. God was awesome and I still doubted him. I learned to obey God no matter how it looked. The biggest lesson was that God would do the work, not me, so just obey and trust Him to do the rest. I pray that everyone in that room that day got to know that God answers prayer as they witnessed His answer with their own eyes, and that the mother was also touched by God's healing power, being mindful that God answers prayer.

50. "Bed Bugs" and Head Lice

When we came home from Bible study on Wednesday evenings, we found our children who were old enough to take care of themselves, sleeping. They left little notes and messages telling us what happened that evening. We kept such late hours as we went out for coffee with a group of friends enjoying our social life as well as the Bible studies. My joy were the little notes that told of the most important events that went on while we were out that night, as well what was needed the next day, either for school or after school. I have the cartoons to this day, and they were called, "Bed Bugs," and I loved their characters and actions. What an artistic way of communicating as it was such a joy to find these notes in the kitchen, or on our bed upon returning home.

I was involved in home-and-school and spent many hours at Greendale Public School on our fundraisers. The home-and-school were responsible for legislating that vehicles should stop when seeing the flashing red lights on a bus. The rule was so new, that one time I didn't stop. The bus had stopped and put its lights on and stop sign out and I just kept going, being horrified that I did. I was so shaken, I would never forget again. Thank the Lord no one was getting off the bus yet.

I did hairdressing out of our home and set up a little "shop," of sorts with two dryer chairs and two workstations. Harry put the salon sink in for me and it made my work so much easier.

Many of the teachers from Greendale were my customers. Every time the school had an outbreak of lice, I received a call to let me know, so I could check my kids when they came home. We never had lice except once when Shawn came home from a hockey tournament late one night.

As he stepped in the door, I asked him why he was scratching his head. He said it was very itchy. I checked his head carefully, right then and there, only to find one louse. We had no lice shampoo at home and the drug stores were not open all night like they are now. I sent Harry and Shawn to the hospital, and they marveled that there was only one louse to be found and they gave them some lice shampoo and sent them home with it. I knew that by morning he could have a head of nits and they would spread like a wildfire.

While they were gone, I woke the girls, stripped the beds, vacuumed and made the girls wash their hair too. Terry and Tammy must have thought I had gone mad with such disturbing action. They were good sports about it as I knew that if there were any eggs left, we would have a mess on our hands, and I would have to sterilize the house from top to bottom especially since I did hair at home. Thinking about it now, they had just come home, and the lice were just coming in with Shawn so I do not think their nits would have been in the house yet. Talk about being paranoid. Sorry girls!

A lot of Saturday afternoons I would make a huge pot of soup with dumplings. The children would have their friends over to ride the minibike or just hang out and we would have three more strangers at our table. I think of them often and I wonder how they are doing. We got to know so many children and loved that they felt at home at our place.

Our children were conscientious about others and appeared to have their own ministry at Greendale School. One day, Terry told me she prayed with someone at the locker as they had confided in her about a problem. They were always inviting kids to come to Sunday school as well as pray for their unsaved family members. I appreciated and treasured my children for the kind of hearts they were cultivating. I knew with God they would become strong at a much earlier age than I.

We would invite my parents to all our children's functions at church. Each of the children asked my dad if he would want to accept God's love. Dad was the kind of man who treated every one of them fairly, but we all knew, for some reason he had a real distaste for things of God. He said no, as he always did many times before. When I talked to him about the Lord, he said he was too bad a person and would go to Hell because of it. I couldn't understand it at that time, but his attitude became clearer to me as time went on.

51. Not Too Young for Baptism

When I was a child, I talked like a child, I thought like a child, I reasoned like a child. When I became a man, I put childish ways behind me.

1 Corinthians 13:11

Our children wanted to get baptized after listening to an evening sermon when God gave them a nudge in that direction. Terry and Tammy got baptized but we felt Shawn was too young and looking back, I think we held his spiritual life hostage by telling him to wait. We should be aware that God speaks to our children at an early age, and it helps them to grow and know they are following His commands when we encourage and let them obey. I was grateful that Shawn grew in the Lord and His ways and developed a strong walk with God, despite us.

Of course, none of us would purposely deny our children to follow God. Sometimes we hinder them, just because we think something doesn't fall into our thought and time frame of how life should progress. He got baptized eventually, but it took a few years for him to listen to God about this subject again.

There are things I would do differently today, and I pray that what I did wrong God would change and use to His glory. I do know that when parents fail, our children decide to be better parents themselves in those same ways. This is what I had done. Life has taught me so much and so have my children. Even when our children are Godly children, accept and understand that God has a plan for them, it might not be your plan. If there are any steps towards God that you can help them take, do it as they are on their way to becoming Godly adults. Even though we did things wrong in raising our children, I am truly in awe of God who has grown them to be strong Christian adults.

52. Learning to Obey God's Voice

Since we have these promises, dear friends, let us purify ourselves from everything that contaminates body and spirit, perfecting holiness out of reverence for God.

2 Corinthians 7:1

Our neighbor used to call out to me from her bedroom window and I could hear her through my kitchen window as it was directly across from her bedroom. Even though she was a lovely kind neighbor, it irritated me at the times when I was busy getting dinner for my family. I reluctantly stood in the kitchen window in front of the sink for fear of being noticed and called. When I was in the kitchen it was my busy time either preparing or cleaning up from supper.

I had not heard from her in a couple of weeks and was prompted to call her more than a few times. I argued the fact and I dismissed the thought only for it to return repeatedly. One day, Louise called from the window again and told me she almost died of an aneurysm and had to have emergency surgery. She felt so forgotten as not one neighbor came to see her in the hospital.

Wow, did I feel bad, and I apologized and told her I was sorry that I did not know. God was trying to tell me, but I was not listening. I was so thankful the surgery was successful, and she was on the mend. It was a life lesson from God, and I should have passed, but instead I failed miserably. It taught and demonstrated to me to purposely listen to that quiet, consistent, and inciteful voice that keeps on trying to prompt you to step out for Him. God not only speaks to us but lets us in on things we know nothing about. He was trying to prompt me to intervene on His behalf in Louise's life. I repented and tried to be aware of God's voice. The supernatural power of

God can guide you about things you are ignorant or uninformed about. God knows everything and we must trust Him on that.

Another time, God stopped me in my tracks. We went camping a lot in those days and it was stressful to get the packing done, as I worked all day in my salon and wanted to be ready to go when Harry got home from work. Then the trailer would be hooked up and away we would go. I asked the children to take their little baskets of clothes to the trailer for me, but Shawn loved to play as he was only five. Shawn hadn't done as he was told, and I could see his basket of clothes still sitting in the living room.

I took him by the shoulders and shook him only once. God stopped me cold as I looked down at his little strained face. What was I doing? I never did that before or ever again and was so sorry as I remorsefully hugged him tightly. He had such energy, and it was difficult to harness when you wanted to, and I usually loved that in him. I had a lesson on control that I will never forget, as God is such an expert teacher to prick my conscience quietly or let me hit a brick wall and bring change into my character. I was learning to be more obedient to God. It does not mean I never failed, but I continually tried over again to learn from my Provider and Teacher.

53. Listen to God

What, then, shall we say in response to this? If God is for us, who can be against us?

Romans 8:31

Harry and I were asked to do a Sunday school seminar for our church. We did one segment having to do with Junior Highs. I gathered my materials and props and had one regarding Abraham. I could not find one small important prop.

I was frantic and asked God as I often did, to show me where it was. God answered as clear as could be and communicated to me that it was on top of the china cabinet. I had looked there again and again as I thought that it should be there but knew enough to look once more when prompted. I had to investigate and search every crack, as I knew God did not send me on a wild goose chase. There it was stuck and tucked in between the crown molding and the cabinet. I was so grateful to God for His continuous guidance. Nothing was too small a task for Him to direct my path. It was from then on that whenever I needed to find something in the house, or shop for an item, I would automatically ask God to direct me.

When He spoke, it was as real as if I heard him out loud but didn't. I do not know how it is possible, but that is what I heard. It was not audible, but as real as hearing a voice. My confidence in God had become the bottom line for everything. The seminar turned out well and we had lots of material to share.

When they became teens, Terry and Tammy took our car to youth and took Shawn with them. Shawn was able to stay out longer and go to a lot of places because he always had a willing ride with his sisters. Our children loved going to youth together and would never miss, unless necessary.

We would have kids over all the time whenever the kids wanted. In those days I had a guest book and love reading it to this day. I don't know how I had the energy for the traffic that passed through our home. At times our large foyer floor was covered with shoes and the house became wall to wall teens. When they left there was never a thing out of place, and they made sure they left a clean house behind. Only twice did we miss a Teddy Bear and baby Jesus. The bear belonged to Shawn and his name was Zeddy. He became somewhat of a mascot to some of the teens and one day was kidnapped. We had our suspicions as to who had him but had to wait quite some time for Zeddy to return to his rightful owner. The kids would toilet paper those homes and properties of only people they admired. This became natural as a thing to do for many years and gave excitement to the owners of the property. How can you blame someone for doing that when you know they did it to show you they love you!

Every Christmas I put a nativity set in our spacious foyer and it was always moved around by the teens. Sometime before Christmas, our baby Jesus disappeared out of the manger. We searched everywhere to no avail. Jesus reappeared before his birth on Christmas Eve, and we were delighted for his reappearance. I still have the same nativity and it was used on Christmas Eve for fifty years, to tell the Christmas story, in our home.

John Counsel influenced and motivated the youth of Central, both physically and spiritually. It took a lot of energy and time on John's and his wife Heather's part to accomplish all that they did. We helped along with other adults and devoted many hours with the youth as it was a rewarding time in our lives. Our teens became strong under their ministry and flourished as they stepped out and grew in God.

Shawn was looking for a good friend in youth and we prayed God would send one for him and shortly after that prayer, two brothers, Irv and Marco appeared in youth. Irv was the same age as Shawn and Marco was older. Their dad was raising them as a single parent, and they didn't have deep roots and had restless spirits. We believed God answered and sent Shawn a friend. Their friendship led into Irv living with us for a few years. We enjoyed his interactive presence in our home and Shawn and Irv enjoyed their music and had many jam sessions together, and both played in the worship team at youth. He fit in very well with our teens and it made for an interesting household.

God has answered so many prayers and I was so glad that our son could also experience this, firsthand.

I think of a morning when I got up and saw two older teen boys sleeping on our couch. I woke Harry and asked him to check them out and find out who they were before he went to work. Of course, he was stumped too and did exactly that. They were from Ottawa and were told if you are ever in St. Catharines go to the Lecwez house and look under the front door mat for the key and you will be welcome there. They were welcome but it was kind of unnerving to have two strangers sleeping in your house all night. We were glad to help them out and they were on their way the next day.

Often there would be tents pitched on our property when we rose in the morning, and they disappeared soon after sunrise.

We had some great trips with the family. Florida, and of course Disney World were the earliest ones. We went with the Schultz family, and we all wore red Central Jackets, looking like a gang.

In those days we were on a budget, and I canned some meats, sauces, and so on to take on the trip. They made quick meals after we spent all day in the Magic Kingdom, and we camped in our little camper. Shawn loved hanging out with Scott and Todd looking forward to many hours together.

We called our camper Big Blue, and Cookie and Ernie's was called Shamrock. They were excellent holidays from beginning to end. We made wonderful memories for both of our families.

Our kids travelled well, and we were off to the East Coast of Canada. It is wonderful looking at new places through children's eyes. It magnifies the experience a hundred-fold, enlarging it and making a full color dimensional picture. Time on the east coast gave us opportunity to see the fishing boats come in and enjoyed fresh lobster and clams in our trailer, as well as sight-seeing, viewing some of the most beautiful, peaceful scenery. Our family enjoyed their lives except for the odd unkind interruption to our tranquil home.

Mom and Dad would be unsettling as they dropped by many times during the years our children were growing up. My mom would unload her angry feelings on me, and sometimes she would yell and scream and bring me to tears and then she would abruptly leave. I really think it was a way she thought she could control me and of course, I was left upset every time, and she was controlling me.

On one of these occasions Harry came home after 9 from choir practice. He found his family in an uproar, crying. The children were upset because Mom came in the house and started yelling at me very loudly with angry words. It frightened the children and I started to cry as she was out of control, and I did not know what to do to calm her. Dad had left the house to sit in his car, as he didn't want to be a part of this scene.

When Harry came home, he piled us all into the car. I had no idea what was going to happen when we got to my parent's house. Harry sat Mom down and spoke very quietly but sternly. He was there because of what happened to his family when Mom visited, and it was going to stop. After a lengthy talk as Mom and Dad didn't say much, Harry prayed, and we left to go home. Mom never did that again and had a new respect for Harry and his household. Harry used wisdom in that he made it a time of healing instead of putting fuel on the fire or building unbreakable walls. He had set his boundaries and they were respected from then on. As much as Mom loved our children, her actions made it difficult for them to cherish her feelings as she portrayed moods of anger and judgments towards them throughout her life.

Our trip out west was one of my very favorites. The girls were finished public school. We loved crossing the country, experiencing the western towns and the rodeos. The badlands captivated our attention.

The west coast was special as the Hildebrandt family lived there. This was Harry's sister Lena, her husband, and children. Ricky, our nephew was the girls' age, and it had been a while since we saw him. We decided to take Ricky back to Ontario with us and it was a little more crowded in both the vehicle and the camper. The kids didn't seem to mind, and never complained as we had a great time travelling together and making memories.

Ricky also visited and spent time with his cousin Larry, also his age. Ricky wasn't a teen of many words, and we hoped he had a good time in

Ontario with all his cousins.

Terry will never forget that she lost her wallet and spending money at Walldrug in the bathroom travelling from British Columbia. She went back within minutes, but they were gone, and it left a distasteful memory for her.

Since I am reporting on vacations, let me tell you about one from hell. We thought it would be nice to take a family vacation before the girls went to university. We booked a trip to Puerto Vallarta, and we were going to meet the Mouck family there. Our teens were excited as this was the first time we were away at Christmas.

At the airport, we were called over to a desk and they told us they had over booked the flight by five people. They showed us a two-page brochure of an all-inclusive resort that was offered to us as an upgrade. It cost more than we could ever have afforded, and our family would fly first class. We wondered what we should do as the kids did not want to trade but meet their friends. The offered trip included everything we could think of, so after much debate we accepted it. The flight was great, and they treated us royally.

Arriving at the airport in Mexico we wondered why there were so many police on guard with their weapons drawn. People waiting to board the plane were waving for us to go back and we did not understand what they were trying to say.

On arrival at the resort, we were invited to have as much tequila as we wanted, but we just wanted to get settled and get on with the surprise of a holiday. We were told we could not use the elevator although we were on the tenth floor, as it was not working, but they said it would be fixed soon. There were a lot of stairs to climb but we could not wait, and the workers at the resort brought our luggage up to us.

By this time, we entered our room with apprehension. As we walked in, we could see that the outside wall was not finished, and the sky lay in full view before us. There were men still putting blocks in to finish our wall. We could not believe it.

Relieved that they were done by the end of the day we were secure in knowing we were safe from the outdoor elements.

Our lamp shades were water stained and we had no toilet seat on our toilet. The bedding looked old and stained but clean. We decided to go for a walk around this resort, as we hoped that it had to be better than our room. The resort was disgusting and horrible with the pools full of garbage and not useable. The resort was in total disarray!

After many inquiries we found there was no way out of there, so we would have to try and make the best of it. There were no planes or ships that were going to Puerto Vallarta. We orientated ourselves and went to bed. Our mattress kept waking us up all night as it stunk so badly that in the morning, we threw it off the balcony down to the rest of the garbage below. They brought us another one, which didn't keep us awake. We would have to see how well we fared under adverse conditions.

The food as well as the smell coming from the kitchen made us feel sick every time, we passed the kitchen fans. Sadly, it was the only way to get to the dining room.

There were mostly doctors and lawyers at this resort as it was very expensive and they were in an uproar, taking names so they could sue after their horrific vacation.

We decided to find other things to do. The town was within walking distance, so we watched the local children's smash open piñatas and enjoyed the celebration of Christmas with a Mexican flavor. We found a great pizza place with hundreds of record albums hanging from the ceiling. The city La Paz was a gratifying place to pass time especially since it was Christmas, and we experienced Mexican culture and the children as they celebrated and observed their traditions.

We scaled and climbed over some dunes and wandered onto a deserted beach where we found some dried scorpions and wondered if we would see some live ones. It was an awesome beach but very deserted, so we didn't spend much time there although it was a lovely sunny warm day.

A taxi was hired to take us horseback riding and as he drove, we enjoyed the scenery. Upon arriving we saw the horses in the corral area, but no one came to take us riding. The taxi driver was having a drink at the bar, so we asked the owner and bartender where the horseback riding was. The owner said he did not offer horseback riding as his horses were too spirited.

Harry was annoyed and asked to be taken back to the resort. We drove back and the driver insisted on us paying for horseback riding, but Harry was willing to pay him for a tour and gas but that was all. The man jumped out of the car at the resort and started yelling for the police. Our tour representative just happened to walk by, and we called out to her, she said a few words to the driver when he left very quickly. I thought Harry was going to end up in jail and we were so frightened at this upsetting scene, although it turned out okay.

Venturing out again, we travelled to Cabos St. Lucas, dare I say, by taxi. It was a wonderful day excursion where we swam and went into a glass bottom boat to see the reef. Eating dinner at a lovely restaurant on the beach, completed our day as even the taxi driver was pleasant and did not over charge. We ended up having a wonderful as well as memorable time learning about Mexico from a non-touristy point of view.

When we got home, I wrote a letter to the tour company saying we were not given what they promised in the brochure. They had asked us to change flights as they had over booked knowing that this resort was still in shambles. We demanded our money back for not only the trip but also time we could not retrieve, as the girls were now going on with their education in Bible School.

Thank goodness, we got every penny back. The other resort guests unfortunately did not. Money was not plentiful for us in those days. We would not be able to make a redo with our family any time soon to regain our lost time. Our family made the best of a bad situation and enjoyed Mexico and its culture in a different way than we would have imagined, and it gave us great stories to tell in our future.

In the early months of Bible School Tammy totaled our Mazda. The cars ahead of her stopped and she ran into the car trying to brake. She said it was like going in slow motion while stepping on the brakes. We were glad they were all unhurt. Terry and Mike, Terry's boyfriend, were also in the car. The money we got back from the trip from hell to Mexico, paid for another car so they could get back and forth to Bible school. It was important to us that our girls were able to get back and forth as we wanted them to feel the connection of our home, family, and their friends.

I am getting ahead of myself. As the kids grew up, I felt like a chauffeur, counselor, time manager, cook, hairdresser, secretary, and wife, and not all in that order. I felt many times that life was going too fast, and I could not maintain life at this pace. I needed to run away but did not know where to run, so I ran to God. My prayer life was never ending, and God and I had a remarkable time together.

54. Intercession

O Lord, you have searched me, and you know me. You know when I sit and when I rise; you perceive my thoughts from afar. You discern my going out and my lying down; you are familiar with all my ways. Before a word is on my tongue you know it completely, O Lord.

Psalm 139:1-4

One warm summer morning I was busy doing my chores as I had customers coming later that day. I was clearly impressed by God to pray for my brother Will. I did not know what to pray for, so I went to my bedroom and prayed in the spirit. I call it that as I did not know what I should pray for and what his need was. In a while, one of the girls banged on my bedroom door. She said Will was on the phone and needed to speak to me. My brother sounded so upset and panicked! He did not know what to do but reach out for help. I told him to come over as I had already been praying for him.

It gave him comfort to know God was having someone pray for him and he would try to make it over to our place. He was so upset that he did not know if he would be able to drive. I kept on praying as I did not know his problem.

There was a knock on the door. One of the girls said my brother was there very upset.

I went to see him in the foyer where he was breathing erratically and clearly not doing well. I took him to my bedroom where we could be alone as our house was a busy one. After settling down, he told me he didn't remember how he got to our place, and he thought he was having a heart attack.

We prayed first, then I told him again that God knew what he was feeling and was taking care of him. God had prayer cover him while he was making his way over. He was going through a breakup with his girlfriend and having a terrible time keeping it together and in perspective.

I prayed God would give me the right words. I encouraged him to get as close to God as he could and live for God, whether he had his girlfriend in his life or not. I did not say he would never have her in his life but told him he had to learn to live for God on his own. It seemed to encourage him.

The hard work continually leaning on God, as well as time, gave him a new perspective. He worked diligently at becoming strong in the Lord and we could see his growth as we spent many hours and days with him. He and his girlfriend got together again but he was then a stronger, godlier man. He had so much more to give as a boyfriend, husband, and some day, father. Will let God be number one in his life. As God led him, Will flourished, and he and Helen married and live a successful Christian life together.

I experienced firsthand how God knew all that was happening. He knew about my brother's crisis, and not only that, but had someone pray to help him through it. How awesome is this God we serve? No one could make this stuff up. God carries us in ways we can't imagine, as he did for my brother that day.

My life was radically changed after having a crippling experience, as well as a liberating one. It was a time when I was having an intimate exchange with God on many topics, but I was still living a lot of my Christian values through Harry's strength, in that I did not trust myself to be who God wanted me to be. He taught me many things so personally, and they made such an impact in my life regarding trusting Him; He spoke to me, and I would try to follow God's prompting.

I was still so fearful to step out in so many ways. I had decided to read the Bible through from beginning to end many times to find out what secrets were still unknown to me. I was on a God mission, to find out what He would reveal to me, to totally free me.

Reading the Bible was a daily event and especially talking to God. After reading a few verses, I would be automatically falling into talking to

God about my previous readings. It took discipline to force myself not to get lost in prayer. It was an exciting and emotional time with God, and I felt like I was growing spiritually.

My need was great, and I had so many questions because of my triggers and feelings. I was feeling more than ever before, and that made it more difficult to overcome some of my triggers. I wanted to know why I felt like I did and needed God to show me.

I got the Bible on tape and listened to it when I chauffeured the kids, and for quiet minutes in the afternoons, when time permitted.

55. Fear Broken

When I am afraid, I will trust in you. In God, whose word I praise, in God I trust; I will not be afraid. What can mortal man do to me?

Psalm 56:3-4

While on my quest for answers, reading the Bible one day, I was overcome with a terrible fear that Harry would die. Harry got skin cancer and it was not serious. Maybe it triggered this fear in me, I don't know. I do know that it was crippling. I did not tell him as I withdrew again. It became obsessing and I could not get away from it, as fear haunted me.

I stopped praying and reading for fear God would confirm the fact that Harry was dying. It was a time of confusion and deep pain. Carrying this for months, I finally felt compelled to speak with Pastor Topping about this. After making the appointment I showed up, and being the first time, I spoke of this, I totally fell apart. As I blubbered all the way through, he listened compassionately. He did not say you should not feel this way or don't be silly, or God will help you if you ask Him.

He zeroed in on the problem, and said he thought Satan was using the spirit of fear to cripple what God wanted to do in my life. It registered deep within me, and it was why I did not want to read the word and pray. I let Satan stop me with fear. It stunted growth in God. Pastor Topping prayed for the spirit of fear to leave me, and it did immediately. I was so free! I could feel the heavy dark cloud lift from over me and the sun was shining in my heart. I had heard of people saying how it felt when something was lifted off them, but always imagined they were exaggerating. I can tell you from personal experience they are not, and it feels just like that. The cloud over your head parts and you see and feel the sunshine on you as freedom. How did I not know this? Again, God led me to the right person to discern the truth, so God could move my spiritual life forward. I thank God for Godly men who hear His voice when we are too confused.

God directed me to someone with insight and discernment. I felt liberated and free to grow in God again. I spoke to Harry about my feelings as soon as he got home from work as Pastor Topping suggested. Harry was understanding as usual and was very favorable with me confiding in someone that I felt trustworthy, also being grateful that I confided in him too, and now we could finally navigate our marriage without fear.

I thought back to how fear affected me up to that point in my life. Fear was a good friend of mine, ever since I could remember. It was always there, walking along side of me with my other friend God walking on the other side. You might find that strange, but that is how it felt from the early days of my life until then. In my life fear showed itself in many simple ways as I battled between God and fear, both trying to become my master.

If you ever get to a point where something is stopping you from praying or reading God's word, you know you are giving in to the wrong master. This is what I had done. I should have known I was being lied to when I was afraid to read and pray.

During the first years of my life my fear family grew, and I adopted a cousin of fear, guilt. I never felt accomplished and deserving of good marks, doing good housework, fulfilling expectations, feeling pretty, having friends, speaking my mind, being happy, being a good sister, a good daughter, a good wife, lover, and mother. Worst of all, although God was my saving grace, I felt I did not deserve God's love.

You know, by now God became a very important standard in my life, even though I did not have it all in perspective. I know I loved Him and felt close to Him, and Jesus became my best friend who I could confide in about everything. I learned to lean on Jesus while reading through my Bible many times and especially a couple of times looking for what Jesus said, did, and wanted. Learning what His position was in the trinity made an interesting read and learning experience.

Failing many times, I tried to live according to God's laws. I learned to lean on Jesus who helped me in my time of need. He helped me make decisions as a child that I lived out as an adult. This was an awesome strength throughout my life, to have decisions made long before they became reality. It was like God knitting a strong fiber into my life. I couldn't see the purpose of these fibers until much later. I only saw single strands, some frayed and some knotted. I couldn't see that almost finished beautifully woven product, soft and textured with God's design.

My opinions were never heard, unlike now. Those around me thought of me as very boring, having no opinions of my own and it was true. I became very introverted, as I was afraid to speak. My Jesus gave me fortitude to successfully free my thoughts and opinions and gave me the resilience and courage to speak them.

Jesus became the silent partner, the strength in my life. His name was still very precious to me as I got to know Him as my personal savior as well as learning the power in the name of Jesus. This would be invaluable in my future. I learned slowly that it was not who I was, but who God was that made me worthy. Jesus became my strength and my shield as well as the lifter of my head. I still love the sound of His name and the feel of His arms around me or the touch of Him when I pray.

God gave me foresight regarding marrying Harry so I would not fear but learn to trust him. I found I had a hard time trusting an authority figure especially a male, but I loved being married, and I felt like I was in a strange land and didn't know how I got there. I liken it to a piece of lava erupted and hurled into the sea, enjoying the lapping cool waves but not at all in its familiar shape or surroundings. If only I had known, then that I would grow into a productive person.

I had a difficult time being vulnerable and Harry's approach to intimacy became critically important. I learned to share my feelings and we worked together on how to make our intimacy easier for me. As I became stronger and now didn't tune out, I found there were more and more triggers. I felt like running away so many times but didn't know where to go except to my Comforter. God was so gracious to us supporting and guiding every step of the way.

I wanted to please Harry and be a good lover, so I fought every inclination and terrible feeling I had despite the triggers. I remembered over and over how God gave me Harry and provided the right man for my circumstance. I was so grateful to God who knew me, before I was shaped in my mother's womb, and cared for me in such a real way all my life.

Of course, it took time and much patience on Harry's part as I got to the point of telling him about my every feeling and I continually expressed myself.

We enjoyed each other in so many ways, as well as sexually. I learned to have confidence to be a great lover and wife as well as mother. I was not afraid to step out and make myself vulnerable and used my creative mind to enhance many aspects of marriage and home. I created rooms for intimacy, mental and physical as well as many surprises for Harry on specific occasions. The creativity God placed within me was used in many interesting ways in our private times together as well as in our family life.

Even though life was good, we were left still stumped as to why I felt the way I did but did not let it stop us from living life to the fullest. We were not as knowledgeable then as we are now about these things and did not know where all this came from. It was common back then to keep your private life to yourself, and that is what we did.

I still continually pleaded to God to reveal to me the reasons of my feelings. I wanted to remember my honeymoon and I wanted to become free from my nightmares. The fact that fear was gone opened the door for me to want to know many truths about my life. I was free to know more about myself without fear. Freedom from fear left me strong and I wanted God to release all those confusing feelings within me. I needed all those secrets inside me to be exposed. By now I know that God's timing is always perfect, but back then it was difficult to wait for His perfect timing.

Until then we would keep busy with life, and we were going to move to a new home we built in St. Catharines. It had five bedrooms and all the kids would finally have their own rooms. It was a lovely family home, and we would be close to church.

Irv was living with us too, and he would also have his own room. The young adults had a part in the decor and furniture of their rooms as they made them their own.

God given creativity was visible in my home as far as decor and I loved designing our home as well as decorating it. My children have also fallen victim to some of these creative adventures. They have inherited these genes, as they were expressed in their homes, marriages, and while raising their families.

Back then, they were independent and working and going to school. The girls attended Brock University and the boys were finishing high school at St. Catharines Collegiate. All was well until I started having my nightmares very often, almost nightly.

I would see a face, but it had no features as usual, and it looked blank and yet familiar. I would feel like I was drowning and woke up coughing many times. It was such a shocking intense feeling that I continuously woke with my heart racing.

The girls ended up getting married before they finished school and that was fine with us. We desired for them to finish their education even though married and having the responsibility of being new wives. They did not disappoint and took their rolls as student wives very seriously. Terry married Dave at Christmas and Tammy married Brad in June just six months later.

I had such a wonderful time going shopping with them for their wedding dresses and all that went with the wedding plans. I must say even on a budget, they both did a fantastic job in preparing a beautiful wedding. We were so proud of our daughters' choices in not only their husbands, but also life choices they made.

They both did well and kept up their good marks. Harry was so disappointed that his daughters didn't graduate with the name Ledwez. He was proud that they went to university and graduated with honors. We were super charged and very proud of Terry and Tammy for receiving their teaching degrees while maintaining a healthy marriage.

It was around the time of getting Tammy's wedding plans organized that I started to have much clearer dreams. Over and over, I would dream of the same thing and try to see the whole face. It was frustrating, but I wanted to see it. I was not fearful of knowing who the face was and what it was about.

56. Facing My Past

I was aware that God had done a careful slow archaeological excavation of my soul. He transformed this barren heart into one of memories, giving sight to ruins of rooms and walls of the past years of my life. God did this with care, so as not to destroy what He had created me to be, but gently brushed the earth and painful parts away to reveal His creation. He was now revealing the foundation of all my pain with secrets exposed, showing me exactly where my hurts began.

One night, I finally remembered the first time the man in my recurring dream walked through the door with the light behind him, making him a dark, shadowy and obscure figure. I recognized his face. I wasn't scared. It was good to know my dad was there, even though my mother was in the hospital having a baby. I was told she would bring the baby home when she returned to us. Dad was still wearing his white shirt and black semi-dress pants, with big pleats in them. I felt secure and safe with Dad there.

He walked up to me, and I thought he was going to give me a good night kiss. Instead, he put his hands on a part of his body that I had not seen before. I felt fear and wanted my mother. As he neared, I started to cry.

I felt I was dying and choking. What I felt was so ugly and dark, it overwhelmed me. I felt the zipper as it scraped my face. When he was done, he took his handkerchief from his pocket and wiped my mouth. I could smell the sperm, the aftershave, and the tobacco. He bit my nipples or that is how it seemed to me. I couldn't handle any more, so I blocked to protect myself from the world I was now experiencing.

When in our seventies, my brother Mat spent some time thinking back to that time in our lives. He remembers the drive and taking Mom to the hospital. Afterwards, Dad, Mat and myself were home listening to the radio. Dad said he would put me to bed. He told Mat to stay downstairs and listen to the radio and not come upstairs, even if I cried. He remembers playing with the radio and even taking something apart on it. He heard me cry but was commanded to stay downstairs which he did.

Mat was not responsible for what happened. He was only a little more than a year older than I was, a young child.

All those triggers made sense now. I learned to hate the smell of Pop's after shave and cigarette scent. That was why I stopped kissing him. I didn't get close to him when I was able to stay away when I got older as it was an instinctive move to protect myself.

The next time I was not in my crib, but in a bed that had no rails. It was worse than before. He bit my nipples hard first, and I was overwhelmingly petrified. I felt like I was dying, and I let my emotions go elsewhere. No wonder I felt trapped, scared and helpless when in vulnerable positions during sex in my marriage. I also had flashbacks of other occasions with my dad, which brought revelation to why I felt as I did. I finally knew I was not strange and that I was normal with past secrets of abuse. Dad had taken so much away from me, and I didn't know if I could ever recover.

It took a few weeks of just talking to Harry about what I knew and time for me to adjust to that knowledge, as well as manage the pain. It just had never entered my mind back then, that I was sexually abused. How could I not remember that? Could you block something like that?

I learned all I could about abuse and read books on the topic. I learned that it happened so often to so many innocent young girls and boys. I read about people who blocked abuse as they could not handle the emotions. I never ever suspected such a thing existed and educated myself. I got comfortable enough talking about it and I told my girls and their significant others. I don't even remember the words or anything I told them. I pray it all made sense.

We had services at church regarding abuse and we happened to have some special speakers in around that time. The services helped me to heal some of my pain and get a new Godly perspective. I know my feelings were justified but I would have to deal with them.

Eternity kept nagging at me concerning my dad. The fact that Dad said, he was a bad man and would go to hell, haunted me. No wonder he said that. I wasn't strong enough to do anything about that yet. How could I be?

We went to visit Mom and Dad after weeks and I sat so I didn't have to look at Dad. When I looked at Dad, and into his eyes, they were the eyes of the man who abused me. I tried so hard to be there but after a while gave Harry the eye that we should leave. We did, and I barely made it into the car before I was out of control, sobbing and crying.

This was too hard, and I knew I couldn't talk to Dad until I was able to do it coherently. I knew I had to get to that point and Harry and my kids were there to be supportive and help me.

I didn't tell Irv what was going on. He caught me crying in my room one day, not knowing why, and he felt so bad that he gave me a card to cheer me up. That was sweet of him, and I recall wishing a card would make it all go away. There lay a massive obstacle and job ahead of me that looked humanly impossible, as every time I saw my dad, I saw him through child-like eyes. His face was the one I saw as a child, and I did not want to see it.

I spoke to my family doctor and he encouraged me to go to group therapy. It just wasn't me. I wasn't ready to tell the world. I also wanted to be careful to have God's perspective on my next steps. I thought I should speak to a Christian counselor.

Harry and Shawn were going on a mission's trip with the church, and I thought that it was good as I needed time by myself. I needed to talk to God whenever I wanted and a psychiatrist when I got appointments. I had some time to myself, and the first day I didn't make it. I called Ann, my sister-in-law and George's wife and got to Niagara Falls very upset. She was good company for the evening, and I felt much better after some conversation. Home again, I went to sleep after talking to God. The next evening God sent Alice and Wally over for company. I guessed by now I knew I was not ready to be alone. I knew there were more times of abuse. I remember threats of driving me into the canal if I told anyone.

I wonder if Dad was forcibly taken to the hospital when my sister was three, for a reason. Did Mom foresee something she wanted to prevent in the future? Did he touch my girls when my parents babysat? I asked my girls, and they have no recollection of abuse or triggers to make that suspect and I was so thankful to God.

Remembering has helped me more than you can imagine. I now know that I am not weird and know why I have felt the way I have all these years. It was like a box was opened and the contents were revealed. I know and understand myself better than I could ever have realized. I do not look through the eyes of a wounded child now, but through the eyes of the emotionally mature person that I have become. I have been able to always, live in the present, enjoying the wonderful memories with Harry and our family. I am in awe of the keeping power of my God which can make right so many wrongs. I would never take back the horrors of my life and lose all those valuable and cherished lessons that God has taught me. God has turned something unbearable into something overwhelmingly beautiful and everlasting. How could I ever want to change that and not tell of His glory and power.

57. Forgiveness

Do not conform any longer to the pattern of this world but be transformed by the renewing of your mind. Then you will be able to rest and approve what God's will is, his good, pleasing and perfect will.

Romans 12:2

As time went on, I had a strong urgency to forgive my dad, but I couldn't find it within myself. My merciless feelings left nothing to forgive with. I decided to forgive with God's help. He would have to do it in me or through me. I just couldn't. After that, I started praying for God to do this work of forgiveness in me. I could do no more than to will forgiveness to my dad as every time I thought of what he did, it seemed impossible, so I willed to forgive him with God's help. So far God helped me through everything, so He would do the work this time. I would wait and see.

I spoke to the psychiatrist a couple of times and felt validated. It is so interesting when something like that happens to you, you need to be validated.

I called a number on a book from Rich Buhler. He had a hot line you could call and talk to a professional about your situation, as many times as needed. After I told him my story we talked about my triggers, and he gave me insight to feel a lot better, as I wasn't crazy, and there were reasons for my feelings. I was told that my husband would have to be an exceptional man, to make me feel secure enough to let my past abuse release and be remembered at this time in my life. He said most victims that blocked in this way, never figured it out. He also said we must have a good marriage to be in this recovery position. I agreed totally, knowing who Harry was and what he contributed towards my healing. No one had to tell me, and I was very aware of the man God gave me. Perhaps it would have been nice for Harry to hear that all his good and timely actions were commendable. I had so many times of sadness that he probably thought he was a failure. God and I know better. I began to heal and found it easier to talk about.

One day without even realizing, I thought of my dad and saw a pitiful old man who needed salvation. The one I used to see who hurt me was gone. This is when I decided to go talk to Dad. God's timing is perfect as Mom was not home. She was on a trip to Germany. She was not the forgiving, understanding kind of person, and I do not know what would have happened if she was confronted with the facts. I know she knew something. I went to see Dad and we sat in their living room. Since he was alone, I took him some homemade soup which I put in the kitchen for him.

As we sat in the living room, I started by telling him what happened to me trying to articulate carefully, as I had not ever had this kind of discussion or mentioned sex to him before. I asked if he knew someone that would do that. He looked straight ahead and not at me and said, "No."

I sat beside him facing him as I wanted to see his every move and expression.

I said, "Well what I want, is for that person to know that I forgive them, and God forgives them."

He kept looking forward instead of at me and started talking. He opened up for the first time in our lives. He began with the fact that I, and later Helen, would make him sexually aroused. When he was playing and wrestled with us in the evening, he became so sexually stimulated that Mom would see his arousal. Mom was angry when she noticed this. Then he asked me, "Are you going to tell your mother?" I said I did not think it was a good idea as she was very unpredictable and unforgiving. He agreed and went on talking. Pop said he did not know why he did this to me as he knew he shouldn't and felt terrible but could not stop. At this point I realized why my mother blamed me. I did not realize for what until that time. She was always angry and unloving to me and made me feel like it was my fault. I was now very aware of the fact that none of this was my fault, and I was totally innocent.

We talked about going to the hospital when Mom committed him and how he had shock treatments and it helped him to forget a lot of his past. He insinuated that his pain wasn't as deep now as it had been years before. I told him I wanted to forget the past too and I forgave him. He just sat quietly and nodded. I can still see him, as I had a compulsion to watch and scrutinize his every move. We talked for a couple of hours until we felt it was all said for both of us.

In the light of eternity, I think it was the best time and action to forgive my dad. He considered himself to be such a terrible person that he would go to hell. I felt I released him to be a better man that day, as what is forgiven on earth is forgiven in heaven. I found in my life, what I declared or lost on earth was transformed to a spiritual victory in the future and prayed this would follow through with my dad.

At Mom's deathbed Dad had a chance to accept the Lord as his personal savior. Pastor Topping was visiting Mom and asked Dad if he wanted to accept Jesus while Mom was still on earth and could probably still hear him.

He said, "No, maybe later."

Pastor Topping told him a little story and asked him a question. Peter, if you saw a one-hundred-dollar bill lying on the side of the road, would you say, "I will come back tomorrow to pick it up"?

Pop laughed in his usual little chuckle and said, "No, it will not be there.

I would pick it up right now," Dad replied.

David said, "Well, it is the same with salvation Peter. It might not be there tomorrow."

Dave did not know Pop was such a cheap man, but God did, and God knew what would resonate with Dad.

Pop understood clearly as he was the guy that gave our kids two dollars for birthday gifts. He was a very cheap man with his money and knew to lose one hundred dollars would have almost killed him. He would accept Christ now. He said the sinner's prayer as David led him. Pop was happy Mom had still been there to hear it although she was not speaking any more. Pastor Topping told him to tell someone when he got home.

I received a call that evening from Pop, saying what he did. He had accepted forgiveness from God, and could he come to church on Sunday? I was so shocked and almost didn't know what to say. We said *of course* and he should sit with us.

We waited many years for our father to feel worthy of God. After this he was faithful to God until he died. He went to church smelling like moth balls, but we loved that he loved being there. That doesn't mean his mind was clear all the time, but he knew he was going to heaven. It was so nice after all the years of praying to see him have confidence in God's grace. I believe that he was set free by being forgiven and in turn he forgave himself and accepted the forgiveness of Christ. Again, I say, what is set free on earth is set free in heaven.

58. Darkness Returns

That at the name of Jesus every knee should bow, in heaven and on earth and under the earth.

Philippians 2:10

Harry wasn't home yet, and the house was quiet. Some time after I had spoken to my dad, and found peace in my soul about so much in my life, and not thinking about my past anymore, as I lay in bed, I suddenly felt the bed shake violently. I opened my eyes to see dark foggy figures standing around my bed as it shook. I could hardly get the words out, but I instinctively called on the name of Jesus and rebuked them in his powerful name. I remember it was difficult to even speak the name of Jesus but also knew God to be the more powerful force. I knew and could feel they were from the dark side and their presence was evil. They instantly left at the sound of the name of Jesus, never to return. What a wonderful name, the name of my best friend, "Jesus." I was not afraid but so confident in Christ, who I trusted in all things. I have since learned this force has tried to come back to many people, only to be turned away by the name of Jesus. This evil force would like to cripple you once again with fear, so you cannot be who God has designed you to be.

We had so many valuable family times, and I was totally aware of them all. I can remember most details and don't tune out for either good or bad. I feel like I am a part of the real world. I voice my opinion often and maybe too much and Harry wonders where that quiet non-confronting Marg disappeared to.

I am still here and still developing as God sees fit. His timing is perfect as is His will. We strive for perfection, we will never achieve, but with God's help we will continue to grow in Him. As much as my dad took away from me, God has given back more than I could ask or think. I would never exchange my life's circumstances for the God lessons I had learned to this point in my life. I was continuing my healing journey.

Shawn was getting married, and Irv went to Bible school where he would meet his future wife. Nerissa, Shawn's wife to be, asked me to help with the wedding plans and I was delighted. She too would go to university as a married woman and graduate, but as a Ledwez. My children were happy, and on their way to enjoying their independence. The house was empty, and I didn't enjoy an empty house.

Even though I forgave Pop and he accepted Christ, I would watch that he was not alone with any children. An abuser does not usually abuse just one time. I was told this by the counselor and never forgot it. He said to continually be on guard against abuse, just in case. God's changing power gave me continuous hope as I watched Pop lean on and grow in God.

59. Hope for You

Why, my soul, are you downcast? Why so disturbed within me? Put your hope in God, for I will yet praise him, my savior and my God.

Psalm 42:5

I entered an era of such great understanding of my feelings, and it healed how I dealt with the triggers. It was good to disassociate them from Harry and put them in their rightful place, the past. That didn't mean the work was over, but little by little I found myself letting go of triggers formed by my past. I had continuously pushed them down without knowing their origin, and now I let go of them, knowing where they came from, as I knew where they belonged; while I learned to accept intimacy for what it was meant to be—beautiful, without the continuous struggles I dealt with.

I still deal with some things when they take me by surprise, but my recovery is so quick at those times that Harry wouldn't even know. Being all too familiar with these triggers he does not always see their effects anymore.

I am careful not to lie to myself, and sometimes am way too truthful. Truth was so difficult to achieve in my life and I honor God for it. Knowing God's truth for what it is, sets it apart from just assuming something is true.

I also learned compulsive lying is a sign of abuse. That doesn't mean you should accept it and not change that part of your life. If you know someone that is a compulsive liar or a child that is having problems knowing truth from a lie, don't judge them. Try to find out what the underlying problem is and help them to be released. That does not mean that every child that lies has signs of abuse as other things come into play.

I find it easy to forgive others now and thank God for that too. Always forgive when asked to. Although it is the most difficult of all to do, always forgive yourself.

I can trust the people I love and am so grateful to God for His grace to me, as He has been more than enough, throughout my life. God has been so faithful, and the lifter of my head.

This is only part of my life story. It was the part with a great deal of pain and confusion. With this story I was able to relay my struggles, as well as the awesome leading and healing God provided for me. If you have pain that is indescribable, not knowing where it comes from, ask God to reveal the root of it to you.

Find someone reliable to talk to. They can walk through it with you to a point of healing. If you have unforgiveness in your life, let God do this miracle of forgiveness through you. He is able when we are weak. My prayer is that you might learn something about this great God through my story. I pray it gives you hope, healing and knowledge to know what God can do if you let Him.

This is a story of my life and the many people that have been a part of it. Most importantly it is how God has been there every step of the way and has never left me–not for one second. He has brought me from a fear-filled victim to a confident, self-accepting victor, leaning on the Lord!!

Epilogue

Since completing this autobiography, I have made some new and interesting discoveries. As you have read, there is a special unknown man who picked my brother and I up for Sunday school at the Grace Lutheran Church weekly. He has been with me in thought for many years. Since I entered my seventies, my desire to find and thank him has grown considerably. My brother and I could not remember his name, but I could picture his face from all those years ago.

I had been in contact with a friend Heidi, who also attends the Grace Lutheran Church. One day in January of 2022, the thought came to me that the church might have records of parishioners who once worked for the church. I gave Heidi a quick call, and she informed me she did not know, but she still had an old directory with photos of the families that attended in 1969, and offered it to me, as maybe it would help me find this man. Harry quickly went to retrieve it from her, and we couldn't wait to start our search. I knew he and his family would have to be a little older in this directory, since he had picked us up as young children.

I scanned through the photos without names under them, thinking perhaps I might recognize him. One page, then another, and another… and there he was, just like I remembered him! I flipped to the back where the names and addresses were listed. I was so elated to find Doug Wachs' picture with his family and was euphoric to finally know his name. I thought it was him—and the fact that he had a daughter named Alice confirmed the fact. Somehow, I remembered that he had a daughter by that name.

We searched for him online and found an obituary for Doug's deceased wife Alma, and it gave the information that he had lived in St. Catharines years ago, and now lived in British Columbia. His daughter Kathy also lives in B.C., and it seemed like she might be his caregiver.

I asked her to be my friend on Facebook and posted a note that I was looking for Doug. It wasn't long before I got word from Kathy, and I relayed that I was looking for Doug as he was so important, to who I was today. I wanted to thank her father for his kindness in picking us up as well as teaching the class that I accepted God in. This had radically changed my life forever. I wanted to thank him in person, but he is well over ninety, and was not able to speak to me on the phone. He could recall picking us up after all these years and I was overjoyed at this.

I wanted to know how he came to pick us up and how he knew us. His reply to Kathy, when she relayed my question, was that he didn't know us at all. His passion for the lost and the growth of the church made him knock on doors to find people to pick up. Our mother thought it would be good as she attended a Lutheran church in Germany, and she let us go with him. He was faithful in giving us rides, until his family grew so much that they could not manage without Doug on a Sunday. We had moved further out into the country and further from the church. With no ride I was devastated, too young to know that God was still in control, and I ended up living right beside a church, in our new neighborhood. Doug's faith and loyalty to God changed my life in ways that he will never know. I am so grateful to him for all he did and especially for introducing me to my now best friend, Jesus. I pray that Doug's most senior years are elevated with and bathed in God's love, feeling His nearness as I do, thanks to his faith and loyalty. Thank you, Doug, you will always be in my heart.

My siblings and their families are thriving. They have shared my life with me, and in turn I have shared part of it with you. Can I say they are still some of my favorite people and I still love taking life's journey with them? They have all married and are serving God. Their spouses have become a vital part of our family as well. We love to sit around a table of good food and enjoy our differences of opinions. We are quick to give our view of the truth as we see it, and do not always agree, but always love each other no matter what. God has been good to all of us, and we are not afraid to voice that either.

It has been many years since my story began. My children have all married, and we have six grandchildren. Most of them are married, but all are serving God. Our great granddaughter Lily, one year old, is such a joy. She has a little new girl cousin who loves smiling. Haidyn, also born this year (2022). They are both waiting for their boy cousin (Jack) who will arrive soon! Life is awesome even though COVID has tried to stop us, and at times life became debilitating and other times totally immobilized our freedom. We are blessed and give God the praise He deserves for caring for us through whatever life throws at us. It amazes me to this day how one man's faith and loyalty to God can be responsible for changing so many people that I deeply love.

Acknowledgments

This has been a lifelong journey that I have not conquered unaccompanied, as Harry has been there from our teen years, through the good and bad, never leaving my side but rather holding me up when I was not able to stand on my own. No one will ever know how much he has done to stabilize my life, so I could merge and then speed into reality. My life has been a painful agonizing walk through the fire at times, creating unsightly, even crippling ugly scars, making me hide from others and myself. Through it all, with Harry by my side I learned to embrace my scars, enjoying life, like a cooling refreshing swim, and appreciating the lapping waves. At times the turmoil of those strong crashing waves, forced me to a place that I didn't want to go, but with Harry's help I survived those storms. Some were strong enough to push me out into the deep waters, further than I would have liked, but Harry was there ready to rescue me. Other times we were gently refreshed while we enjoyed our lives together. Harry has been my strength to fight the current, when I had none of my own. He has no idea what his trustworthiness and stability mean to me.

Thank you for believing in me. You spent a lifetime with me, putting the puzzle of our lives together, until all the missing pieces were found, creating a beautiful God honouring life, family and legacy. The inspiration you gave me to write, has been noteworthy, as you have without fail encouraged me to keep on going. Writing has taken a chunk of our time and life together, but you sat with me through hours and hours of editing and proofreading my books, and there are no words that can express this enough; but thank you! You tower high above all the men in my life, and I thank you for loving me this much.

My children: they also were, and still are such a powerful force in my life. I loved them from the time they were born when my eyes fell on their small fragile frames. I grew up with them and they empowered me to find myself, all the while learning to be their mother. They were delightful and gratifying to parent, and I relished and savored every bit of it as I lived life in full colour with them. Terry, Tammy and Shawn, in order of their birth, have added a layer of honour to my life, that every mother desires. You made me look like a successful mom and I thank you for this undeserving honour, as you accepted and learned well how to live life as a family. I thank you for being who God wanted you to be.

I am so proud of my grandchildren. They are over-commers and inspire me in so many ways. They love God, work hard, achieve lots, live large, and love me, Oma. What more could a grandmother ever want. Thank you for being the best grandchildren and living your lives with integrity. I love the additions you have added to our family tree and giving us the feeling of "greatness." Being called, a great grandmother, or "great Oma," is a blessed name I am so proud to carry and will be in awe of what this next generation will achieve.

Heidi's skills in the German language are so appreciated as she has corrected my hit and miss German spelling. I am so grateful to have known Heidi since we were young teens and appreciate her many interests and pre-reading my books.

Thank you to those special people who pre-read *From Victim To Victory*, even in the early stages when the book still needed a lot of work and editing. Your time has been so appreciated as well as your encouragement and wise counsel as to how the delicate contents should be expressed. You, my prudent and knowledgeable group of pre-readers, are respected for your opinions, exceptional insight, and encouragement throughout the process of refining this book. May *From Victim To Victory* challenge readers and encourage them to find freedom.

Elm Grove Publishing has worked with me through the publishing of my now four books. I appreciate their guidance in editing, layout, and cover design of my previous books, using the photos Shawn, my son, captured. They have been consistently outstanding to work with and I thank you, Diane and Mick Prodger. You helped me journey through that desired learning curve as it became reality.

Finally, I thank the One who always knew me, stood with me, held me, and continued to love me. You talked to me when I had no one and were my guide when I had nowhere to turn.

God brought me through years of turbulence into a place of trust and peace. Thank you, God, for being the lifter of my head. I honour you with this book.

About the Author

Margarete Ledwez was born in Germany, emigrating to Canada with her parents and brother when she was just a year old. She quickly developed a longing to create, which has eventually manifested itself in her writing. She lives in St. Catharines, Ontario with her husband, Harry.

From Victim to Victory is Margarete Ledwez' fourth book. More information can be found at:

http://www.margareteledwezwrites.ca

CPSIA information can be obtained
at www.ICGtesting.com
Printed in the USA
LVHW040710300323
742983LV00010B/15

9 781958 407066